HAUNTED EMPIRE

T0270538

A volume in the NIU Series in
Slavic, East European, and Eurasian Studies
Edited by Christine D. Worobec

For a list of books in the series, visit our website at cornellpress.cornell.edu.

HAUNTED EMPIRE

GOTHIC AND THE RUSSIAN IMPERIAL UNCANNY

VALERIA SOBOL

NORTHERN ILLINOIS UNIVERSITY PRESS
AN IMPRINT OF CORNELL UNIVERSITY PRESS
Ithaca and London

Open access edition funded by the National Endowment
for the Humanities.

First published 2020 by Cornell University Press

Library of Congress Cataloging-in-Publication Data

Names: Sobol, Valeria, author.
Title: Haunted empire : Gothic and the Russian imperial
    uncanny / Valeria Sobol.
Description: Ithaca [New York] : Cornell University Press,
    2020. | Series: NIU series in Slavic, East European, and
    Eurasian studies | Includes bibliographical references
    and index.
Identifiers: LCCN 2019050549 (print) | LCCN 2019050550
    (ebook) | ISBN 9781501750571 (hardcover) |
    ISBN 9781501750595 (pdf) | ISBN 9781501750588 (ebook)
Subjects: LCSH: Gothic fiction (Literary genre), Russian—
    History and criticism. | Gothic fiction (Literary genre)—
    History and criticism. | Ukrainian fiction—History and
    criticism. | Imperialism in literature. | Uncanny, The
    (Psychoanalysis), in literature.
Classification: LCC PG3098.G68 S63 2020 (print) |
    LCC PG3098.G68 (ebook) | DDC 891.73/08729—dc23
LC record available at https://lccn.loc.gov/2019050549
LC ebook record available at https://lccn.loc.
    gov/2019050550

Cover photograph courtesy of Tretyakov Gallery, Moscow,
Russia. Vasily Vereshchagin, *The Apotheosis of War*, 1871.
Oil on canvas, 127 cm. (50 in.) x 197 cm. (77.5 in.).

To David, Nika, and Lana

CONTENTS

ACKNOWLEDGMENTS

This project was several years in the making, and I am indebted to many institutions and individuals for their support. The sabbatical leave granted by the University of Illinois back in 2012 enabled me to conduct preliminary research in my native Kyiv and to outline the scope of this book. The National Endowment for the Humanities awarded this project both a summer stipend and a year-long fellowship, which allowed me to conduct additional research in Moscow and to spend an entire year working exclusively on this book. The University of Illinois Center for Advanced Study's appointment provided me with an additional semester of invaluable teaching release, while the Campus Research Board award and an International Program and Studies Travel Research Grant, also at the University of Illinois, further supported my research for this project.

I want to thank my former and current colleagues at the University of Illinois, Urbana-Champaign, who have responded to parts of this book at its various stages or simply offered their collegiality and friendship on a daily basis: Laura Davies Brenier, Michael Finke, George Gasyna, Roman Ivashkiv, Lilya Kaganovsky, Harriet Murav, Richard Tempest, Gene Avrutin, Diane Koenker, John Randolph, Mark Steinberg, Craig Koslofsky, Laurie Johnson, and Anke Pinkert. I am grateful to the late Nancy Abelmann who, in her capacity as the then associate vice chancellor for research, helped me not only create a successful grant proposal but also shape this book in a more meaningful way. The University of Illinois Slavic Reference Service provided me with prompt access to any materials I requested, whether I was overseas or at home, in Urbana—thank you, Joe Lenkart. I also thank my graduate research assistants—Irina Avkhimovich, Serenity Stanton Orengo, and LeiAnna Hamel—for their conscientious work.

I am indebted to the invaluable advice and expertise of my colleagues in the field, with whom I have collaborated on publications and conference panels related to nineteenth-century Russian prose, Gothic literature, empire, and Ukrainian studies or who have supported my work on this book in other ways: Katherine Bowers, Nancy Condee, Alexander Etkind,

Tetyana Dzyadevych, Katya Hokanson, Yuliya Ilchuk, Ingrid Kleespies, Ilya Kliger, Ani Kokobobo, Oleh Ilnytzkyj, Roman Koropeckyj, Svitlana Krys, Anne Lounsbery, Robin Feuer Miller, Sarah Pratt, Robert Romanchuk, Dirk Uffelmann, Ilya Vinitsky, and Oleksandra Wallo (this list is incomplete, of course). I also want to thank Vitaly Chernetsky for guiding me through my studies of Ukrainian literature back in graduate school—all that work came in handy for this book. Special thanks go to Lucy Parts for being such a wonderful colleague and friend over all these years.

It was a pleasure working with Amy Farranto at the Northern Illinois University Press at a time when publishing literary studies has become particularly challenging. I am thankful to the NIU series editor Christine Worobec for her encouragement, as well as to my two manuscript readers for the Press, Edyta Bojanowska and Olga Maiorova, whose insightful comments helped me strengthen the book's argument and (hopefully) broaden its reach. I also want to thank the Cornell University Press team who made this book a physical reality: Karen Laun, Irina Burns, and Sarah Noell.

I was fortunate to have been able to present portions of this book at various venues, nationally and internationally, and to receive invaluable comments and suggestions. I benefited immensely from all the feedback offered.

Chapter 1 is based on a portion of my article "'Komu ot chuzhikh, a nam ot svoikh': variazhskoe prizvanie v russkoi literature kontsa XVIII veka," in *Tam, vnutri. Praktiki vnutrennei kolonizatsii v kul'turnoi istorii Rossii*, edited by A. Etkind, D. Uffel'mann, and I. Kukulin (Moscow: Novoe literaturnoe obozrenie, 2012), 186–216. An earlier version of chapter 5 first appeared as the article "On Mimicry and Ukrainians: The Imperial Gothic in Pogorelsky's *Monastyrka*" in *Skhid-Zakhid: Istoryko-kul'turolohichnyi zbirnyk* (a predecessor of *East/West: Journal of Ukrainian Studies*, www.ewjus.com) 16–17 (2013): 369–87. Chapter 6 is an expanded version of my article "'Tis Eighty Years Since: Panteleimon Kulish's Gothic Ukraine," published in *Slavic Review* 78, no. 3 (Summer 2019): 390–409. I am thankful to the journals and their editors for granting permission to republish these materials here.

Last but not least, I thank my family: my parents whose sense of humor and youthful optimism have uplifted me throughout my life and career; my daughters, Nika and Lana, whose busy and creative lives give a sense of balance to my own; my dog Roxie who kept me company during many lonely days of writing; and above all, my husband and colleague David Cooper who stoically has read every word of this manuscript more than once and offered innumerable helpful suggestions, both editorial and conceptual—in addition to his unfailing emotional and everyday support. This book is dedicated to David, Nika, and Lana, and this dedication is only a token recognition of what they mean to me.

Note on Transliteration and Translation

In transliterating Cyrillic text, I have used a modified Library of Congress system, except for last names ending in -skii, which I transliterate as -sky to comply with the tradition of rendering such names in English (for example, "Pogorel'sky" instead of "Pogorel'skii"). I have also kept some authors' names in the form more familiar to the English-speaking reader: for example, Gogol, rather than Gogol'. When giving bibliographical information, however, I have adhered to the Library of Congress system throughout. As for Ukrainian proper names, I have used the Ukrainian transliteration throughout except for fictional characters' names from Russian-language sources (e.g., Mikhailo Charnyshenko, rather than Mykhailo). I have kept the more traditional transliteration for some historical or geographical forms, such as Kievan Rus' (but Kyiv instead of Kiev) and Galicia (rather than Halychyna). For the names of German literary characters and places in chapter 2, I have used the German spelling when available. All translations into English are mine unless otherwise specified.

HAUNTED EMPIRE

FIGURE 1. Map of Russia. *Alden's Handy Atlas of the World* (New York: J.B. Alden, 1887), 35.

Introduction
From the Island of Bornholm to Taman':
The Literary Trajectory of the Russian
Imperial Uncanny

In Mikhail Lermontov's novel *A Hero of Our Time* (1839–40), the Russian officer from St. Petersburg Grigorii Pechorin, traveling to the Caucasus, arrives in the small frontier town of Taman'. Trying to find lodging late at night, he ends up staying in a little house of questionable reputation where he faces danger from the outlaws who occupy it. Pechorin is warned by a local Cossack that the place is "unclean," and indeed his first encounter with one of the inhabitants immediately raises suspicions:

> Finally a boy of about fourteen crept out from the inner porch.
> "Where's the master?" I asked.
> "Not here (Nema)," answered the boy in Ukrainian.
> "You mean there isn't a master at all?"
> "Not at all (Sovsim)."
> "Well, where's the mistress?"
> "Gone to the village (Pobigla v slobodku)."
> "Who'll open the door for me then?" I asked, giving it a kick. The door opened by itself, and a dank smell came from within. I lit a sulphur match and held it up to the boy's face. Its light showed a pair of wall-eyes: he was blind, totally blind from birth. He stood before me without moving, and I had a good look at his face.

> I confess I'm strongly prejudiced against the blind, one-eyed, deaf, dumb, legless, armless, hunch-backed, and so on. I've noticed there's always some odd link between a person's outward appearance and his inner self, as though with loss of the limb, our soul loses some feeling as well.[1]

The narrator attempts to "study" the blind boy's face and notices his faint smile, which strikes him as suspicious and makes him wonder whether the youth is in fact blind. The Russian-Ukrainian conversation is then resumed, in the course of which the youth denies being the son of the mistress of the house; her only daughter, he says, had fled home with a Crimean Tartar.

Travel to an unknown land gone awry; an overnight stay in a dangerous house; the uncertainty, suspense, and dark atmosphere of this encounter—these are recognizable tropes of Gothic literature, a type of fiction that dominated the European literary scene between the 1790s and the 1820s. The motif of sulfur, with its demonic connotations, further contributes to the eerie effect of this scene. It is important to note that what Lermontov describes here is also a colonial encounter, which takes place on the margin of the Russian Empire and involves the somewhat subhuman local boy who "creeps out" of the hut, speaks a different language, has a physical disability easily interpreted by the Russian traveling officer as a potential moral or emotional deficiency, and serves as an immobile object of Pechorin's prejudiced gaze. It is this juncture of the literary Gothic tradition and the imperial context into which it is inscribed that constitutes the primary focus of this book. Though it may be tempting to interpret Lermontov's use of Gothic tropes as a travesty of the popular genre (the decrepit hut of "Taman'" can be easily construed as a parody of the traditional Gothic castle), I argue that the Gothic trappings of the novella tap into deeper imperial anxieties. By examining several literary works produced in the Russian Empire during this period that relied extensively on Gothic clichés, I show that these attributes of the Gothic genre are far from being mere decorations or a tribute to a popular literary form. Instead, they channel some of the central ideological, historical, and sometimes philosophical concerns of each particular work and are deeply intertwined with the peculiarities of the Russian imperial situation.

Lermontov quickly dispels the mystery of 'Taman' as the intriguing residents of the little house—a sinister old woman, who is selectively deaf; the boy who may or may not be blind and who speaks now Ukrainian, now Russian; and a beautiful but treacherous young "mermaid" who converses in folkloric riddles—turn out to be mere smugglers and the narrator luckily escapes them and destroys their "nest." This outcome does not cancel the fact that Pechorin nearly met his death there, in the small god-forsaken coastal town.[2] It is in this drab place—rather than in the exotic war-ridden Caucasus, where highlanders were fiercely resisting the Russian occupation—that the greatest dangers await the protagonist, as the beautiful "mermaid" almost succeeds in drowning him, and the blind boy steals his valuables. As I argue elsewhere, what makes Taman' such a suitable venue for some of the most suspenseful and threatening events of the entire novel has to do with the town's liminality, the uncertainty of the locals' identities, and the complex interplay between "self" and "other" characteristic of the Russian colonial experience.[3] The officer arriving from the empire's capital and equipped with the necessary bureaucratic documentation encounters a radically unstable space on the imperial frontier, where the smugglers' ethnic identities, native languages, kinship, and even physical disabilities are constantly called into question and where the outlaws exhibit a greater degree of freedom and mobility than the itinerant official. The "uncleanness" of the place refers not only to the demonic connotations of the locals but also to the anthropological concept of "dirt" defined by Mary Douglas as "essentially disorder."[4] The imperial order seems to disintegrate in this liminal space, and the inevitable questions of how Russian that little town of Taman' is and how stable the boundaries of the empire are create an unsettling sense of the unfamiliarity of a location that should be safe, familiar, and domestic.

FIGURE 2. Mikhail Lermontov, *Taman'*, 1837. Drawing, 24.2 cm x 14.8 cm (9.5 in x 5.8 in). Institute of Russian Literature, St. Petersburg.

Pechorin's experience in Taman' exemplifies what I call "the imperial uncanny"—instability in the categories of one's own and the foreign, the familiar and the strange, self and other, a confusion resulting from the threatening ambiguity of the Russian imperial space. At the literary level, this disorienting effect is accomplished by conventional Gothic tropes that take on a new meaning when placed in a specific geographical and historical context. This book thus reads the Gothic as a key literary form that enacts historical and cultural tensions that arise from Russia's idiosyncratic imperial experience.[5]

The Gothic Tradition

The term "Gothic" began to be associated with a particular literary genre after the publication of Horace Walpole's novel *The Castle of Otranto: A Gothic Story* in 1764. Set sometime between the late eleventh and mid-thirteenth century, the novel introduced key characteristics of the genre: a remote time period; an exotic (often southern European) location; a suspenseful atmosphere; a supernatural intervention; the trope of the castle, with its subterranean passages, as the site of an ancient transgression; and the figure of the Gothic villain persecuting an innocent maiden.[6] For Walpole and his contemporaries, the term "Gothic" primarily meant "medieval," through its association with Gothic architecture which, in turn, was linked to the Germanic tribes that sacked Rome in the fifth century CE. However, the reference to the Middle Ages in eighteenth-century Britain was not merely temporal, just as the connection to the Goths had not been purely geographical for the Renaissance humanists. The latter applied the term, used in a pejorative sense, to the medieval architectural style. For them, Gothic meant everything that harmonious classical antiquity was not: barbaric, uncivilized, uncultured, whimsical, and ornate. Similar "negative aesthetics," to use Fred Botting's phrase, define the Gothic genre in eighteenth-century literature. Indeed, if the Enlightenment is the "Age of Reason," Gothic fiction's Catholic setting and its focus on the irrational and supernatural (or superstitious) could be construed as harking back to the "dark ages" of European history. As David Punter puts it, "Gothic stood for the old-fashioned as opposed to the modern; the barbaric as opposed to the civilized; crudity as opposed to elegance. . . . Gothic was the archaic, the pagan, that which was prior to, or was opposed to, or resisted the establishment of civilised values and a well-regulated society."[7] Because of its focus on the irrational sphere, Gothic literature also signaled a crisis of the Enlightenment, revealing the limitations of its epistemological optimism and scientific rationalism.

After the success of Walpole's work, a wave of Gothic novels in Britain followed, reaching its peak in the 1790s–1810s, a fact unanimously interpreted as a literary response to the French Revolution, the Terror, and the disturbing uncertainties of the Napoleonic era. These decades witnessed development of two main trends within this increasingly popular genre, termed alternatively as "the literature of terror" versus that of "horror," or "sentimental" Gothic versus "frenetic" Gothic.[8] These two trends are exemplified by Ann Radcliffe's more subdued and refined Gothic novels, such as *The Mysteries of Udolpho* (1794), and Matthew G. Lewis's much darker *The Monk* (1796?), which scandalously portrayed rape, incest, and the pact with the devil.[9] Despite the differences in Radcliffe's and Lewis's takes on the Gothic genre, the scholars agree that their works arise from the same cultural and political context and share an essential thematic core, specifically the tension between the individual's desire to escape the constraints of society into the world of imagination and at the same time his or her external compliance with the "bonds of convention and repression."[10]

As the genre develops and its popularity soars, the arsenal of Gothic tropes broadens, with an abbey, monastery, or convent added as alternative settings, the sublime landscape emerging as a staple of Radcliffe's Gothic novels, while the supernatural element becomes optional: still present in many Gothic works, it typically received a rational explanation in Radcliffe's fiction. Inevitably, the vogue for the Gothic genre and its ubiquitous presence on the literary market made it a subject of travesties and parodies (most notably, in Jane Austen's *Northanger Abbey*, 1818). The genre continued to thrive, as evidenced by the publication of Mary Shelley's *Frankenstein* in 1818 and especially Charles Maturin's *Melmoth the Wanderer* in 1820. After that, the Gothic novel as a distinct genre waned, but its elements, or what is referred to as "the Gothic mode"—a persistent deployment of recognizably Gothic tropes and narrative techniques in connection to the dominant Gothic themes of irrationality, transgression, past history haunting the present, and barbarism lurking behind under the veneer of civilization—continue to reemerge throughout the nineteenth century across Europe and beyond. The lasting legacy of the Gothic tradition manifests itself more explicitly in Gothic-fantastic works by E. T. A. Hoffmann and Edgar Allan Poe but also can be discerned in the sisters Brontë's villains and bleak northern landscapes, Charles Dickens's grim urban setting, and Fedor Dostoevsky's claustrophobic spaces. The late 1800s witnessed an energetic comeback of the Gothic genre as exemplified by Stevenson's *The Strange Case of Dr. Jekyll and Mr. Hyde* (1886) and Bram Stoker's *Dracula* (1897). The influence of the Gothic continues well beyond the nineteenth century: its elements are dispersed in the twentieth-century science fiction tradition, the popular culture of horror, and the more recent "cybergothic" fiction and film.[11]

In the literature of the Russian Empire, the Gothic genre makes a relatively early appearance in Nikolai Karamzin's novella "The Island of Bornholm" (1793)—subject of a closer examination in chapter 1. Along with this original experiment in the genre, Gothic fiction swept the literary scene in the form of numerous translations and adaptations, as well as parodies and travesties, during the first decades of the nineteenth century. Predictably, Radcliffe enjoyed the greatest popularity, to the extent that when the Russian translation of Lewis's *The Monk* came out in 1802, it was attributed to Radcliffe, not in the least for marketing reasons.[12] A mocking recipe for a "novel à la Radcliffe" was published by Orest Somov as early as 1816, and the term "Radcliffism" or "Radcliffian" would be used in critical reviews well into the 1840s, often condescendingly, as a shortcut for "Gothic."[13]

The nineteenth-century Russian critics' somewhat dismissive attitude toward the Gothic tradition as a largely borrowed, sensationalist, and popular "low" literature was later adopted by Soviet literary scholars. For the latter this tradition also embodied an ideologically suspicious literary trend preoccupied with the irrational and (supposedly) divorced from social reality. With some exceptions, Soviet critics either ignored the Gothic legacy in Russian literature, subsuming it under the discussion of pre-Romantic and Romantic literature, or studied individual Russian authors' borrowing from Gothic authors within the framework of literary influence.[14] A more systematic examination of the Russian Gothic tradition began in Western scholarship, where it was also scarce, although instrumental for the future development of this line of critical inquiry.[15] By contrast, Gothic literature in English has been subject of many theoretically diverse studies that opened up numerous avenues for exploring this literary tradition—from psychoanalytical interpretations that treat Gothic tropes as an externalization of the unconscious or a metaphor of a repressive society, to postcolonial analyses that read Gothic horrors and plots as reflecting on British imperial expansion and the fear of the other.[16] These approaches have been extended to a broader pan-European context to challenge the Anglo-American monopoly (or even "tyranny") of the literary Gothic.[17] The literary Gothic tradition, with its emphasis on alterity, provided a fertile ground for colonial and postcolonial readings in the Western European context, because of the challenge this tradition posed to Enlightenment categories and hierarchies, among them race, ethnicity, and the very distinction between human and nonhuman.[18] The Russian Gothic is still to be read through the colonial lens, which is my approach in this book.

Since the beginning of the twenty-first century, the reception and trans-formation of the Gothic tradition in the Russian Empire, as well as in Soviet and post-Soviet literature, has begun to receive serious scholarly attention. Vatsuro's seminal book on the history of the Gothic novel in Russia (a 2002 posthumous publication of his previous and unfinished studies of this sub-ject) was followed by an edited volume on the Gothic tradition in Russian literature.[19] In the English-language scholarship, significant contributions to the Gothic studies in nineteenth-century Russian literature have been made by Alessandra Tosi, Robin Miller, and Katherine Bowers.[20] Muireann Magu-ire's 2012 monograph, building on Eric Naiman's earlier exploration of the "NEP Gothic," discovered the persistent Gothic substratum within both the Socialist Realist canon and the more alternative literature of the period.[21] Dina Khapaeva has proposed the term "Gothic aesthetics" to characterize contemporary culture that aims to recreate the effect of a nightmare and centers on dehumanization and violence.[22] A breakthrough has also occurred in the studies of the Ukrainian Gothic, with Svitlana Krys's contributions and the publication of the forum "Rethinking the Gothic in Ukraine."[23]

This book contributes to this "Gothic turn" in studies of Russian and Ukrainian literatures. It is important to underscore that I do not attempt a genre study; rather, I investigate the Gothic mode in the prose of the pre-Romantic and primarily Romantic period, focusing on the nexus of the Gothic and empire. Several scholars of the Gothic have insisted on the need to distin-guish between works that borrow elements of the Gothic genre and those that truly belong to the Gothic tradition.[24] I agree that the use of a Gothic element does not automatically inscribe the work into this literary tradition. Yet my understanding of the "Gothic mode" is broader than that of some scholars (e.g., Vatsuro or Malkina and Poliakova). In my approach, each Gothic trope or element can invoke the entire tradition as long as it is linked with the ideologi-cal and thematic "Gothic complex."

Because the rise of the Walter Scottian historical novel overlapped with the continuing popularity of Gothic fiction, critics often treated histori-cal and geographical settings in these two traditions differently. The ten-dency was to regard history and geography in Gothic fiction as mere props intended to invoke the largely imagined Middle Ages or an exotic southern European locale; as Alfred Tresidder Sheppard harshly remarks, it is "false geography" and "spurious history."[25] Most Gothic fiction lacks the historical specificity and ethnographic detail of Scott's historical novels (themselves not immune to Gothic influence). Still, it does not mean that the Gothic literary mode is profoundly ahistorical.[26] As Punter observes in connection to *The Castle of Otranto*, from its beginnings Gothic fiction is pervaded by a sense of history: "Walpole is quite unconcerned with the details of life in the Middle Ages; what he is concerned with is conjuring a general sense of 'past-ness' by the occasional insertion of costume detail or its equivalent. And yet, in another sense, *Otranto* is serious about history. For whatever its shortcomings and infelicities, it does give evidence of an eighteenth-century view of feudalism and the aristocracy, and in doing so originates what was to become perhaps the most prevalent theme in Gothic fiction: the revisiting of the sins of the fathers upon their children."[27]

Mikhail Bakhtin makes a similar point in his brief discussion of the chronotope of a Gothic castle: "The castle is saturated through and through with a time that is historical in the narrow sense of the word, that is, the time of the historical past. The castle is the place where the lords of the feudal era lived (and consequently also the place of historical figures of the past) . . . And finally legends and traditions animate every corner of the castle and its environs through their constant reminders of past events. It is this quality that gives rise to the specific kind of narrative inherent in castles and that is then worked out in Gothic novels."[28] Bakhtin argues for the continuity between the Gothic genre and the historical novel because of the historicity of the castle as a setting, with its peculiar fusion of temporal and spatial characteristics.[29]

One of the premises of this book is that it matters where, in terms of Russian imperial geography, Gothic encounters take place, what the participants' ethnicities are, and in what historical context Gothic tropes are deployed. It is significant that the inhabitants of the suspicious house in Taman' speak Ukrainian (which Lermontov takes pains to transcribe in the original Russian text of the novel), and that this encounter takes place in a frontier Cossack settlement on the southern margin of the Russian Empire. In his polemics with ahistorical or psychoanalytical readings of Gothic fiction, the British Gothic scholar Robert Mighall claims, referring to the etymology of the term, "The 'Gothic' by definition is about history and geography."[30] Significantly, when Russian poets created their adaptations of Gottfried August Bürger's famous Gothic ballad "Lenore" (1773) about a maiden who rides with her ghostly groom to the grave, they changed the historical context and the geography of the German source. While in Bürger, the dead groom returns from the Seven Years' War, in Vasilii Zhukovsky's "Liudmila" (1808) and Pavel Katenin's "Olga" (1816) he arrives from military campaigns fought in Russia's borderlands—the sixteenth-century Livonian War and the 1709 Battle of Poltava, respectively.[31] These two locations, the Baltic North and Ukraine, correspond to the two poles of the Russian imperial Gothic examined in this book.

When analyzing literary texts, I do not take the location or historical references for granted or dismiss them as part of the Gothic paraphernalia. That Karamzin's narrator is stranded on the island of Bornholm, and not any other Scandinavian or Baltic island vaguely described in Ossianic terms, is significant.[32] The fact that the convent graduate's adventures, in Antonii Pogorel'sky's eponymous novel, unfold on the territory of the former Hetmanate in Left-Bank Ukraine gives us an insight into the novel's deep overriding anxieties; and Mikhailo Charnyshenko's participation in the infamous Holstein campaign launched by Peter III, narrated in Panteleimon Kulish's first novel, is not simply a plot device to get the hero out of the house, as some critics have claimed.[33] Deeply rooted in time and space, Gothic tropes serve as vehicles of expressing and addressing profound imperial and national anxieties and traumas. Gothic literature does offer seemingly paradoxical portrayals of some regions as existing outside of history, as was the case with Finland in the Russian literary and ethnographic imagination. It does not mean, however, that the Gothic mode is unconcerned with history. On the contrary, because this literature is so intensely engaged with historicity, the denial of history to some imperial locales becomes marked and betrays itself as a strategy of Russian colonial discourse. This strategy allows Russia to highlight its image as a modern empire and justify its rule over the supposedly "backward" and "stagnant" territories, even those that were simultaneously admired for their modernity and high level of "development." History, whether present or conspicuously absent, along with geography, are key to my reconstruction of the Russian imperial imagination through the literary Gothic tradition. This pan-European literary form assumed new relevance in the context of nineteenth-century Russia, where its conventional tropes, somewhat removed from their original well-defined genre setting, now served to address a range of issues particular to the Russian imperial situation.

The Imperial Uncanny

It has become commonplace in the studies of the Russian Empire to invoke its peculiarity as a vast continental empire.[34] Because of Russia's gradual expansion into contiguous territories, scholars typically contrast its imperial experience to that of Britain and France, with their exotic overseas colonies (although British colonization of Scotland, Ireland, and Wales exhibits some productive parallels with the situation of Ukraine in the Russian Empire).[35] Russia's somewhat idiosyncratic development as an empire gave rise to a set of persistent ideological concerns and cultural anxieties, which are addressed in literature indirectly through the Gothic mode.

One such concern is the lack of clear differentiation between the Russian imperial and national identities, a phenomenon that is typical of contiguous empires in general, but that seems to be particularly prominent in the Russian case.[36] Some scholars suggest that for various reasons—mainly related to its status as a land empire—Russia failed to create a nation altogether, and its intellectual and political elite were imperialist rather than nationalist.[37] Conversely, Mark Bassin argues for the fusion of imperialism and nationalism in Russia, where the national sentiment did not preclude a full endorsement of Russia's political and territorial expansion into non-Russian areas; rather, it was seen as "as an important part of [the nationalists'] program of national advancement and renewal."[38] Olga Maiorova, while contesting the assumption that Russian national identity was overshadowed or even subsumed by that of the empire, admits the overlap between the two, a "peculiar blend of national sentiment and imperial pride," characteristic of nineteenth-century Russian nationalist discourse.[39] It is this overlap that is relevant for my purpose; rather than taking sides in this debate I focus on the disorienting effect of this fluid sense of Russianness. As Bassin puts it, as a result of this symbiosis between the nationalist and imperial projects and the unclear nature of Russia's geographical contours, "the question 'where is Russia?' . . . was neither elementary nor self-evident, but instead one which had no commonly accepted answer."[40] In his *Atlas of the European Novel, 1800–1900*, Franco Moretti observes that in Jane Austen's novels, the marriage market connecting differing counties in a particular part of England could work only if "women feel 'at home,'" "can feel nation-state as a true homeland."[41] In the Russian case, this sense of the nation-state within the empire was muddled at best, and the literary characters I examine do not quite feel at home in the Russian imperial peripheries or even in its problematic center, St. Petersburg.

A blurred distinction between the center and periphery in the Russian Empire contributed to that sense of disorientation. A hierarchical, inequitable relationship between the metropole and the periphery marked by difference (ethnic, geographical, social, or administrative) is essential to the concept of the empire.[42] Yet in the Russian case this relationship proved rather unstable, as did the markers of difference, especially at a symbolic level of representation. As Mikhail Epshtein observes, "in Russian history even the capital not infrequently was transformed into a province, since the sovereign would transfer his seat to a specially created or minimally populated center. . . . The Russian autocracy obsessively strove to settle outside of its own state (derzhava), so it could keep it at its side as a province. . . . As a result, even Moscow, and later St. Petersburg as well, were turned into provinces in relation to the ever-elusive, transcendent imperial power."[43] Anne Lounsbery attributes "Russia's sense of its own provinciality less to the nature of the autocratic state than to the educated elites' strained relationship to European culture."[44] Indeed, Russia's proverbial cultural dependence on the West, resulting from Peter I's reforms and becoming an acute source of anxiety already in the late eighteenth century, only added to the complexity of the situation. As Katya Hokanson reminds us, even if the imperial capital, St. Petersburg, preserved all the characteristics of a classical metropole, its location on the periphery of Europe made this centrality questionable.[45] Gogol's works, according to Lounsbery, eliminate the dichotomy of the capital versus the provinces: "they are ultimately *the same*" repositories of emptiness.[46] Whether we are dealing with the imperial peripheries (discussed by Hokanson) or deep Russian provinces (analyzed by Lounsbery), their distinction from the center appears highly problematic. As a result of Russia's lack of unique national culture, as perceived by many intellectuals, the imperial centers seemed to be provincial in relation to the West and lacking in originality and specifically Russian identity. To quote Hokanson, "in Russia, even the center is fraught with emptiness, shot through with the same absences as the vast reaches between the major cities."[47] This symbolic emptiness of Russia translated in some texts into an uncanny void, a source of Gothic terror that breaks through the veneer of a seemingly entertaining and conventional adventure narrative. Such is the case of Pogorel'sky's *The Convent Graduate*, with its several layers of imperial and colonial anxieties associated with the lack of a national and cultural core of both the colonizers and the colonized.

One feature of Russia's empire-building, singled out by several theoreticians and historians of the empire, is the deliberate and pragmatically driven inconsistency of its imperial policies.[48] Russia dealt with newly acquired territories and their populations on an ad hoc basis. It sometimes granted its colonized elites greater privileges than those enjoyed by the Russian nobility (e.g., giving a constitution to the Poles), integrating some of the territories into the administrative structure of the empire (as was the case of Ukraine eventually), or preserving their political autonomy (Poland and Finland). An inconsistent application of the principle of differentiation versus homogenization created a vast realm for various colonial ambiguities and paradoxes. For example, a "colonized" Swedish nobleman of Finland enjoyed greater political autonomy than a member of the Russian gentry; the native population of the empire (Russian peasants) was often enserfed by the nobility of a foreign or at least mixed origin who came from the territories occupied by the Russian Empire (e.g., Polish, Ukrainian, Baltic German, Tartar); some non-Russian ethnic groups were exempt from military service and serfdom. The elites from the territories added to the Russian Empire—Baltic Germans and Ukrainians, for instance—were coopted and often entrusted with leading administrative positions. Their role in implementing the imperial project not only placed them in a position of power within the empire, thus challenging the colonizer/colonized dichotomy. It also potentially put them at odds with the Romantic nationalist ideals of their native culture, as was the case with some Ukrainian writers I explore here. Elaborating on this strategy of co-option and integration in Russian empire-building, historian Geoffrey Hosking observes the absence of the "distinction between metropolis and colonies" as one of the defining features of the Russian Empire.[49] Vera Tolz also notes that "at the level of government bureaucracy, no clear distinction existed between colonial administration and internal Russian policy."[50]

This blurring of the boundaries between the colonizer and the colonized—a system of difference critical to the empire-building process in modern Europe and yet often muddled in the Russian case—is particularly important for my project.[51] This distinction was also problematic in geographical terms, given the fluidity of both external and internal borders in Russia. The new imperial center, St. Petersburg, was not only located on the periphery of Europe; it was built on a freshly annexed territory (Ingria), as the Russo-Swedish war was still raging. The capital of the empire was created in its colony—an example of the shifting external borders and elusive sense of the Russian imperial realm. Nikolai Karamzin's *Letters of a Russian Traveler* (*Pis'ma russkogo puteshestvennika*, 1791–95) capture this elusiveness, as the narrator crosses into the Baltic lands, annexed during the same military campaign, the Great Northern War won by Peter I, and observes: "The German part of Narva, or so-called Narva proper, consists primarily of stone buildings; part, separated by a river, is called Ivan-gorod. In the first part everything has a German character, in the other—a Russian character. This used to be our border—oh, Peter, Peter!"[52]

The lack of "hard" internal borders, typical of contiguous empires, complicated the differentiation between the colonizer and the colonized even more—especially because the expansion of the Russian Empire involved annexation of adjacent East Slavic territories or those regions that were included into "the Russian identity" through mythological or historical connections, as was Finland.[53] As Alexander Etkind asks provocatively in his essay dedicated to internal colonization, "When did Russian colonization begin—with the occupation of ethnically alien Kazan' or ethnically close Novgorod? Where were Russian colonies—in the lands of the Chud', in Ural and Siberia, where a classic process of intermingling between migrants and locals was taking place, or in Little Russia where everything was reversed and where the population, ethnically similar to that of the metropolis, formed cultural and political differences that would prove decisive?"[54] Etkind's questions highlight the complexity of the Russian imperial situation, with its unstable borders, an empty center, a lack of a clear notion of what "Russia" really means—in a geographical, ethnic, and cultural sense—aggravated by the problematic differentiation between self and other. All these factors are at play in the literature of the imperial uncanny that I examine.

Key to Freud's definition of the uncanny is the dissolution of boundaries between what is home and what is not. A large portion of his essay "The Uncanny" (1919) is dedicated to the etymology of the German term *unheimlich*, which invokes the idea of being "not like at home," or unfamiliar.[55] As Freud shows, its opposite—*heimlich*, something homey, comfortable, and cozy—also develops the meaning of unfamiliar and threatening through its association with being concealed from outsiders, mysterious, and esoteric. In other words, the binary of the familiar and unfamiliar, or one may say, self and other, collapse, as the eerie, the strange, and the uneasy already resides in the familiar, or heimlich. Freud explores this idea at the level of an individual psyche, where a seemingly new, unfamiliar experience haunting the self turns out to be an earlier trauma repressed into the subconscious. But it also has implications for cultural analyses of alterity and (post)colonial studies. Julia Kristeva applies the notion of the unheimlich to the psychological experience of an encounter with the other, which proves unsettling as it reminds us of our fragmented nature: "Uncanny, foreignness is within us: we are our own foreigners, we are divided."[56] This psychological experience has direct ethical and political implications: recognizing one's uncanny strangeness challenges the division between "us" and "them," "natives" and "foreigners," and opens the possibility of a tolerant and cosmopolitan coexistence in contemporary society. Drawing on Freud's unheimlich, Homi Bhabha defines "unhomeliness" as "a paradigmatic colonial and post-colonial condition" that involves an uncanny disorientation caused by the collapse of boundaries between private and public, home and the outside world, self and other.[57] For Bhabha, "colonialism uncannily returns to unsettle modernity" by destabilizing its sense of monolithic one-ness and uniqueness through doubling, repetition, and mimicry.[58]

Scholars of the Gothic, even those who resist the purely psychoanalytical approach to the genre, have productively engaged with the concept of the uncanny as the return of the repressed.[59] In Mighall's discussion of the geography of the British Gothic novel, the uncanny is at work when geography and history merge, or rather history becomes displaced onto geography.

In British literature, the Gothic setting often represents an other that is a suppressed part of the self; a successfully overcome darkness of the bygone time displaced into a different geographical region. English Protestant travelers of the late eighteenth century tended to depict their visits to southern Catholic countries as a sort of time travel, a shocking discovery of still existing medieval barbarism and backwardness, from which they felt fortunate to have been liberated by the Reformation. To quote Mighall, "the past has often been referred to as a foreign country, but in [travel writing] and in the early Gothic novels, certain foreign countries become the past."[60] Moretti makes a similar point about historical novels, except that "journey into the past" is possible in the proximity of the internal borders: for example, by crossing into the Scottish Highlands in Walter Scott's *Waverley.*[61] In the texts of the Russian imperial Gothic (often indebted to the Walter Scottian historical novel as much as to the Gothic tradition proper), it is the colonized contiguous territories intimately connected to Russia's cultural mythology of origins and primordial authenticity that become loci of this return of the repressed, be it the ghost of glorious independent Ukraine revisiting its subdued provincial present or dark and irrational Finland confronting Russia's modernization. In my investigation of the Russian Gothic, I follow the classic British "North/South" axis, but this imaginative geography takes on a different significance in the specific context of the Russian Empire.

The Geography of the Russian Gothic and the Structure of This Book

The North/South opposition is inherent in the Gothic genre. The term "Gothic" was first associated with the northern barbaric tribe that sacked a sophisticated southern civilization, but it underwent an ironic reversal in the eighteenth century. Many early British Gothic novels—*The Castle of Otranto, The Mysteries of Udolpho, The Monk* (as well as a large part of the later *Melmoth the Wanderer*), to name just a few—are set in southern Catholic countries viewed as an epitome of medieval superstition and barbaric backwardness.[62] The opening of Lewis's *The Monk*, for example, immediately mentions its setting—Madrid, which is characterized as a city "where superstition reigns with a . . . despotic sway."[63] For the British Gothic, then, the South became a space into which the fears of the irrational, of the "dark" Catholic past and medieval barbaric cruelty were displaced. Although the Catholic versus Protestant opposition is hardly relevant to the Russian case, the general North/South paradigm has proven productive for my investigation of the Russian imperial Gothic.

Since Russian and Eastern European studies engaged with Edward Said's theory of Orientalism, much scholarly attention has been focused on the applicability of this theory to the region, as well as on the conceptualization of Russia's place and identity "between East and West" in its intellectual tradition.[64] Russia's self-positioning vis-à-vis North and South, by contrast, has been somewhat neglected, although several scholars have stressed the status of the Russian South (Crimea and the Caucasus) as an equivalent of the East in Romantic Orientalism.[65] Larry Wolff argues that the East/West division emerged during the Enlightenment era and replaced the hitherto dominant North/South geographical perspective.[66] Although the latter model still appeared in the eighteenth century as a rhetorical form, Wolff argues, it became increasingly anachronistic. However, the North/South axis preserved its significance for the imaginative geography of the Gothic genre and, in the case of Russia's self-identification with the North, it was more than a rhetorical form.[67] Russia's historical development and its colonial expansion in the eighteenth century as a result of the Great Northern War and Russo-Turkish campaigns contributed to the enduring relevance of the North/South paradigm at least into the Romantic period. Moreover, as Edith Clowes reminds us, the metaphorical North/South axis is critical to postcolonial thought, where the colonizing center is usually located in the north, sapping the resources from the southern periphery, relying on the old "civilization/barbarism" opposition.[68] The multivalence of this model, combining the geographical "memory" of the genre, the specifics of Russia's development as an empire, and postcolonial symbolic geography, makes it a productive lens for exploring the Gothic mode in its imperial context in this book.

Starting with the legendary medieval account of the "invitation of the Varangians" and well into Russia's modern imperial period marked by the construction of a new capital on the Gulf of Finland by Peter I, the North remained at the core of Russian state and imperial identity. In Petrine times, according to Otto Boele, the East held connotations of the old, regressive, and religious, leading to a reorientation toward the North, which connoted the new, European Russian identity.[69] Similarly, W. Gareth Jones points out that Catherine II embraced Gothic architecture and English gardens because of the Nordic association of the Gothic style. She wanted to send a message of Russia's cultural belonging to Northern Europe, with its characteristics of "uncorrupted strength, vitality and vigour," in opposition to the Ottoman Turkey she was fighting at the empire's southern limit.[70] The cultural self-identification with the North, both geographical and symbolic, can be observed in Karamzin's works from the late eighteenth century.

The narrator of his *Letters of a Russian Traveler*—an educated Russian nobleman visiting Western Europe during the early years of the French Revolution—constructs the image of Russia as a Northern civilization, an organic part of a larger community of nations that also includes Sweden, Denmark, and England.[71] Karamzin's pre-Romantic novella "Sierra Morena" (1793) concludes with the narrator returning to the "land of the melancholy North," after the grand passions and tragedies he experienced in southern Spain.[72] During the Romantic period, the association with the North becomes the foundation of Russia's unique national identity, not in the least under the influence of Montesquieu's climatological doctrine.[73] In his poem "To Ovid" ("K Ovidiiu," 1821), Aleksandr Pushkin, whose poetry typically contrasts his native North to the South of his exile, fashions his lyrical persona as a "severe Slav" (surovyi slavianin), in contrast to the Roman poet who had perceived the Moldavian landscape as Northern, harsh, and uninviting.[74] Lermontov's Pechorin, who in *A Hero of Our Time* travels from St. Petersburg to the Caucasus, identifies with the Northern imperial center: in Taman', as he observes the turbulent sea, its monotonous murmur reminds him of a big city's noise, and his memories take him back to "the North, to our cold capital."[75] The most influential literary critic of the period, Vissarion Belinsky developed an entire theory of the superiority of the northern races over the southern ones, identifying Russia with the former: "Its cradle was not Kyiv, but Novgorod."[76]

The competition between the two cities, northern Novgorod and southern Kyiv, as Russia's "cradles" goes back to the two key "tales of origin," found in the medieval *Primary Chronicle* (*Povest' vremennykh let*, 1113): the "calling" of the rulers from Scandinavia (the "invitation of the Varangians") in the ninth century and the adoption of Byzantine Christianity by Kievan Prince Vladimir in the tenth. As Richard Wortman points out, claiming descent from a foreign ruler acquired particular prestige in the Russian monarchs' "scenarios of power."[77] Foreignness, thus, lay at the core of the Russian foundation narratives, a feature that contributed to the uncanny quality of the regions I discuss.

According to *The Primary Chronicle*, in the ninth century Slavic and Finno-Ugric peoples in what is now northern Russia invited the "Varangian" prince Riurik and his brothers to rule over them and bring order to the chaotic land. Later historians have been divided as to what exact ethnicity the Varangians belonged to (various theories suggested Swedes, Finns, Prussians, or Slavs) and what the nature of that "invitation" was (an invasion, a usurpation or indeed a legal acceptance of the authority). However, the "Norman" theory of the provenance of the Russian state, as it became known, has proven influential and linked the origins of Russia's statehood to the Scandinavian world.[78] The Baltic provinces and Finland had become part of the Russian Empire as a result of the Russo-Swedish wars of the eighteenth and early nineteenth centuries. Still, in the Russian historical imagination Russia's ties to the region go back to the legendary early Middle Ages. The construction of St. Petersburg in the early eighteenth century on Finnish territory annexed from Sweden, moreover, inextricably ties the foundational myth of Russian modernity to Finland and Scandinavia—a connection explored in Odoevsky's *The Salamander* (1844). The Baltic territories acquired by Russia during the first quarter of the eighteenth century, for all their "German" feel, were reimagined, in the "Livonian tales" of the 1820s, as an integral part of Russian medieval history.[79] Even the supposedly foreign and exotic Danish island of Bornholm in Karamzin's novella (discussed in chapter 1) proves connected to the Slavic world. The island becomes a setting for imagining Russia's alternative history in the Gothic vein. The first part of the book thus focuses on the way the Baltic and Scandinavian North figures in the Russian Gothic, and what I find particularly important is that this region appears simultaneously as alien to and inextricably entwined with the Russian sense of selfhood. The interplay between the exoticism of these regions (as expressed, for example, in the Western medieval architecture of Baltic cities or the Finnish gloomy sublime landscape) and their supposed historical affinity with Russia transformed these territories—especially Finland—into a fertile ground for the Russian imperial uncanny.

Similar ambiguity applies to the South in the literature of the Russian imperial Gothic. In Russian Romantic literature, the South has been examined through the Orientalist lens with the focus on the exotic Caucasus and Crimea. However, my focus is primarily on a more problematic Southern other.[80] The South in this book is represented by Ukraine, often referred to in the nineteenth century as "Southern Rus'" and frequently presented in the literature as a Southern "double" of the Russian imperial self—or even directly as "primeval [*pervobytnaia*] Southern Russia."[81] Imperial Russia traced its origin to Kievan Rus', a medieval state with the center in Kiev (now Kyiv), the site of the introduction of Orthodox Christianity to Eastern Slavs in 988. Claiming historical and cultural continuity with Kievan Rus' was of great symbolic importance, given the prominent role Orthodox Christianity held for the Russian identity.[82] Between the decline of Kievan Rus' and the rise of Muscovy to prominence, Ukraine took a separate trajectory of development: it belonged to the Polish-Lithuanian Commonwealth, experienced significant Catholic influence, developed a separate language, and witnessed bloody Cossack independence wars and uprisings. When, after

a series of treaties and policies of integration, Ukraine was fully incorporated into the Russian Empire, it emerged as another uncanny presence—a
closely related Slavic nation with a supposedly shared historical and cultural
origin but its own political history, language, and distinct folk culture. As
many scholars point out, in the Romantic era Ukraine was both exotic,
almost foreign, and familiar; nearly self but undoubtedly other.[83] The blind
boy in Lermontov's "Taman'" represents this ambiguity as he switches to
Ukrainian to underscore his otherness and to build a barrier between his
world and the representative of the imperial authority (while speaking in
Russian with his fellow smugglers, as the protagonist discovers with surprise
and growing suspicion).

Many Romantic-era writers with personal ties to Ukraine, most promi-
nently Gogol, exploited both the Russian vogue for "Little Russia's" exoticism and Ukraine's own rich demonological folk tradition. What interests
me, however, is less the actual diabolic Gothic-fantastic tales set in Ukraine
than Ukraine itself as both Russia's uncanny double and a Gothic setting
haunted by its colonial history.[84] The writers included in the "Ukrainian" section of this book were intimately connected to Ukraine and acutely aware of
its distinct history and culture. Yet, they all took part in the Russian imperial
project in various capacities, as was typical of Russia's co-optive colonizing
practices. These writers produced poignant literary works that tried to cope
with this ambivalence, not in the least through employing Gothic tropes. To
an extent, then, this book is also about the Ukrainian (and "Little Russian")
Gothic as part of Russian imperial literature.[85] In that sense, this project is
somewhat asymmetrical: it does not give a similar voice to writers representing the northern imperial peripheries (Finland or Baltic regions).[86] Instead,
the Gothic North appears as it was perceived and constructed by Russian
cultural figures. But because Russian writers felt ambivalent about their status as imperial agents and their cultural belonging, parallels are manifested
between the works from the "Northern" and "Southern" sections of the
book where Gothic tropes are employed to address the complex problems of
cultural assimilation and modernization.

The Russian imperialist discourse exhibits remarkable consistency,
whether it invokes Russia's northern Baltic possessions or "Little Russia"/
Ukraine, even though some peculiarities remain. This discursive uniformity
is particularly curious given that Russian imperial policies differed substan-
tially in the two regions, with far greater autonomy granted to Baltic provinces and especially Finland, as opposed to Ukraine, where the prevailing
approach was that of integration and assimilation. However, symbolic strategies of "mental appropriation," to use Karsten Brüggemann's term, were

similar. When trying to justify continued Russian domination in ethnically non-Russian territories, "Russian intellectuals preferred to use historical and cultural arguments . . ., rather than explain autocratic power simply with reference to divine right."[87] Russia claimed (and still does, as the annexation of Crimea has shown) its right over certain territories by asserting the regions' "primordial" belonging to the Russian sphere; it ostensibly reclaimed what had "historically" already belonged to it, rather than conquered a new land. This tendency explains why the narratives of origins associated both with the Baltic North and Kievan Rus' are of such great importance for the formation of the Russian imperial uncanny. Geographical arguments of Russia's "manifest destiny"—for example, its expansion up to its "natural" border at the shore of the Baltic Sea—were also at work, although they seemed to be invoked more consistently with regard to Russia's expansion eastward.[88] The historical and geographical argumentation often took precedence over the more traditional *mission civilisatrice* doctrine, which would be harder to justify in the case of some Western possessions of the empire along its North-South axis, perceived as more "modern" and better educated than the Russian core. Nonetheless the Russian imperialist discourse appealed to the civilizational benefit of Russian rule, often by portraying Russia's rivals over these territories (Danes, Germans, Swedes, and Poles) as savage and cruel and by focusing on particularly "dark" periods of these regions' histories before their inclusion into the Russian Empire (the bloody Middle Ages in the Baltics, the "chaos" of the Ukrainian Cossack past, or, in Finland's extreme case, a lack of history altogether). Gothic tropes of medieval barbarity combined with the Romantic discourse of primitivism came in handy for this process of "mental appropriation" of the imperial North and South. No matter how impressively literate the Finnish population might have been or how much Western, Jesuit-style, education might have spread in Ukraine during its time as part of the Polish-Lithuanian Commonwealth, the dominant discourse neglected this factual and historical reality and constructed a "reality" of its own, mainly relying on the arsenal of the literary Gothic tradition. Attention to this alternative reality, the imaginative workings of the Russian Empire, can enrich and complicate the findings of purely historical studies of the same subject. The reconstruction of this discursive "reality" is one of the primary goals of this book.

Like any division, the North/South dichotomy I offer here is somewhat schematic and therefore open to criticism. By focusing on this paradigm I am not suggesting that it is necessarily more productive than the East/West one or that the two are mutually exclusive. Far from that: their configurations often intersect, as is evident from Boele's discussion of the eighteenth-century concept of the "North" arisen as an alternative to Russia's "Eastern" identity. The "North" and the "West" as standing for "Europe" could be used interchangeably at different points of Russian intellectual history: in fact, the Slavophiles (Mikhail Pogodin in particular) perceived the Varangians as "Western" rulers.[89]

The fruitful interaction between the two paradigms can be observed in literary examples: in Karamzin's "Russian traveler" fashioning himself as a "Northerner" but also as a "Scythian" in Western Europe; in the Orientalization of Serbs in Kulish's *Mikhailo Charnyshenko* set in Ukraine during the imperial northern campaign; or the anxiety over Westernization in Odoevsky's "Finnish" tale *The Salamander*. Much of the uncertainty in the Russian imperial and national identities that seeped through the Gothic tropes I explore stems from Russia's cultural dependence on the West. My favoring the North/South model does not dismiss the relevance of the East/West axis but rather seeks to restore some balance in our studies of Russia's imperial imagination.

I do not imply that the North/South axis is the exclusive setting for the imperial Gothic and uncanny, as if a literary work cannot depict an uncanny encounter or experience in the Eastern or Western borderlands of the empire, in deep Russian provinces, or within the center. There is an uncanny quality to Pugachev in Pushkin's *The Captain's Daughter* where the events mainly unfold on Russia's Eurasian frontier, as well as to the Gogolian provinces, while a number of Gothic-fantastic tales from the period are set in Moscow. The advantage of the North/South lens is that these settings powerfully invoke Russia's imperial legacy, while preserving a more immediate connection to the actual European Gothic literary tradition, reproducing its typical tropes and loci, such as medieval castles in Bestuzhev-Marlinsky's Livonian tales or ancestral home ruins depicted by Kulish. They are productive focal points for studying the intersection of the literary and political, Gothic and empire, which is the main goal of this book.

More important, both regions, the Baltic north and the Ukrainian south, are integral to the Russian narratives of selfhood, while preserving their disturbing otherness. The writer and literary critic Nikolai Polevoi perceived this otherness beneath the surface of integration, co-option, and Russification. In his 1830 review of Dmitrii Bantysh-Kamenskii's *History of Little Russia*, he describes the colonization of Ukraine and northern territories as follows:

We treated both the regions that were once Russian (the Dnieper area and Volyn') and the regions that had not been Russian before (the

Ostsee [Baltic] region, Lithuania, Finland, Little Russia) the way victors treat the lands they have conquered. We have *Russified* their aristocrats, we have little by little done away with their local autonomy, we have introduced our laws, our beliefs, we ourselves have mingled with their lower-class local populations, and yet we have failed to Russify the locals themselves, as we have failed to Russify Tartars, Buriats, and Samoyeds. They do not have their political individuality and cannot have it—and yet, again, they are *ours*, but they are not *us* (oni nashi, a ne my).[90]

Unlike some of his contemporaries, Polevoi does not claim most of these territories as originally Russian. Yet his formula "they are *ours*, but they are not *us*" betrays anxiety about the imperial possessions along the North-South axis, which I explore through an analysis of the Gothic mode in literary works.

The North/South paradigm functions in the book not as a dominant theme of each case I examine but as an imaginative mapping of the Russian Gothic viewed in its imperial context. From a practical point of view, the North/South axis has also proven useful as a criterion for my material selection and as an organizing principle of the book structure. The chapters are grouped into two parts, "The North" and "The South," each organized both chronologically and conceptually. The first two chapters focus on Gothic texts that, while not explicitly concerned with the empire, lay the foundation for the development of the imperial uncanny in later works. Chapter 1 examines the earliest and the most "classical" Gothic tale in Russian literature—Nikolai Karamzin's "The Island of Bornholm" (1793) where the Russian traveler, stranded on a mysterious Danish island, is surprised to learn that the island used to be populated by Slavs. The fictional traveler's investigation of the mysteries of the island (deriving from possible incest and the resulting punishment) becomes a journey back to the dark pagan origins of Russian history and a Gothic prelude to Karamzin's later historical project. Chapter 2 analyzes the Livonian tales of the 1820s penned by future Decembrists and set in medieval times in what would later become the Baltic provinces of the Russian Empire. This setting provided the Russian Romantics of a liberal political leaning with "access" to the European Middle Ages. It also allowed them to explore the bloody legacy of feudalism, which they were intent on fighting at home. Despite their subtle critique of contemporary Russia in these tales, the Decembrists' imperial imagination fully justifies the Russian expansion in the region by contrasting the Baltics' "dark" and "savage" medieval past to their benign present in the Russian Empire, by emphasizing historical ties between the then German-dominated Livonia and its East Slavic neighbors, and, in some cases, by reclaiming the Baltics as an originally "Russian" domain. Chapter 3 draws on a variety of sources, from ethnographic publications in contemporary journals to Romantic novellas and historical novels that construct the image of the "wild" but docile Gothic Finland that is finally included in history and civilization through its incorporation into the Russian Empire. Both ethnographic and literary texts depict the Finns as a magic-prone, semi-mythological people destined by both history and geography to be ruled by others and enthusiastically embracing the Russian civilizational mission. Odoevsky's Gothic novella *The Salamander* stands in stark contrast to these optimistic interpretations of the annexation of Finland. It offers a dark story of a failed conversion where "natural," intuitive and irrational Finland (embodied by the heroine Elsa) resists the mechanistic spirit of Petrine Russia and ultimately wreaks vengeance on the Russified Finnish hero.

Part II, "The South," opens with chapter 4, which introduces Ukraine as the quintessential locale of the Russian imperial uncanny. The topic of Ukraine in the Russian imperialist discourse and Gogol's complicated relationship to his Ukrainian and Russian "selves" have been sufficiently addressed in scholarship. Thus this chapter only outlines the major factors that contributed to the image of Gothic Ukraine in the Russian literary imagination as its uncanny double and briefly discusses Gogol's stories "The Night before Christmas" and "A Terrible Vengeance" (1832) as case studies. Chapter 5 examines Pogorel'sky's novel *The Convent Graduate* (1830–33), set in Ukraine. The novel mockingly plays with the clichés of the Gothic tradition to subtly point to the true threat—the "menace of mimicry," to use Bhabha's terminology. Ukrainian mimicry, ruthlessly satirized in the novel, exposes its very object, the Russian imperial self, as a simulacrum, and thus calls into question the Russian colonial strategy of assimilation. Chapter 6 gives voice to Ukraine by focusing on the Ukrainian writer and scholar Panteleimon Kulish's historical novel *Mikhailo Charnyshenko, or Little Russia Eighty Years Ago* published in Russian in 1843. I show that multiple Gothic tropes employed in the novel—from "medieval" ruins and towers to exotic demonic villains and supernatural phantoms—produce an intricate play of temporalities. Moreover, they create an ambivalent vision of the Ukrainian heroic past, as both an object of Romantic nostalgia and a dangerous period of chaos overcome by the country's incorporation into the Russian Empire. Kulish's extensive use of the Gothic mode, when analyzed closely, reveals his profound ambiguity about Ukraine's imperial present haunted by the ghosts of its autonomous heroic past.

The concluding section reflects on the contemporary moment, which has witnessed a revival of Russia's expansionist and imperial discourse. Ultimately, this book reconstructs a coherent tradition of the Russian imperial uncanny—a fictional space into which the Russian Empire projected its colonial fantasies and anxieties and where it created its monsters and doubles that continue to haunt the Russian historical imagination.

PART I

The North

CHAPTER 1

A Gothic Prelude

Nikolai Karamzin's "The Island of Bornholm"

My reconstruction of the Russian imperial uncanny begins in 1794, when Nikolai Karamzin, the Russian leading Sentimentalist writer, journalist, and future official historian, published an enigmatic Gothic tale, titled "The Island of Bornholm" ("Ostrov Borngol'm," 1793). In this story, the narrator, an educated Russian nobleman, recounts an episode that occurred as he was returning from England to Russia by sea, after an extensive voyage around Western Europe. During the ship's stop in Gravesend, the traveler encounters a ghost-like, emaciated young man who sings a melancholy song in Danish; the song mentions the Danish island of Bornholm and some illicit love that prompted the young man's exile from Denmark, a result of "a parental curse."[1] The narrator is deeply moved by the young Dane's lot and is intrigued by the secret to which the song alludes. As he continues his sea journey back to Russia, his ship makes a stop near that very island, described by the captain as "a dangerous place," because of its shoals and underwater rocks. Undeterred by these warnings, the Russian traveler sails to the island where his curiosity is rewarded: he is invited to spend the night at the castle and eventually discovers a young woman imprisoned in a cave. She turns out to be the young Dane's beloved mentioned in the song. From an old man, the castle's owner, the narrator learns the lovers' "horrible secret" (673), which is not revealed to the reader.[2]

This story is framed as the narrator's recollection, in the circle of close friends, of his past travels: "You know that I have traveled in foreign parts, far, far away from my fatherland, far from you, who are so dear to my heart; I have seen many marvelous things, have heard many astounding tales; I have told you a great deal, but I could not tell you all that happened to me" (661). By alluding to a journey reported previously to his friends, the narrator links himself to the quasi-autobiographical sentimental narrative persona of Karamzin's travelogue *Letters of a Russian Traveler*.[3] The *Letters* end with the traveler returning from England to Russia by boat, where he, quite appropriately, reads "Ossian" while the ship approaches Scandinavia; after a brief mention of the ship's stop near Copenhagen, the narrative fast-forwards to the traveler's arrival in Russia. Both the *Letters* and the story describe the narrator's seasickness with the waves "baptizing" him, literally and not just metaphorically, as he emphasizes in both cases. In a way, "The Island of Bornholm" fills a gap in the *Letters'* description of the traveler's journey home.

Karamzin's travelogue constitutes an essential background to his Gothic tale: the Russian traveler of the *Letters* repeatedly stresses Russia's "Northern" identity and, more generally, actively engages with a plethora of historical, political, philosophical, and cultural issues.[4] In "The Island of Bornholm," these issues are overshadowed by the story's Gothic paraphernalia—the dramatic cliffs, the dangerous stormy sea, the gloomy and terrifying castle, and an allusion to a horrible secret it harbors, possibly incest. As a result, some scholars saw its significance merely in introducing "the gothic manner" into Russian literature and considered it less interesting compared to Karamzin's later prose works.[5] By contrast, in one of the earliest in-depth analyses of "The Island of Bornholm," Vadim Vatsuro emphasized its philosophical aspect, particularly Karamzin's engagement with the philosophy of history in the aftermath of the French Revolution.[6] According to Vatsuro, the tale was not only an early Russian experiment in the Gothic genre but also "the first harbinger of budding historicism," anticipating the exploration of the role of history in shaping the human mind and behavior in the Russian literature of the 1820s and 1830s.[7] In this chapter, I explore a different aspect of this entwinement of the Gothic mode and historicity in "The Island of Bornholm." By focusing on the ambivalent representation of the story's eponymous setting as both foreign/Scandinavian and Slavic, as well as on the island's historical ties to Russia established in the text, I demonstrate that this early text of the Russian Gothic lays the foundation for the later development of the tradition of the imperial uncanny in Russian literature.

Although produced in a different literary and cultural atmosphere and dissimilar in terms of plot and style, in many respects Karamzin's story anticipates one of the key texts of the Russian imperial uncanny, Lermontov's "Taman'." "The Island of Bornholm" is also narrated in the first person, by a traveler who finds himself in an unknown, mysterious location marked by geographical liminality. His lodging also has bad repute with the local population: in "The Island of Bornholm," the local boy describes the castle to the traveler in these terms: "We don't go there. . . . And God knows what's going on there" (666). In each work, the narrator experiences nightmares and wakes up in the middle of the night; prompted by his curiosity, he leaves the house and encounters a mysterious woman. Both protagonists are trying to solve an enigma, and at the end of the work leave by boat.

At first glance, the two works' geographical settings could not be more different: Taman' (a "disgusting little town," in Pechorin's words) is a small Cossack settlement located on the frontier of the Russian Empire, whereas the majestic Danish island of Bornholm is a territory of a foreign state. However, in each case we observe a similar conflation of the categories of native and foreign (svoe and chuzhoe). In "Taman'," the seemingly familiar (the Russian town and its residents alternatively speaking Ukrainian and Russian) turns out to be confusing, unfamiliar, and threatening for the narrator, while in Karamzin's story we find an opposite mechanism at work: what is supposed to be foreign and exotic is unexpectedly revealed to have kinship with the traveler and the world he comes from. The uncanny effect in each work derives precisely from such ambiguity.

The narrator of "The Island of Bornholm" repeatedly underscores the distant and exotic nature of his journey, describing his travels to "foreign" / "other" lands, "far" from his home country (in fact, the word "far" is used thrice in one sentence). The island's inhabitants consistently address the Russian traveler as a "foreigner" (chuzhezemets, literally "the dweller of the other lands"), stressing thereby his otherness.[8] The established cultural and geographical distance, however, is dismantled throughout the story. The Russian traveler happens to be fluent in Danish. Upon hearing the melancholy song of the Danish lover in England, he understands every word and offers a poetic rendition of this song in Russian. He informs the readers that he had learned the language in Geneva from his Danish friend Dr NN (the readers of the *Letters of a Russian Traveler* will recognize Danish Doctor Gottfried Bekker whom the biographical Karamzin met during his travels and who frequently appears on the pages of Karamzin's travelogue).

The aura of danger associated with the island, too, dispels quickly. When the ship, carried by a strong wind, approaches the island, Bornholm presents a dreadful if sublime picture: "We could already see its fearsome rocks, from where the roiling streams hurled themselves, with roar and froth, into the depths of the sea. The island seemed inaccessible from all sides, enclosed from all sides by the hand of sublime nature; nothing but terror appeared on its gray cliffs. With horror I saw there an image of cold and silent eternity, an image of implacable death."[9] The wind soon quiets down, and despite the captain's warning about the hidden perils of travel to the island, the narrator's boat trip and his disembarkment are strikingly uneventful: "We sailed and safely landed in a small, peaceful bay" (665). The fishermen of Bornholm who greet him there, while "crude and wild people, . . . unfamiliar with the smile of a friendly greeting," turn out to be "not cunning or malicious" (665–66)—unlike the treacherous smugglers in Taman'. Thus, the element of danger and threat set up by the Gothic description of the island and its otherness is consistently undermined by the subtle twists of the narrative, even as its external Gothic trappings continue to evoke the horrors associated with this genre.[10]

The suspenseful atmosphere of the story builds up, as the local boy who accompanies the narrator to the castle trembles with unexplainable fear, implores him to turn back, and disappears as soon as the narrator enters the castle. A tall, silent man in black with a piercing gaze leads the visitor through "gloomy and empty" rooms of the crumbling castle to meet an old man, the castle's owner (667). As was the case with the arrival on the island

FIGURE 3.   Georg Emil Libert, *Landscape with the Ruins of Castle Hammershus, Bornholm*, date unknown (no later than 1908). Oil on canvas, 33 cm × 44 cm (13 in × 17.3 in). Private collection.

by boat, the effect of danger and dread the castle emanates is undone: far from a typical Gothic villain, the old man strikes a friendly if melancholy figure. He warmly greets his guest and engages him in a lengthy conversation about the European past and present. The encounter between the castle's owner and the curious traveler might feel somewhat anticlimactic, at least according to the Gothic genre expectations. Both thematically and stylistically it is more in line with Karamzin's *Letters of a Russian Traveler*, full of intellectual debates, than with the story about a mysterious castle, hiding some horrible secret. Let us take a closer look at this odd disruption of the Gothic flow of the narrative.[11]

In the beginning of the encounter, the old man addresses his visitor as a foreigner (chuzhezemets) but then immediately adopts the Enlightenment's universalist perspective: "Foreigner! I do not know you but you are a human being—in my dying heart a love for people is still alive—my house and my embrace are open to you" (667). The binary opposition, native/foreigner, established between the two interlocutors is undone by their common humanity, as well as by their shared discourse of the Enlightenment. When responding to the old man's inquiry about the situation in the contemporary world, the Russian traveler relies heavily on Enlightenment symbolism, even as he questions the triumph of this worldview: "The light of the sciences . . . is spreading more and more, but human blood still flows on the earth—the tears of the unfortunate are still shed—the name of virtue is praised while its essence is debated" (668). Both Vatsuro and Derek Offord read this exchange as reflecting a crisis in Karamzin's Enlightenment values prompted by the French Revolution. Such a crisis, they argued, is also echoed in the tale's Gothic plot, with its unresolved conflict between nature and law ("the laws condemn the object of my love," sings the young Dane in the story).[12]

The conversation, however, does not stop here and soon turns to a more specific historical subject. Once the traveler's nationality is mentioned, the old man seems to abandon his ahistorical universalism and delivers a monologue on the history of the island and its ties to the Slavic world. Characteristically, in this part of the conversation, the Enlightenment's "light of the sciences" is replaced by the medieval "light of Christianity":

> Upon learning that I was a Russian (rossiianin), he said, "We descend from the same people as you. The ancient inhabitants of Rügen and Bornholm islands were Slavs. But you were illuminated by the light of Christianity before us. While in your parts, magnificent temples dedicated to the one God were already rising to the clouds, we, in

the darkness of idolatry, offered bloody sacrifices to insensitive idols. You already celebrated the creator of the universe in solemn hymns, while we, blinded by error, praised the idols of myth in disharmonious songs."—The old man spoke to me about the history of the northern peoples, the events of antiquity and modern times, and spoke in such a way that I could not help but marvel at his intelligence, his knowledge, and even his eloquence. (668)

After that excursus, the narrative returns to its Gothic register and does not explicitly revisit the questions raised in this brief interlude.

Scholarly studies of "The Island of Bornholm" have paid scarce attention to this episode. Vatsuro interprets the figure of the old man as an embodiment, for Karamzin, of his era's erroneous concept of virtue, resulting in the "medieval barbarity" of the punishment he metes out. In this context, the scholar briefly mentions the "historical past looming over the inhabitants of Bornholm and Rügen," which reinforces the medieval associations of this character.[13] Offord offers the most detailed reading of the scene and suggests that, by asserting the superiority of the civilization of the Eastern Slavs, Karamzin separates Russia from the realm of Gothic horrors, represented by Bornholm, as well as from the social cataclysms of the late eighteenth century. "The Russians, a subtext of 'The Island of Bornholm' seems to tell us, are one of the northern peoples whose historical moment is approaching and who, even among the northern peoples themselves, enjoy pride of place by virtue of their spiritual heritage."[14]

I read this scene somewhat less optimistically, as focusing more on the dark past than the bright future and more on the uncanny relatedness of the Russians and the locals than their separation. The established exoticism of the mysterious foreign island and the cultural and ethnic distance between the visitor and its population is now undermined not only by their common humanity but also by their shared ethnic origin. Thus, on the way home, the Russian traveler is already "at home," as it were—if not in a literal, then in a historical sense. Therefore, by learning about the island's past and the secret it harbors, our traveler discovers something about his own culture's historical past.

An association between Russia and Bornholm also can be inferred from Karamzin's later curious reference to his story. In a letter to Empress Mariia Fedorovna dated August 16, 1815, he offers a joking "happy ending" to the tale:

[The young woman] suddenly saw the light and the Gravesend melancholic who threw himself into her embrace with the exclamation, "You're not my sister but my wife!" They exited the cave [and] became conjoined in a lawful marriage. The old master, admiring the now law-ful love of his daughter and son-in-law, gives balls and himself dances a polonaise, while the dark cave, where the pale and languid beauty used to be imprisoned, is being prepared for yellow and fat Napoleon, should a storm strand him on Bornholm. This is the report I got from Denmark.[15]

Despite its mocking tone, this summary reinforces the relevance of history to the tale's Gothic plot. The joke refers to Napoleon's sea journey to his exile on St. Helena, which was in progress when the letter was written. The mention of the Gothic cave of the story, now potentially serving as a place of the defeated emperor's imprisonment, highlights the entwinement of the story's romantic plane and broader historical concerns. The reference to Napoleon's capture, moreover, indirectly invokes Russia's victory over the French army.

The text of the story, however, is more concerned with Russia's distant past. The Scandinavian setting of the work and the reference to early Slavic history in the conversation between the castle's owner and the visitor may allude to the famous "Norman" or "Varangian" theory of the origin of "Russian" statehood, which was passionately debated in eighteenth-century historiography and which Karamzin would canonize in his *History of the Russian State*.[16] The island of Rügen, mentioned by the old man along with Bornholm, was populated by Baltic Slavs in the early Middle Ages.[17] The eighteenth-century poet and theorist Vasilii Trediakovskii, in his tract *Three Discourses on Three Principal Russian Antiquities* (*Tri rassuzhdeniia o trekh glavneishikh drevnostiakh rossiiskikh* [1755]), claimed that the Varangians were Baltic Slavs ("*rugii*") and that the legendary prince Riurik, the founder of the ruling dynasty in ancient Rus', came from Rügen and thus was of Slavic origin.[18] In the first volume of his *History of the Russian State* (*Istoriia gosudarstva Rossiiskogo*, 1816–29), Karamzin concludes, by contrast, that the Varangians mentioned in the East Slavic medieval chronicles are Scandinavians, most specifically the Swedes.[19] Although he does not include direct ruminations on the provenance of the Russian ruling dynasty in his Gothic story, it can be argued that his ambivalent portrayal of the Danish island off the Swedish shore in uncanny terms, as both Scandinavian and Slavic, dangerous and tame, reflects contemporary anxieties over Russia's uncertain origins—the anxieties explored, albeit in a different context, in Vladimir Odoevsky's "Finnish" Gothic novella *The Salamander*.

The entwinement of history with the Gothic plot in "The Island of Bornholm" is enacted in the description of the narrator's nocturnal experience, immediately following his conversation with the old man. The Russian traveler spends the night in a room surrounded by "ancient" armor on the walls, which conjures up in his imagination "the past times," the history witnessed by this "ancient" castle. At the final moment of his wakefulness he has a vision of the melancholy "Gravesend stranger," and then he drifts off to sleep. In his consciousness, then, a private story of illicit love merges with the ancient history of the island, a move facilitated by the polysemy of the Russian word *istoriia*, referring both to "story" and "history" (the word istoriia in both meanings recurs throughout the text). "Will I ever learn his story?" the narrator wonders after his encounter with the young Dane (665). "Perhaps you know my story, but if you do not know it, then don't ask me," exclaims the young woman locked up in a dungeon (671). The old owner of the castle, as I already mentioned, talked to the narrator "about the history of the northern people" and at the end tells him "a most horrible story," which revealed the melancholy Dane's "terrible secret" (673). Significantly, neither istoriia is reported to the reader—the ancient history of the northern peoples remains untold, as does the story of the unfortunate lovers.

The narrator's dream also conflates story and history. In this nightmare, the suits of armor hanging on the wall come to life as knights who surround the traveler with their bare swords: "How did you dare land on our island? . . . How did you dare enter the terrible sanctuary of this castle? . . . Insolent man! Die for this pernicious curiosity!" (669). In the earlier scenes of the work, the narrator insists on stepping his foot on the island, despite the captain's advice, and he enters the castle, ignoring the local boy's warnings. Moreover, while before he seemed driven only by his obsession with the mystery of the young Dane and his unfortunate love, his dream reveals another dimension of his transgressive desire—his pursuit of history in a broader sense. The knights from his nightmare, the figures from the castle's medieval past, who are threatening to punish him for crossing boundaries, seem to guard an ancient secret rather than merely a late eighteenth-century romantic transgression. The mysterious Gothic atmosphere of the island has to do not only with the horrible family secret but also with the island's historical past. It is indicative that when, upon awakening, the traveler enters a dark alley (which will eventually lead him to the dungeon where the young woman is imprisoned, that is, closer to the revelation of the family secret), he begins to think about the pagan history of the island: "A thought about druids arose in my soul—and it appeared to me that I was approaching that sanctuary where all the mysteries and horrors of their worship were preserved" (669). In other words, as the narrator comes closer to the revelation of the young Dane's secret, he moves further back in history, from the "terrible sanctuary" of the medieval castle to the sanctuary of ancient druid rituals and from one horrible "mystery" to another.

The story of transgressive love can be read as an external manifestation of the work's subplot—the dark history of the island which, according to the old man, is part of the history of the ancient Slavs.[20] The narrator's encounter with the horrors of Bornholm, in their various historical incarnations—pagan, medieval, and contemporary—functions as his confrontation with Russia's alternative history. This history turns out to be too terrifying, and the Karamzinian narrator, while narrowing the distance between him and the inhabitants of Bornholm and while crossing further into its space and time, also reestablishes the divide and eventually leaves the island for his true homeland.[21] In the end, the ancient Slavs of Bornholm and Rügen, who dwelt in the "darkness of idolatry," are presented more as dark twins of the Eastern Slavs than as their historical brothers.

The word *istoriia* appears twice toward the end of the tale. As we recall, the old man tells the traveler "a most terrible story—a story, which you will not hear now, my friends," the narrator stresses; "it will remain to be told some other time" (673). The readers do not find out what exactly happened to the inhabitants of the mysterious castle on the island of Bornholm, but Karamzin fulfills his promise to tell another story—*The History of the Russian State (Istoriia gosudarstva Rossiiskogo)*, his monumental study of the Russian past from antiquity to the early seventeenth-century "Time of Troubles." In light of Karamzin's future historical endeavors, "The Island of Bornholm" can be read as his earlier metaphorical journey, represented in a Gothic mode, to the origins of Russian history. The work's uncanny setting—the Danish/or Slavic island, simultaneously exotic and familiar, distant and closely related, threatening and hospitable—creates an atmosphere of disturbing ambiguity and uncertainty, which also marks the semi-mythological "beginning" of Russian history.

"The Island of Bornholm" remained an isolated phenomenon in late eighteenth-century Russian literature, unique for its complex fusing of Gothic tropes and historical concerns. Although not yet explicitly engaged with the imperial thematics, beyond the issue of uncertain origins, this text demonstrated the uncanny potential of the northern setting, as well as the relevance of seemingly distant Western medieval culture to vital questions of Russia's historical self-definition. These potentialities are developed in the Livonian tales of the 1820s, where the "budding historicism" of Karamzin's story moves to the foreground of Russia's cultural and political preoccupations and their literary explorations.

CHAPTER 2

In Search of the Russian Middle Ages

The Livonian Tales of the 1820s

If we have become so fond of all things Gothic; if, with such avid curiosity, we examine the monuments of feudal times and, listening to the legends completely alien to us, we forget our Russian antiquity, then do we really need to leave the borders of our fatherland to have that experience? We will find all of this not far from our parts: go to Livonia, to Estonia—there an admirer of the Scottish bard will quiver with delight upon seeing what a luxurious feast is offered to his gaze and imagination.[1]

This statement, belonging to the minor Romantic writer Aleksei Bochkov (1803–72), reflects the near-obsession with the Baltic provinces in Russian prose fiction and travel literature of the 1820s. This passage lays out the main reasons for this obsession: the Romantics' fascination with the Middle Ages imagined as an era of grand passions, heroism, and national specificity; the rise of the Walter Scottian historical novel, which overlapped with the still influential Gothic literary tradition (the "Gothic" in this quote most likely refers to the Western European Middle Ages but also implies the literary Gothic); and the accessibility of this medieval Europe within the borders of the Russian Empire. It is this last factor that made Livonia, with its Gothic castles and history of knightly tournaments and heroic battles, more than just a popular setting for Russian Romantic writers. Its ambivalent position as part of Russia's imperial present but with a distinct medieval past and at the same time with a long history of contacts with East Slavic territories contributed to the "Livonian theme" becoming a critical stage in the development of the tradition of the imperial uncanny in Russian literature.

The term "Livonia" was a Latinized form of the name the Germans gave to the Baltic settlements of the Finno-Ugric tribe of Livs. Later, it was expanded to refer to the area corresponding roughly to modern-day Latvia and Estonia.[2] Its early history is marked by close contacts with both Vikings and Slavs who tried to take control over the eastern Baltic coast; the region held strategic importance as a key trade transit between medieval Rus', Byzantium, and Scandinavia. The late 1100s marked the beginning of the prevailing German influence in the region (although northern Estonia remained under Danish rule until the mid-fourteenth century). In the thirteenth century, German knights undertook crusades against the Baltic pagans, Christianized the local population, and eventually formed the Livonian order (an autonomous branch within the order of the Teutonic Knights) in these territories. The region was ruled by German nobility and clergy who left a lasting influence, having built medieval castles, manors, and cathedrals, with German serving as the language of the elites. The dissolution of the order in the sixteenth century did not end the dominance of the Baltic German clergy and nobility, which introduced Lutheranism in the region, converted most of the Latvian and Estonian peasants, and spread literacy among the lower classes, in stark contrast to the rest of the Russian Empire, with the notable exception of Finland.[3] Despite the shared religion, in the Baltic region "for nearly six centuries these two groups, a foreign upper crust . . . and a subjugated native peasantry . . ., coexisted with each other in what was essentially a colonial relationship."[4]

German rule in Livonia did not remain uncontested by surrounding powers, and this contestation manifested itself in the prolonged "Livonian Wars" of the sixteenth century. During these wars Muscovy, ruled by Ivan the Terrible, made significant territorial gains in Livonia only to lose them all as a result of a series of defeats against the joint forces of Sweden and the Polish-Lithuanian Commonwealth. The relatively brief period of Swedish control of the region was later fondly remembered by Estonians and Latvians as rather liberal and reform-minded, compared to more oppressive German and then Russian rule.[5]

It was not until Russia's victory in the Great Northern War (1700–1721) that the lands of the former Livonian order—by then Livland and Estland, two separate dominions of the Swedish crown—were incorporated into the Russian Empire.[6] Russian rulers, up to a certain point, tended to view the well-educated Baltic German nobility as a loyal and model subject of the empire and granted this elite group a significant degree of autonomy. The orderly and relatively modernized Baltic provinces, moreover, raised Russia's prestige, justifying its claim to the status of a "European empire." The region was viewed in the first half of the nineteenth century as "the most treasured possession of the Empire," "a balcony" for the emperor, from which he could observe the developments in Europe, and a valuable source of German Enlightenment.[7] This benevolent view of the Baltic otherness will change dramatically over the course of the century, with the rising nationalism in Russian imperial policy and the fear provoked by the unification of Germany in 1871. This process will reach its peak under Alexander III, when Baltic Germans will be seen with increasing suspicion and distrust, and the government's attempts to Russify the region, both symbolically and legislatively, will intensify.[8]

Travel to Livonia: A Journey in Time

For the Romantic writers of the 1820s, the main appeal of the region had little to do with the idea of Enlightenment. By contrast, the Baltic possessions provided an opportunity for them to experience the European Middle Ages—a historical stage, which, they believed, Russia missed as a result of its isolation from the West. To quote Belinsky, "We, the Russians, who entered the arena of moral and spiritual development later than others, did not have a Middle Ages."[9] With the acquisition of the Baltic provinces, the European Middle Ages were now readily available—indeed, just "a quick trip away" from St. Petersburg.

In 1820, the Russian writer and future Decembrist Aleksandr Bestuzhev undertook such a trip, and a year later published his literary account of it. *A Journey to Revel* ("Poezdka v Revel'"—now Tallinn) enjoyed great success at the time and inaugurated the Livonian theme in Russian Romantic literature.[10] This travelogue did not merely introduce an attractive new setting and employ its Romantic potential; it articulated a thinly veiled ideological agenda, in which the author's political and humanistic concerns as a future Decembrist were entwined with his imperial vision of the region. In other words, Bestuzhev did not only "discover" Livonia for the Romantically inclined Russian audience but also reappropriated it as part of medieval "Russian" history, displaced it into the past and thus legitimized Russia's imperial rule over it.[11]

Written in the form of letters to friends that frequently evoked emotional distance, *A Journey to Revel* was influenced by Karamzin's Sentimentalist travelogue.[12] Karamzin's Gothic tale "The Island of Bornholm," framed as a stop on the Russian traveler's journey back home, also served as an essential background for Bestuzhev's travel narrative. Indeed, the entwinement of the Gothic mode and history—and, specifically, Russian history—is prominent in Bestuzhev's entire "Livonian corpus."[13] In *A Journey to Revel*, the narrator constantly seeks vestiges of the past historical events, which the ruins of medieval castles and the gloomy steeples of Gothic churches readily provide (or, if the ruins are absent, the originals could be easily imagined). The "no longer existent walls" of the town of Yamburg (now Kingisepp), for example, witnessed numerous attacks by the Teutonic knights and victories and losses of the Russians; the "half-ruined" castle of Wesenberg tells the story of the Novgorodians' and Pskovians' confrontations with Teutonic knights in the thirteenth century; the remains of a church near Maholm bring to mind Ivan III's battles with the Livonian order; and the ruins of castle Vegfeuer testify to the internal conflicts between the Livonian bishops and knights.[14]

Even though the narrator at times mocks the clichés of the supernatural Gothic (as when he describes the St. Brigitta convent and ironically observes that "a belatedly superstitious" person will certainly imagine ghosts that wander around its dungeons), Bestuzhev's crossing into and out of Estonia is marked by an unmistakably Gothic atmosphere.[15] This atmosphere pervades his description of the town of Narva, to which Karamzin referred in his travelogue as Russia's former border. Bestuzhev, too, stresses the town's liminal location, in addition to its Gothic characteristics. "Beyond Narva," he states, "Estonia begins": "The black towers of the castle loomed on the cliffs; here and there walls trampled by time hung over Narva, and, above the spires of the towers and Gothic churches, the darkness of night spread its wings."[16] When leaving Estonia, the traveler notes the "gigantic castles" Ivangorod and Vyshgorod, situated across from Narva, whose "darkened high walls and jagged towers . . ., rocks and cliffs hanging over the river, and all the Gothic antiquity of military architecture instill some gloomy and dejected feeling."[17]

Framed by these two descriptions almost literally as its border "checkpoints," Estonia emerges as a dark Gothic realm of the past. Although the narrator describes its present in idyllic, or even utopian, terms as a perfect, natural society, this positive picture is overshadowed by the travelogue's overarching focus on the region's gory history and its general medieval aura.[18] Revel strikes the narrator by its winding streets and Gothic irregularity, which he finds strangely attractive. The view of the city covered in snow arouses "Ossianic meditations" in the traveler and leads him to immerse himself in the past and forget the present.[19] What follows is a lengthy narrative of the city's history—as if Revel itself is a ruin invoking the past.

The interactions between Livonia and what would become Russia are the focus of this history—a relationship that culminates in Peter I's triumphant victory over Sweden and the incorporation of Livonia into the Russian Empire. In contrast to the cruelty of Danish crusaders and the despotic rule of the German knights, the Russian presence in the region almost invariably appears in a positive light (with the notable exceptions of Revel's resistance to

Ivan the Terrible, as well as the author's admiration for Wolter von Pletten-berg's leadership in Livonia).[20] Bestuzhev, for example, stresses the alliance between the Estonians and the Rus' tribes in their fight against the Teutonic knights, an alliance that existed in the thirteenth century.[21] Less historically objective is his portrayal of medieval Muscovy as an enlightened state where foreign poets and scholars thrive, in stark contrast to Livonia ruled by igno-rant and decadent knights. The Livonian order finally disappears in a truly Gothic way, "like a terrifying apparition," and ultimately Russian imperial rule, in this rather biased narrative, brings peace to this long-suffering land and the moral improvement of the once primitive and animalistic indige-nous population.[22] The author's tendency to reverse the prevailing Western view of medieval Muscovy as "savage" and "barbaric" and project it onto the medieval West can be explained as a compensatory mechanism, revealing Bestuzhev's anxiety about Russia's questionable "Westernness." Even more important, this strategy allows Bestuzhev to retrospectively justify Russian imperial rule over the Baltics in his own time.

In keeping with the tendency of the Russian imperialist discourse, Bestu-zhev's travelogue legitimizes Russia's (and Rus''s) claims over the region by stressing its original belonging to the East Slavic domain. In the travelogue's historical section, the appearance of the Danish crusaders in Livonia causes the following reaction among the Rus': "The Russians [sic]—who had con-sidered Livonia their own territory for a long time, had been sending hunt-ers there, had a fortress on the Dvina (Kukeinos), and collected tribute from its residents, from the German knights themselves . . .—were greatly sur-prised at the unexpected Danish domination." This passage preserves the dis-tance between the Russians and the traveler's position, whereas Bestuzhev's description of the Swedish control over Livonia, prior to the Great Northern War, is less ambiguous: "For a century and a half the Swedes controlled this ancient domain of Russia. Through Estonia, like through a gate, they invaded the heart of our fatherland, penetrated as far as beyond Novgorod and harvested with the sword what the Polish fire forgot to destroy."[23] In the concluding part of the historical excursus, the narrator, somewhat more carefully, discusses the city's history as intrinsically connected to that of Russia and elaborates on the Romantic appeal of its medieval heritage:

> Thus ends the memorable chronicle of the Estonian capital! It doubt-less deserves a place in the chronicles of our fatherland, for it had a significant impact on the destiny of [Russia's] northern regions; in addition, our [former] proximity to the Knights of the cross and the sword . . . endows the city with some special charm, some Romantic

character, perhaps insufficient for the mind but still rich for the imagination. These towers coddled by centuries, these loopholes in the wall overgrown by the moss of antiquity, these ruins of the knightly castles scattered around Revel—they unwittingly immerse one in meditation; the bygone ages rush by in fogs of recollection and with them, a melancholy anticipation of the future flickers in the soul.[24]

The passage above sums up not only the history of Revel as presented by Bestuzhev but also the dual status of Livonia. On the one hand, it is an imagined "other" space filled with romantic ruins and a past sunk in the "fogs of recollection"; on the other, it is a region directly involved in Russia's history because of its geographical proximity to the East Slavic north.

In addition to these Romantic, historical, and medieval associations, Livonia held particular political significance to Bestuzhev as an active member of the Secret Society of future Decembrists, whose goal was to transform Russia into a liberal state where autocracy and serfdom would be abolished. As some scholars point out, the Livonian theme in Russian literature is primarily explored by Decembrist writers, such as Nikolai Bestuzhev (Aleksandr's brother) and Vil'gel'm Kiukhel'beker.[25] There were at least two reasons for the Decembrists' intense interest in Livonia, beyond the general Romantic fascination. In 1816–19, the Russian government carried out a series of reforms in the Ostsee (Baltic) lands, granting local serfs personal freedom and courts but without the redistribution of land. The impetus for the reforms was Catherine II's trip to the provinces in 1764 when she was "appalled by Baltic landlords' 'despotic and cruel' treatment of their serfs," an impression that might have contributed to the vilifying of the Baltic Germanic nobility in the literature of the Livonian corpus.[26] The empress urged the Baltic landlords to improve the situation of their serfs, but little changed until Alexander I's rule. Despite the limited benefit of his emancipation effort in the region, the Decembrists viewed the reforms as a hopeful development to be extended to the rest of Russia.[27]

In *A Journey to Revel*, the traveler repeatedly praises Alexander I's reforms and comments on the significant improvement of the Estonian peasants' both physical and moral condition as a result of the "wise" Russian government's policies. Andreas Schönle notes that this optimistic picture did not correspond to historical reality (the change for the better that the Estonian population experienced in the early nineteenth century, for example, was not due to the limited reforms). Instead, he observes, "in magnifying the effect to which the emancipation act enhanced the peasants' living conditions, Bestuzhev was evidently striving to make the economic case for generalizing this policy to the rest of the Russian Empire."[28] Moreover, the intriguing gap in Bestuzhev's travelogue between the reign of Peter I (which concludes its historical section) and the highly idealized present conveniently excludes the more recent Russian imperial policy in Livonia, often detrimental to Livonia's low classes. As Schönle argues, such omissions and exaggerations may have stemmed from Bestuzhev's programmatic goals as a Decembrist and his desire to provide Alexander I with the model of enlightened governance. However, they also indisputably serve to justify Russian imperial rule as bringing enlightenment and overall improvement to the Estonian population, described, in typical colonial terms, as dirty, ignorant, animal-like, and even "black" (from tar).[29] Bestuzhev's sympathy for the subjugated Estonian peasants as a class seems to be at odds with his imperial perspective—a contradiction typical for the Decembrists more generally.[30]

Another reason for the specific Decembrist interest in Livonia was that it provided easy access to the horrors of the feudal past. Bestuzhev's travelogue frequently addresses the cruelty and lawlessness of Danish and German rule precisely as products of feudalism, and the tyrannical and bloodthirsty Livonian knight becomes a typical variation on the traditional Gothic villain figure in the Russian Livonian tales.[31] The themes of tyranny and lawlessness resonated powerfully with the Decembrists' political program. At the same time, the emphasis on Livonia's "dark" medieval past, facilitated by the deployment of a range of Gothic tropes, had an imperial agenda. The Gothicizing of the Baltics symbolically deprived the provinces of their Western modernity—the quality that made them such an attractive possession in the eyes of the Russian rulers and intellectuals. Instead, it is Russia that emerged in these narratives as a force of enlightenment and civilization that justifiably controlled the once unruly region—even as the same Russia is implicitly cautioned against slipping toward "savage" feudalism.

Toward the end of *A Journey to Revel*, this paradox is laid bare, as the political and Gothic motifs merge in a particularly evocative way. After leaving the historical boundaries of Livonia, the traveler offers an emotional summary of the history of this land that "served as a boulevard to the northern peoples that strove to ransack Russia" and "left History a bloody memory."[32] The attacks by external invaders; the internal subjugation of the vassals and the torturing of the peasants by the knights; the fires of incessant wars, the bloody tears of the population, plague and famine—all these "horrors," the traveler claims, are now over. "The castles that had burdened the land no longer exist; *feudalism lies under their ruins*; peace brings Estonia to life, and she is slowly gathering her powers exhausted by seven centuries of hardships."[33] The presence of the Gothic ruins challenges the finality of this statement.

Evoking the past within the present and possessing "a sort of half-life, the power to inspire and frighten," to quote Peter Fritzsche, the ruins undermine this idea of the dreadful past irrevocably gone.[34] The violence and chaos of the past seep into the seemingly benign imperial present.

In Bestuzhev's travelogue, then, the Gothic horrors are not the ghosts wandering the dungeons of an abbey but the bloody history of the region that continues to haunt the Russian present (recall his comparison of the Livonian order to a "terrifying apparition [*groznoe prividenie*]"). *A Journey to Revel* masterfully conflated the Gothic mode with historical narrative, affirmed Russian imperial rule in the region by appealing to its medieval history and established the region's relevance for Russia's self-exploration. By doing so, Bestuzhev set the paradigm for the "Livonian Gothic" in Russian literature, which would be richly developed in the 1820s.

Fiction: The Decembrists' "Livonian Tales"

By the 1820s, the Livonian setting offered a Russian Romantic author a whole bouquet of resonant cultural associations and literary themes, from its northern "Ossianic" feel to the Gothic ruins of medieval castles and the stories of knightly tournaments, cruel tyrants, and bloody vengeance—stories readily available in German chronicles and French historical sources.[35] The Russian imperial conquest of Livonia allowed the writers to partake both in the Western Gothic tradition and the historical Middle Ages without leaving the comfort of home.[36] In the context of the Decembrists' ideology, moreover, the figure of the medieval tyrant could serve as an invective to the feudalist system that they were intent on fighting at home.

Nikolai Bestuzhev's novella "Hugo von Bracht" (Gugo fon Brakht, 1823), with a characteristic subtitle, "An Incident from the Fourteenth Century," makes ample use of Livonia's Gothic potential. The story opens with a dramatic description of a castle on the island of Werder, overlooking the green waters of the Gulf of Riga—a castle that has now turned into "a scourge of the land and the sea, a brigands' den," since its owner, Hugo von Bracht, a formerly noble and generous man, became a vindictive and bloodthirsty pirate.[37] Such a transformation was provoked by the following: during von Bracht's pilgrimage to Palestine, his neighbor knight von Keller tried to seduce von Bracht's wife Ildegerda; after Ildegerda rejected him, he falsely accused both von Bracht and her of heresy and sorcery. Ildegerda died a torturous death, her niece and the von Brachts' only son disappeared, and their original castle was destroyed. Upon his return, von Bracht brutally murders von Keller and takes over his castle, where he withdraws from any social contact, occupied only by his attacks on passing trade ships. In an ironic (and Gothic) twist of the plot, von Bracht's last victims are his son and niece whom, without recognizing them, he captures and executes by having them thrown into the sea. The morning after horrified Hugo realizes the identity of the young couple (by the jewelry and memorabilia stripped from them), he is found dead. His death is interpreted as the punishment at the hands of Providence.

In addition to the typical Gothic characteristics—the castle and the transgressions associated with it, the tortured Gothic villain, the suspenseful plot development, and the highly emotive and hyperbolic narrative style—the story has an incestuous motif. It appears first in the description of the feelings of von Bracht's son Heinrich (Genrikh) for his cousin Ida whom he, for a long time, believes to be his sister. After fleeing evil von Keller, the two children are adopted by a kind Danish nobleman and only later find out the truth about their past. "My love for my sister," says Heinrich von Bracht, "which secretly rebelled against our tie of kinship, was rewarded by Ida's hand." Even more shocking, after capturing the young couple, Hugo von Bracht chooses Ida as his spoils, and the narrative repeatedly suggests the possibility of him dishonoring her. The reference to Heinrich and Ida as the villain's "misfortunate children" reinforces the incestuous implication of this plot development.[38]

N. Bestuzhev is faithful to the Gothic portrayal of medieval Europe as a realm of darkness, barbarity, and prejudice—this is why von Keller succeeds in condemning the von Brachts with the help of the "Secret Courts" (Vehmgericht, a German variety of Inquisition). The Estonia that appears in "Hugo von Bracht" is decidedly "savage" and dark, plunged in the chaos of internal divisions within the order, skirmishes and plunder, a place where no human compassion can be found and where "force replaces the law" (the recurrent theme of lawlessness is a Decembrist concern).[39] Interestingly and consistent with the Livonian theme in this period, the rule of the Christian German knights fails to civilize this land: "Subjugated by the Germans, Estonia, while losing its freedom, did not abandon its savage condition."[40]

Unlike other fellow Decembrists who wrote on the Livonian theme—his brother Aleksandr Bestuzhev and Vil'gel'm Kiukhel'beker—Nikolai Bestuzhev does not inject commentaries on Russian rule or Russian contacts with Livonia. However, a reference to the Estonian present appears in the final section of the novella:

Centuries passed. Estonia changed its appearance. The earth soaked in blood is buried under waves of yellow wheat. Only the ruins of the Sondenburg castle, like a mark of Cain (pechat' otverzheniia), in the midst of blossoming nature, scream their terrible tale with a voice that will not be silenced. Where the storm cast the bodies of the spouses thrown into the sea, there now stands a hotel for pilgrims and the poor. On Bracht's burial mound, on the elevated windmill, heavy grindstones are turning incessantly over the heart of an unfortunate father, a hardened villain, a terror of humankind![41]

This description alludes to the peaceful and humane present in contrast to the cruel and bloodthirsty past; however, this veneer of civilization appears superficial. Underneath the field of wheat, the earth is soaked with blood, the ruins of the castle serve as a silent witness to the transgression of the past, and the triple invocation of the Gothic villain at the very end of the text asserts his symbolic presence. The archaic style of this passage, replete with Old Church Slavonicisms, along with the symbol of the windmill's rotation imparts a metaphysical and atemporal quality to the novella's conclusion. The ruins of a Gothic castle, not unlike in A. Bestuzhev's "Journey to Revel," challenge the linearity of history and invite the reader to investigate the present through the remnants of a past that does not entirely go away.

In the same year, 1823, Nikolai Bestuzhev's younger brother Aleksandr published his first Livonian tale, "The Castle of Wenden," to be followed by others, which, together with *A Journey to Revel*, made him the most prolific and influential writer on the Livonian theme of the decade. "The Castle of Wenden," written in 1821, reads almost like an episode from A. Bestuzhev's travelogue: the narrator is also an autobiographical figure, a Russian officer stationed in Livonia, fascinated by the medieval castles of the land and the bloody history they invoke. This bloody history seems to follow directly from the violent conquest of Livonia described in unmistakably colonial terms: "The knights, when conquering Livonia and subjugating the savages, had invented everything that afterwards the Spaniards repeated in the New World, to the torment of unarmed humankind . . .; the blood of the innocent flowed under the sword of the warriors and the whips of the masters."[42]

The story, set in the thirteenth century, focuses on the first owner of Wenden, the Master of the Livonian Brothers of the Sword Vinno (Wenno) von Rohrbach, whose despotic rule is challenged by another knight, Vigbert von Serrat. In these "barbarous, unenlightened times" (42), as the narrator comments in a footnote, every offence was resolved by force: insulted by the Master, von Serrat, mistaken for a ghost, penetrates the walls of the castle at night and strangles von Rohrbach. "The Master was no more but his power remained, and the law-usurping murderer, tormented by tortures, died on the wheel" (45). The image of the wheel, not unlike the windmill in N. Bestuzhev's novella, here suggests the timeless quality of the German knight's feudal power, a cycle of violence that perpetuates itself, starting with the bloody conquest of Livonia by the crusaders. As in many scenes from *Journey to Revel* and N. Bestuzhev's "Hugo von Bracht," the rule of the Teutonic/Livonian order in the "wild" region does not bring the benefits of European civilization; instead, it is described as inhumane, barbarous, despotic, and lawless. The cruelty, barbarism, and arrogance of German knights are often contrasted, in A. Bestuzhev's Livonian tales, to the bravery and nobleness of the Russians whose sense of honor is not "[written] on their blazons," but in their hearts (73). Most of these texts stress Livonia's contacts with the East Slavic territories, primarily Novgorod and Pskov, and feature Russian characters.[43] The threat of Russian attacks and the rumors about the Muscovites' cruelty, for example, hover in the background of his novella "The Tournament in Revel" ("Revel'skii turnir," 1825); at the end of the Gothic tale "The Castle of Eisen" ("Zamok Eizen," 1825–27), the Russians appear as the tool of ultimate historical justice.[44] As Isakov points out, Bestuzhev introduces Russians into his tales to "claim" their participation in the "knightly Middle Ages" (rytsarskoe srednevekov'e), so coveted by the Romantics.[45] I assert that the claim was also territorial and imperial. A case in point is Bestuzhev's novella "The Castle Neuhausen" ("Zamok Neigauzen," 1824)—a work that exhibits a particularly close connection to the Gothic literary tradition and in which Russian characters play a central role.[46]

The historical castle Neuhausen, as the narrator reminds us at the end of the story, was erected in the thirteenth century on the eastern boundary between Livonia and the Pskov region, and Bestuzhev uses its location to bring Russians and Livonians into close contact, both familial and hostile.[47] The castle's founder and owner, Evald von Nordek, develops a friendship with his Novgorodian captive Vseslav but then turns against him after another knight, Romuald von Mey, convinces von Nordek that his wife Emma and Vseslav are lovers (in fact, von Mey himself is in love with Emma). With his evil scheming, his "maliciously sparkling eyes, like those of a wolf at the sight of his prey," his readiness (if rhetorical) to make a pact with devil, and his "maliciously joyful" expression, von Mey exhibits traditional characteristics of a Gothic villain (70, 75, 80).[48] Nordek falls into von Mey's trap, lamenting his trust for the "Russian barbarian," confronts Vseslav, and a duel is set between the former friends. However, before the duel Nordek disappears, imprisoned by the Secret Court—a result of Mey's intrigues.[49] Emma is captured and taken on a boat to von Mey.

Vseslav manages to flee and joins a group of Novgorodian merchants led by his brother Andrei. Vseslav's encounter with the Novgorodians is interesting because of the identity confusion it entails—a confusion made possible by the novella's liminal setting. Despite Vseslav speaking Russian to the merchants, they mistake him for a Livonian knight because of his armor. They are reluctant to believe that he is their compatriot until Andrei recognizes him. When he addresses them as zemliaki (compatriots, from zemlia, land or earth), the Novgorodians rudely respond that all people are zemliaki (made from the earth). Besides being a clever pun (Bestuzhev's dialogues tend to be rather witty), this linguistic play also suggests an obliteration of state and ethnic boundaries, a theme that will reemerge at the end of the story.

The Novgorodian merchants, led by Vseslav and his brother Andrei, succeed in rescuing both von Nordek and his wife Emma—who turns out to be Vseslav and Andrei's sister Marfa, kidnapped as a child during one of the Livonian raids. This explains the tender feelings Vseslav and Emma had developed for each other and which jealous von Mey mistook for a romantic attraction (another echo of the incest motif). Von Mey suffers a gruesome death, thrown from a tower window onto the paling of the walls.[50]

The novella's conclusion consists of two parts that differ in terms of both style and their temporal settings. First, in an elevated tone, the narrator addresses his "young, fortunate" characters who have now forged new family ties and recreated those of friendship: "Rush to the coast, the young, fortunate ones! There friendship will greet you and under its shield will guide you to the motherland. Rush on! In Neuhausen joy and celebration await you; and in Novgorod, the hospitality and welcome of rediscovered parents wait for you" (92). It is not clear, however, to which motherland (rodina) this passage refers—von Nordek's (and Emma's, by affiliation) Livonian castle or Vseslav, Andrei, and Emma's northern Russian lands. The border between Livonia and Russia, Neuhausen and Novgorod (both places containing the root "new" in their names) is thus obliterated, and the horrors of Livonia's medieval past are diluted in the joy of the newly discovered kinship.

The immediacy and open-endedness of this passage, with its second-person address and the future tense, contrast to the second part of the ending that establishes a historical and emotional distance between the narrator and the story. Here Bestuzhev introduces the melancholy gaze of a nineteenth-century visitor to the ruins of the medieval castle, once full of life and action.[51] The juxtaposition of the two temporal perspectives makes the ending of the story ambiguous: "The traditional Bestuzhev plot ends happily enough with the family restored to its prenarrative integrity, but the mutability of life and the inevitability of death enter the text from the narrator's temporal frame. He describes the ruined castle as it appears to him in the nineteenth century— harmless and peaceful, rather than the locus of a life-and-death struggle. The past cannot be recaptured from the debris even through the agency of fiction and its fantasies."[52] I would argue that the whole novella recaptured the dramatic and bloody past from the ruins, which problematized the peaceful picture of the present. The description refers to the castle's location and its political significance, made irrelevant by the passage of time: "This castle, which had been built by Walter von Nordek in 1277 and had stepped with its heel on the Russian border, once served as a proof of the [Livonian] Order's might; now it serves as a proof of the power of time" (92). The border that was symbolically and rhetorically blurred within the narrative plot, thanks to the familial ties between the Russians and Livonians, is actually obliterated in the narrator's contemporaneous time frame, as a result of the Russian conquest of Livonia.

While exploring Livonia's Gothic potential as a repository of the bloody feudal past and at times using it as a cautionary case for the Russian present, the Bestuzhev brothers stop short of turning it into a full-fledged site of the imperial uncanny. Aleksandr Bestuzhev destabilizes the idea of Livonia as an autonomous political and geographical formation by focusing on the Russian presence and the fluidity of borders; yet this region still seems too exotic to be perceived as "their own." This "privilege" will be reserved to Finland in the 1830s and 1840s, when the narratives of conversion in the Gothic mode will come to the fore and the imperial conquest of Finland will become incorporated into the explorations of Russia's problematic identity. But before that happens, an important transitional work was penned by yet another Decembrist writer in the 1820s.

Vil'gel'm Kiukhel'beker, a friend of Pushkin and another Decembrist, was born into a Baltic German family and spent his childhood in Estonia. His story "Ado: An Estonian Tale" (1824) is written in his characteristic archaic and elevated style, with substantial use of local ethnographic terms and toponyms.[53] Unlike the brothers Bestuzhev's Livonian tales, "Ado" focuses on pagan Estonians who are resisting the tyrannical rule of the German crusaders. Fleeing the despotic knight Ubald's persecution, the story's titular character, the gloomy and terrible (strashnyi) Ado, and his daughter Maia retreat into the woods. There they are temporarily protected, thanks to the Germans' and Latvians' superstitious fear of Estonian sorcery and contacts with the supernatural (a reputation shared by Finns, Lapps, and Estonians).

Eventually, Ado and other pagan leaders decide to resist the Germans and send Maia's fiancé Nor to Novgorod for military support. The Russian-Estonian historical ties are repeatedly stressed in the novella and include their trade connections, the protection the Rus' princes had traditionally offered to the Chud' tribes, the latter's "admitted dependence on Russia" and, most important, the "ties of friendship" between the two peoples that go back to "pre-Riurik times" and are reinforced by the etymology of *"veny"* (the Estonian term for Russians), meaning "brothers."[54]

When in Novgorod, "the simple son of nature" lives in the house of the Novgorodian merchant Derzhikrai, whose virtues Nor greatly admires.[55] After witnessing the Orthodox service in the St. Sophia cathedral, the young Estonian is impressed by the spirituality and the elevated atmosphere of the ritual and decides to convert to Christianity. The political developments are not in his favor, as the Novgorodian prince cannot come to Estonia's rescue, Nor, now baptized as Yurii, finds solace in his new faith. In the meantime, events in Estonia take a tragic turn: Ubald discovers the identity of the "sorcerer," brutally executes other rebellious leaders, imprisons Ado to put him to a particularly painful death and, struck by Maia's beauty, takes her to his castle. Maia manages to flee and dressed as a young man, finds Yurii in Novgorod.

On Derzhikrai's advice, Yurii and Maia seek help from an Uralic Mordovian tribe, appealing primarily to the linguistic and ethnic commonality between them and the Estonians. The Mordovian attack on Ubald's castle takes place in a decidedly Gothic atmosphere: as Ubald is about to enjoy a bard's singing, the sun begins to set, the wind starts howling in the chimneys of the castle, the light penetrating through the windows turns into a pale flickering, and the portraits of Ubald's ancestors and the armor on the wall seem to come to life in the darkness; no wonder that "some inadvertent fear crept into everybody's heart." The bard sings a song about punishment, a string on his harp breaks, and at this dramatic moment the "savage" throng of the Mordovians breaks in, along with the Estonian rebels, the "terrifying Ado" among them.[56] The bloodthirsty Mordovians and the vindictive Ado are keen on murdering Ubald and his entourage, but Yurii insists on mercy, in keeping with the tenets of his new faith. Eventually Ado, Maia, and Yurii move to Novgorod, where Maia converts to Christianity and, under the new name of Mariia, marries Yurii.

Unlike A. Bestuzhev's happy endings, the finale of Kiukhel'beker's tale is rather dark, despite the three Estonian protagonists' conversion from paganism to Orthodox Christianity—a process associated here with their cultural and spiritual convergence with the Russians, if not a full ethnic conversion.[57] Yurii falls fighting the Germans for Estonia's liberation in the army of prince Iaroslav Vsevolodovich; after his death, Ado converts to Christianity and under the new name of Adam, becomes a monk; Mariia dies in childbirth. Still, the transition of Ado (whose name is evocative of "the inferno," *ad* in Russian) to Adam suggests a relatively satisfying ending.[58] Russian Orthodoxy, with its spirituality and mercifulness, is juxtaposed, in Kiukhel'beker's story, to Estonian and particularly Mordovian bloodthirsty paganism, on the one hand, and to the savagery of Western Christianity represented by the German conquerors, on the other. The element of religious conversion is mainly absent from the Gothic tales of assimilation in the Finnish context, for which nonetheless "Ado" set the stage. The motif of a "simple son of nature" traveling to Russia/Rus', embracing its values, learning the Russian language and Russifying his name, would reemerge in the Russian "Finnish" Gothic in a new imperial framework.

The Livonian theme in Russian literature is not limited to the period discussed in this chapter; it will reappear in the 1830s, in one of the early Russian historical novels, Ivan Lazhechnikov's *The Last Novik, or the Conquest of Livonia during the Reign of Peter the Great* (*Poslednii Novik, ili Zavoevanie Lifliandii v tsarstvovanie Petra Velikogo*, 1831–33). However, the Decembrists' Livonian tales of the 1820s were key for both appropriating this setting for Russian literature and reclaiming the Baltic territories for the Russian Empire. These works did not merely discover and exploit a novel and exotic "medieval" locale, reflecting the typical Romantic fascination with Middle Ages more generally and with Gothic aesthetics in particular. Instead, they inscribed this popular theme into a specifically Russian imperial context, even as they focused on the region's medieval past. This "dark" feudal past is invariably integrated into the present in these texts, both as a warning about the potential excesses of Russian autocracy and as a legitimization of the Russian expansion into the region.

In the Livonian tales, the imperial context remains in the works' subtext, alluded to through the imagery of Gothic ruins, the elegiac gaze of a Russian traveler, or the blood of the past hidden under the veneer of the supposedly enlightened present. By contrast, in the texts exploring Gothic Finland, the empire unapologetically comes to the foreground. It is the explicit incorporation of Gothicized conversion narratives into the framework of Russia's annexation of Finland that separates the works of the 1840s (analyzed in the next chapter) from the Decembrists' Livonian corpus, and especially Kiukhel'beker's "Estonian tale." Unlike the "Livonian Gothic" in Russian

Romantic literature, deeply embedded in history, Gothic Finland will emerge as markedly ahistorical, and the wild natural Finn will prove to be a favorite (but also at times problematic) object of the Russian civilizational mission. Finally, the Finnic/Chud' ethnic proximity to East Slavs, in addition to the construction of the new Russian imperial capital on the "Finnish swamps," will contribute to the role of Finland as a literary setting for the Russian imperial uncanny to unfold.

CHAPTER 3

"Gloomy Finland" and Russian Gothic Tales of Assimilation

Finland occupied a peculiar position in the Russian historical imagination, even more so than the Baltic provinces. On the one hand, Finnic peoples had lived side by side with Eastern Slavs in the areas around and north of Novgorod, Pskov, as well as the Baltic region, Urals, and some others. Thus, they were often included in the Russian historical and literary foundational narratives, ranging from the medieval *Primary Chronicle* to Catherine II's drama *From the Life of Riurik*. On the other hand, they were frequently referred to as the "Chud'"—a term associated with the notion of foreignness and otherness because of its hypothetical etymological connection with *chuzhoi*, a stranger.[1]

Nineteenth-century Russian publications acknowledge a significant Finnish admixture to the Russian ethnicity, while underscoring the "civilizing" Slavic influence on the original Finnish population of contemporary Russia in the process of the formation of the "Great Russian" nationality. An 1845 article in *The Finnish Herald* (*Finskii vestnik*), titled "Chud' i Rus'," poses the question, "to what extent has the Chud', or Finnish, element entered the composition of our nationality?" The article concludes that the population of what eventually became Muscovy is not composed of pure Slavs but of an ethnic mixture of Slavs and the Chud' (the latter absorbed by the superior and more spiritual "Russians" but leaving their "Northern" imprint on their language and culture).[2] In 1847, an ethnographic report on the Baltic population stated that "the so-called Great-Russian variety (ottenok t. naz. Veliko-Rossiiskii) is . . . nothing else than the result of the penetration of the crude Chud' sphere by the edifying Russian element."[3] The same year, another article in *The Finnish Herald* celebrated the complete merging of the Finnish population "with a more independent and clever people, the Slavs; they entered their great family, got accustomed to their language and faith, and, granted citizenship rights, have become Russians."[4] Even when the Finns are recognized as the indigenous population of the "Russian North" and given a special status in connecting Asia and Eastern Europe, their role is still seen as subordinate to the future history of Slavs. The historical "idea" the Finns were "destined to express," according to the Hegelian scheme outlined by *The Finnish Herald*, was to tame the ferocious nature of Eastern Europe before moving further north: to dry its swamps, to cut down the forests, and to cultivate its "wild soil," in order to prepare it for "future generations, namely for the Slavic race (plemeni)."[5]

The Finno-Ugric peoples of the contemporary Russian Empire had long been part of the early history of Eastern Slavs and were perceived as mostly assimilated. However, Finland proper entered the Russian cultural imagination only after its gradual incorporation into the Russian Empire as a result of the Russian-Swedish wars of the eighteenth and early nineteenth centuries. After defeating Sweden in the Great Northern War, Russia, under the 1721 treaty of Nystad, acquired (in addition to Baltic dominions) southeastern Finland, including Ingria, part of Karelia, and some islands. Another slice of Finland, just west of the previous border, went to Russia in 1743 under the Peace of Turku during the reign of Elizabeth I. The Russo-Swedish conflict of 1808–9 resulted in Russia's occupation and annexation of the remaining Finnish territory. Alexander I granted this "New Finland" the status of autonomous Grand Duchy of Finland within the Russian Empire. In 1812, "Old Finland" (the territories acquired in the eighteenth century) was included into the Grand Duchy as well.[6] This autonomous formation preserved its laws, estate privileges, languages (Swedish and Finnish), and Lutheran religion until the 1880s when the Russian government turned to more oppressive and nationalist policies.[7] As was the case with the Baltics, the last decades of the Russian Empire witnessed the imperial government's increasing encroachment on the region's autonomy and attempts at (at least administrative) Russification.[8]

A Nation without History

When Peter I began the construction of St. Petersburg in occupied Ingria, Finland became an inextricable part of the foundational narrative of Russian modernity—the St. Petersburg text. As Otto Boele convincingly demonstrates, in this cultural myth Finns typically embody the realm of chaos and amorphous existence, preceding the cosmic act of creation carried out by Peter on the Finnish swamps. The poor Finnish fisherman epitomized by Pushkin's Finn in the famous opening of *The Bronze Horseman* (*Mednyi vsadnik*, 1833)—"the sad stepson of nature"—is a staple figure in this narrative.[9] Associated with water, the realm of chaos, and fighting inclement nature, the Finnish fisherman (and Finland, more generally) exists outside of history. Caught between Russia's and Sweden's military and political ambitions, the Finn remains a passive onlooker of the battle of the two Northern superpowers raging on his land—as in Lomonosov's portrayal of a battle of the 1741–43 Russo-Swedish War.[10] The Finn's simplicity, closeness to nature, and poverty often acquire idyllic overtones and were idealized in the Romantic period, as in Baratynsky's narrative poem *Eda* (1826).[11] As Boele concludes, in the literary representations of Finland in Russian Romantic literature, the Finns "live in a more or less timeless, pre-historical world where 'nothing really happens'" or happens because of an external, foreign influence.[12]

The Finns' submissiveness, poverty, and historical irrelevance would become commonplace in nineteenth-century historical and ethnographic texts. This perception was not new, however; it goes back to the first century BCE, to the Roman historian Tacitus's description of the Finns in his treatise *On the Origin and Situation of the Germanic Peoples*. In Russia, his characterization was popularized by Karamzin's *History of the Russian State*:

> This people, ancient and numerous, which used to occupy (and still does) such a great area in Europe and Asia, did not have a Historian, for it was never famous for its victories, never took away other people's land but always surrendered its own . . ., and in poverty alone sought its safety: "having (according to Tacitus) neither houses nor horses nor weapons; eating herbs, clothed in animal skins, and hiding from inclement weather under entwined branches." In Tacitus' description of ancient Finns we recognize those of today, especially the Lapps,

who inherited from their ancestors both their poverty, rough mores, and peaceful insouciance of ignorance.[13]

This reputation came in handy in the context of Russia's imperial rule over this well-educated population with long traditions of Western institutions. Iakov Grot, the professor of Russian at Helsingfors University, in his essay on Finnish folk poetry published in the widely read *The Contemporary* (*Sovremennik*) in 1840, also notes the Finns' historical passivity and their "insignificance (nichtozhestvo) in the political world." He explains it as the result of the Finns' introspective nature and their indifference to "everything external": "They have never sought might and power, have never been seduced by the conqueror's glory, have not accomplished great heroic feats, but instead they have withdrawn to themselves and with invariable loyalty submitted themselves to the rule of others. Amidst political changes, their passive (stradatel'nyi) character has remained untouched, and only in such a way could the Finnish nationality emerge intact from the bloody storms of its existence."[14]

Even such a seemingly positive characterization conveniently depicts the Finns as inherently predisposed to being an object of foreign rule and thus indirectly legitimizes Russia's imperial conquest of this land.[15] Another publication in *The Contemporary* from the 1840s adopts a more overtly imperial view, denying Finland any history of its own and reducing its history only to that "of the wars, and more generally, the political relationships between Russia and Sweden."[16] The stereotype of the Finns' lack of heroism and military ambition finds its way into a supposedly scientific publication of the Russian Geographical Society established in 1846. Academic K. M. Ber's article "On Ethnographic Studies in General and in Russia in Particular" refers to the Finns' inherent peacefulness as an example of enrichment through labor rather than through military aggression: "When lacking in military spirit, man seeks enrichment in intense labor; thus, for example, Finnish tribes, according to historical testimony and saga narratives, have practiced animal husbandry and agriculture since ancient times."[17] To cite Nathanaëlle Minard-Törmänen, "Finns as warriors simply did not seem to exist in early nineteenth-century Russian representations."[18] The scholar sees this discursive practice as part of a broader ideological agenda that presented the Russian Empire as "naturally" expanding into underdeveloped neighboring territories.

The myth of passive and submissive Finland was at odds with the historical reality of Russia's military engagement in that country (as well as with the portrayal of the local resistance by Finnish writers).[19] Finland' s occupation in 1808–9 tested Russian cultural presuppositions about this land. Prominent Russian poets, such as Denis Davydov and Konstantin Batiushkov, participated in this military campaign and had to confront both "real" Finland and their imperial mission there. Jacob Emery analyzes Batiushkov's "Excerpt from a Russian Officer's Letters about Finland" (1809), where the poet freely, if erroneously, projects Scandinavian and Celtic mythology, as well as Ossianic motifs, onto his image of Finland.[20] Emery comments on the irony of Batiushkov's position as simultaneously a Romantic poet invoking and identifying with fallen Viking warriors, who were defending their land, and a Russian officer who has invaded that land: "While the living Russian soldier-poet is busy figuratively identifying himself with his eulogized Scandinavian predecessors, Finland passes from the Swedish into the Russian Empire . . ., a regional shift of power that Batiushkov represents as an inheritance rather than an annexation."[21] By tracing the genealogy of Russian poetry to northern skalds in his Scandinavia-themed works and by obliterating boundaries between Russians and Scandinavians (including Finns) more generally—as ancient warriors, dead soldiers, invaders, defenders, and poets—Batiushkov "imagines the conquered territories to the North and West as proper to Russia itself."[22] Such a rhetorical and ideological move is possible because of the mythology of shared origin embedded in Russia's treatment of the North. The coverage of the war by the Russian press relied on the rhetoric of the "brother Finn" and invoked the "Finnish" version of the Varangian narrative, according to which Riurik was partly of Finnish origin. The conquest of Finland thus was presented as a legitimate return of Riurik's homeland to the Russian tsar.[23]

The unexpectedly fierce resistance by the local population, a veritable guerrilla war—reported, among others, by Denis Davydov and Faddei Bulgarin—shattered the image of the timid and passive "brother" Finn welcoming the Russian rule.[24] The publication of Baratynsky's *Eda* during the poet's lifetime did not include its political epilogue, which mentioned the Finns' hostility toward the Russians, as well as their fearless bloody struggle against the invader:

Ty pokorilsia, krai granitnyi,
Rossii moch' izvedal ty,
I ne stolknesh' ee piaty,
Khot' dyshish' k nei vrazhdoiu skrytnoi!
Srok plena vechnogo nastal,
No slava padshemu narodu!

Besstrashno on oboronial
Ugriumykh skal svoikh svobodu.
Iz-za utesistykh gromad
Na nas letel svintsovyi grad;
Vkusit' ne smela kratkoi negi
Rat', utomlennaia ot ran:
Nozh istuplennyi poselian
Okrovovlial ee nochlegi![25]

(You have submitted, the land of granite,
and you have tasted Russia's might;
you will not push its heel away,
even though you are breathing hidden animosity toward it!
The time of eternal captivity has come,
but glory to the fallen people!
It defended courageously the freedom of its gloomy rocks.
From behind the masses of crags, a hail of lead was flying at us.
Our army tired from wounds could not enjoy even a moment of
languid rest—
the ferocious knife of the peasants
covered our camps with blood.)

The contradiction between the official rhetoric of a legitimate and unprob-
lematic annexation of Finland and literary and memoiristic portrayals of
Finnish resistance were reconciled in some texts by a narrative that depicted
a wild Finn from the imperial periphery integrated into civilization by Russia.[26] This narrative—parallel to a similar portrayal of taming "savage" Cossacks by the Russian Empire—serves as a foundation of several texts of the
imperial Gothic discussed in this chapter. The trope of the "submissive" and
passive Finn continued to dominate Russian literary and ethnographic discourse on Finland. The persistence of this trope, despite the alternative narratives of the Finns' resistance and violence, helped "neutralize" the latter by
framing Russia's conquest of Finland as smooth and inevitable.

The military conquest and subsequent annexation of Finland in the early
nineteenth century led to the cultural exploration of this new territory.
Batiushkov's "Excerpt from a Russian Officer's Letters about Finland" was
followed by numerous Russian travel narratives, poetic works, and other publications dedicated to this exotic northern land, whose gloomy granite and
desolate expanses were portrayed as a source of inspiration and dejection

FIGURE 4. Fedor Matveev, *The Imatra Waterfall in Finland*, 1819. Oil on canvas. State Russian Museum, St. Petersburg.

and whose waterfall Imatra was alternatively described as beautiful or sublime.[27] In 1846, *The Finnish Herald* observed the growing fashion for Finland and the changing cultural perception of this region in Russia:

> In the quite recent past, we, the Russians, knew Finland only by its geography and imagined it to be a mysterious and gloomy country populated by a wild, untamed people alien to European civilization. . . .

But the time has come for the kinship (srodstvo) of the Finns and the Russians. . . . Everything that used to seem ridiculous and savage to us has suddenly become full of charm and enchantment, and thousands of St. Petersburg residents have rushed on the waves of the Baltic towards joyful and noisy Helsingfors. Both the Finns' proud poverty and the wild and gloomy nature of this land, which in our imagination chilled our souls,—everything has become charming to us, and with delight we hurry to the Finnish rocks, beginning to understand the magical, striking beauty of this majestic nature.[28]

Until the mid-1830s–early 1840s, Finland was included in the general Scandinavian and Ossianic discourse popular in European pre-Romantic and Romantic literature; like Batiushkov before him, Baratynsky invokes Odin and "skalds" in his 1820 poem "Finland."[29] The situation changed in 1835–36 when Elias Lönnrot, the Finnish medical doctor and philologist, published two volumes of *The Kalevala*—the Finnish national epic based on the folk songs and tales he had collected primarily in Finland and Karelia. The unique Finnish folklore and mythology, distinct from both Norse/Scandinavian and Slavic traditions, were popularized in Russia by Grot, the primary Russian expert on Scandinavia, who moved to Finland in 1840 and became the first professor of Russian literature and history at the Imperial Alexander University in Helsingfors in 1841. Starting in 1839, Grot published prolifically in leading Russian journals, such as *The Contemporary* and *Notes of the Fatherland* (*Otechestvennye zapiski*). His writings introduced the Russian reader to various topics, among them descriptions of the cities and landscape of Finland, the Finnish national character, as well as Finnish folklore, including a detailed summary of and translated excerpts from *The Kalevala*. Contemporaries perceived Grot as a Columbus of his day, discovering a new continent hidden in plain view, "next door" to Russia. Shevyrev, reviewing Odoevsky's novella "The Southern Shore of Finland" (the first part of what would become his diptych *The Salamander*), referred to the work's setting as the "world of poetry, completely new and recently discovered by Mr. Grot next to St. Petersburg: this is the Finnish world."[30] The editor of *The Contemporary* Petr Pletnev, in his letter to Grot in 1847, sums up his friend's contribution, albeit in less exuberant terms: "For all its poverty and gloominess, under your pen, Finland turns into a country worthy of an inquisitive person's study."[31] As is typical of colonial discourse and practices, Finland emerges from barbarity and obscurity only thanks to a Russian expert and his writing about and on behalf of the conquered region.[32]

Grot's copious correspondence with Pletnev shows that the latter perceived Grot's educational mission as part of the Russian imperial enterprise in transforming the Finns into loyal subjects of the empire by educating them in the Russian language, literature, and history. In particular, he suggested teaching the history of the North in Helsingfors in a way that would demonstrate the primordial unity of Northern Europe and the civilizational benefits of its current "reunification." Using separate histories of northern countries as sources, Grot should strive, Pletnev insisted, "to prove mathematically what a blessing it was for the annexed provinces that the Lord gave them this lot." This lot is, of course, their joining Russia, the "most remarkable nation" of our time, to quote Pletnev, who presented Russia as an enlightened and benevolent ruler: "Only sans-culottes shout meaninglessly against conquests. Was Poland really better off before its annexation to Russia, and Finland as well? One should be talking business, not empty phrases. The Frenchmen in England destroyed the language and mores, while we support them everywhere. And if we want our allies to learn Russian, it is only so that they, having gotten to know us more closely, could see for themselves that we are not cannibals, as some believe out of ignorance."[33]

As is clear from this quote, teaching Russian to the Finns was supposed to promote a two-fold goal: the Russian language would serve as a conduit to Russian culture and would assert Russia's high level of civilizational development. At the same time, learning Russian was a vital part of the Finns' cultural conversion: "Remember," writes Pletnev to Grot, "that you were made an apostle of the Russian language in the Finnish land (v chukhonskoi zemle)."[34] This mission, however, was not easy. In his letters, Grot repeatedly complains about the difficulties he encounters as the professor of Russian in Helsingfors in overcoming his students' lack of motivation. The latter, he speculates, is caused by the poverty of Russian literature, the difficulty and "youth" of the language, and "historical hostility" that, in the natural course of things, will take "two or three generations" to disappear.[35] Sensitive to the local perspective, Grot advocates a gradual approach that would refrain from imposing Russian too forcefully but instead involved using the Swedish language to introduce his students to Russian literature and history. Pletnev takes a more aggressive view, suggesting that Grot mix up Swedish and Russian in his lectures and compare the two languages in favor of the latter. "Act as an intelligent, subtle and strategic politician. After all, by trying to make the Finns learn Russian, we are not oppressing or cheating them but rather increasing their interest [in Russian culture]. Are we really not worthy of their study?"[36] Pletnev's overall strategy is to "lure" the Finns into the sphere of Russian culture and language with colorful stories from the Russian past: "for example: [they can read] excerpts from Konysky from Pushkin's *The Contemporary*, about the state of Little Russia under Polish Catholic rule, and from Derzhavin, the ode to Zubov's return from Persia. . . . A voice of talent will silence any historical hostility."[37] The choice of potential episodes from Russian and Ukrainian history is characteristic, especially in the case of the *History of the Rus' or Little Russia (Istoriia Rusov ili Maloi Rossii)*, attributed to Archbishop Heorhii Konysky, which graphically describes the injustices and atrocities of Polish rule in Ukraine before the latter's incorporation into the Russian Empire.[38] Derzhavin's ode, while less explicitly political, paints a portrait of a humane and cordial Russian military leader who "has conquered a kingdom" but should be known primarily for his virtues.

Pletnev assigned literature and history a crucial role in bridging the cultural gap between the Finns and the Russians and in legitimizing the Russian rule over the former Swedish territory. In 1845, a journal dedicated to Finland and the North more generally, is founded in St. Petersburg—*The Finnish Herald*, edited by Fedor Karlovich Derschau and funded by Count Alexander Armfelt, the minister and the secretary of state (stats-sekretar') of the Great Duchy of Finland.[39] Oriented toward the natural school, with its preference for ethnographic discourse, the genre of the physiological sketch, and typological classifications, *The Finnish Herald* nonetheless relied heavily on Romantic and Gothic tropes to describe Finland and the Finnish national character.

Gothic Finland in Russian Literature and Ethnography

Several factors contributed to the portrayal of Finland, both in fiction and in ethnographic sketches, in Gothic terms. On the more obvious level, the Finnish northern, gloomy and menacing landscape invoked Ossianic associations and was a perfect source of the Gothic sublime.[40] The remnants of Gothic architecture in Finland, such as the cathedral in Åbo or the Vyborg castle, provided Romantically inclined Russians with easy access to the legacy of medieval Europe, as was also the case with Baltic provinces.[41] Finland's association in Russian poetry with emptiness, death, and the graveyard, may have also contributed to its Gothic image.[42] A more complex set of factors had to do with the ambiguity of Finland's historical and geographical relation to Russia: Finnish peoples were seen as part of the modern Russian nation, linked to the beginning of Russia's history; yet they were others, with their distinct linguistic, ethnic, and cultural markers, at times resisting assimilation and conversion to Orthodox Christianity. Finland proper, too, was an exotic, unfamiliar country that was linked to Russia through the Varangian myth and on whose territory the symbolic center of Russian modernity and the actual center of the Russian imperial identity, St. Petersburg, was located. When the capital of Finland was transferred to Helsingfors, rebuilt after the model of St. Petersburg, the two capitals could be perceived as uncanny doubles. Grot's description of Helsingfors is characteristic in this regard: "In Helsingfors, next to welcoming art, you see gloomy and menacing nature. Majestic, bright building and towers are looming on gray monstrous masses of granite. Having come from the shores of the Neva, you involuntarily recall them and you think for a moment that you've never parted from them; but suddenly casting your gaze on the array of wild rocks, you realize that you have been transferred to some new realm (tsarstvo)."[43] Helsingfors strikes the Russian visitor by its combination of art and nature. Grot admires the triumph of civilization over bleak nature and barren soil embodied by Helsingfors, reproducing the typical tropes of the Russian St. Petersburg text in his description of the Finnish capital. A "half-savage," "developing beauty"—especially from the point of view of a St. Petersburg dweller used to straight and harmonious lines, Helsingfors emerges as St. Petersburg's savage twin, which enables a Europeanized Russian to assume a position of civilizational superiority.

The persistent theme of the Finns' "wildness" and primitive stage of development—contradicted, paradoxically, by Russian travelers' testimonies of the high level of education in Finland—is closely related to the cultural perception of the Finns existing outside of history discussed by Boele.[44] Grot—who commented with admiration on the widespread literacy of the Finnish lower classes—idealized the Finns for their simpleheartedness and observed that the "daily life of Finnish peasants still exhibits a fairly antiquated character and such features which we would search for in vain in other modern peoples."[45] Odoevsky, a friend of Grot, echoes this description in a lengthy footnote opening his Gothic tale *The Salamander* (*Salamandra*, 1841–44), characterizing the Finns as "an ancient people transferred to our era."[46]

This vision of the Finns' archaic lifestyle untouched by civilization and history is linked to the nearly universal reputation of the Finns as possessing a particular prowess in magic.[47] From Icelandic sagas to a Russian proverb that refers to Finland as "the devil's land" (chertova storonushka), Finns (and Lapps) are portrayed as endowed with esoteric knowledge and a unique ability for (usually dark) magic.[48] Both Lomonosov and Karamzin mention the Finns' reputation for sorcery.[49] Moreover, Pushkin's *Ruslan and Liudmila* (1820) introduces a Finnish sorcerer accompanied by a full arsenal of traditional "Finland" tropes, from the poverty and desolation of this land of fishermen to its "gray-haired wizards" gifted with extraordinary pro-phetic and magical power.[50] This perception assumes particular relevance in the pre-Romantic and Romantic era and paves the way for Gothic Finland in Russian literature. In Nikolai Grech's popular novel *A Woman in Black* (*Chernaia zhenshchina*, 1834), a group of friends gathered in Finland feels predisposed to a melancholy mood by the autumnal Finnish landscape and exchange mystical and supernatural stories; some of them are set in Sweden and involve a Finnish seer.[51]

In the 1840s, the view of Finns' magical power received scholarly legiti-macy, when Grot dedicated a lengthy section of his article on the Finns and their folk poetry to Finnish "wizards" and stressed the Finns' innate poetic and mystical sensibility. Citing Tacitus and a widespread perception of Finns as wizards in medieval Europe, Grot establishes a direct link between this people's disregard for military glory and power and their respect for wis-dom and the word (again, emphasizing the Finns' interiority). Reliance on supernatural forces and esoteric knowledge, Grot speculates, derives from the Finns' history of two-fold struggle—against implacable nature and exter-nal conquerors. Thus the Finnish predilection for the mysterious, magical, and supernatural—the characteristics that contribute to the "Gothicizing" of Finland in Russian literature—appears inextricably linked both to the land's geography and to the history of this people as an object of territorial, reli-gious, and imperial ambitions.

The trope of the superstitious Finn, whose inclination toward magic and mysticism is overdetermined historically and geographically, pervades Russian literary and journalistic discourse of the 1840s. Odoevsky draws on Grot when he observes in *The Salamander*: "Their innate passion for the miraculous is combined with a strong poetic element and a half-savage attachment to their land" (141). Their geographical isolation leads to a dis-torted understanding of world events, which then, processed through the Finnish creative imagination and coupled with their innate talent for story-telling, leads to a mythologized account even of recent events.[52] The Finn, thus, is denied a historical existence, eternally suspended in the realm of the myth.

This view is echoed in ethnographic publications of the 1840s, includ-ing in *The Finnish Herald*, despite its anti-Romantic orientation.[53] The physi-ological sketch "A Shop Assistant" ("Prikashchik" [sic]), for example, offers a quasi-"scientific" classification of various ethnic groups inhabiting Rus-sia, as well as of professions typical of St. Petersburg; in this classification, the Finn is characterized as an ultimate "Northern type" and a "legend

personified."⁵⁴ The same issue of the journal offered the following gener-
alization in the article "On Pietism": "Under the sky of Finland, the sky of
sorcerers and wizards, there is some ineffable tendency towards religious
exaltation: Swedenborgism, illuminism, and mysticism have more than one
follower here."⁵⁵

The theme of Finland as a land of dark superstition, magic, and the supernatural, is explored in the Gothic tale "Lalli, the Twelfth-Century Finn," penned
by Derschau (interestingly, this tale is published not in the literary section of
the journal but in the ethnographic one). The story is loosely based on the
Finnish legend about a Finnish villager named Lalli who murdered Bishop
Henry (Henrik) of Uppsala during the first Swedish crusade.⁵⁶ Derschau rel-
egates the historical context to the end of his narrative, focusing instead on a
tragic love triangle, Finland's Gothic associations, and his demonic protagonist.
The story is set near present-day Åbo, during what the author calls the "pre-
historical" (read "pre-Christian") time, in the mysterious, austere, horrifying,
and "wild" Finnish nature. A direct link is established between this gloomy
yet sublime landscape and the Finnish folk tradition, with the references to
The Kalevala meant to set up a poetic and mythical atmosphere for the story.

In contrast to the meek image of the colonized Finn, "prehistorical" Finns
were typically depicted as brutish and bloodthirsty.⁵⁷ This "savage" aspect of
the Finnish imaginary identity is embodied by the story's eponymous protagonist Lalli who, in the course of the narrative, commits a series of gruesome murders. Lalli is in love with Elli, the daughter of a poor (but proud in
his poverty) blacksmith Jan. Famous for the arrows he produced, Jan nonetheless declined repeated invitations to move to Sweden to work for its army,
out of love for his homeland. Thus, from the outset, Derschau establishes a
tension between Swedes and Finns, which also provides an opportunity for
an ethnographic commentary: "Such was the ancient Finn, and so he appears
to us now: he'd rather experience need on his native cliff than go to seek for-
tune in a foreign land. Can one attribute this sentiment to laziness and passivity?—No! Love, his ardent love for his country alone attaches him to the bare
cliffs with gloomy forests. Not pursuit of glory but a feeling of dignity used
to constitute, and still does, the most important feature of the Finnish character."⁵⁸ Here again we find the motif of timelessness, associated with the
Finnish national character, presented as an ethnographic "fact": the Finn is
the same now as he was centuries ago; therefore, by reading an old "legend"
we learn something important about today's Finn as well. Another trope—
that of Finnish passivity and immobility—is questioned in this description
and reinterpreted as (anti-Swedish) patriotism.

The hostility between Finland and Sweden is reenacted at the plot level of the story, where it is translated into a romantic rivalry between Lalli and the Swede Fabian over Elli's hand. Elli's heart belongs to Fabian, but her father refuses to marry his daughter to a Swede. While Elli is tortured by nightmares about her beloved where "horrible sorcerers created by the superstitious Finns' imagination" take her beloved away from her, her father enlists an actual "Finnish sorcerer" Pavo to conjure up a vision of Elli's destined spouse during an elaborate ritual at a cemetery.[59] The appearance of Lalli, mistaken by them at first for a ghost, seems to suggest that he is Elli's husband desired by the gods. Elli, however, has no feelings for Lalli. The rivalry between her Finnish and Swedish suitors reaches its peak during the village fight contest won by Fabian, which prompts the following reaction from Lalli: "Accursed Swede! It's not the first time that you're an obstacle to my happiness . . .! Be damned, foreign serpent! Be damned all foreigners . . . You're all the cause of my misfortune and grief. Perio seduced my mother, Henrich took my sister across the sea, and Fabian . . ." And upon mentioning his name, Lalli convulsively clenched his fist.[60]

Lalli's hatred for Fabian is part of his broader perception of the threat coming from the outside, from across the sea, from the other. Eventually, he finds Elli and Fabian together on a cliff and, overcome with "jealousy, malice, and hatred," pushes his rival into the "Finnish waters." From this scene, in particular, Lalli emerges as a demonic Gothic villain: after killing Fabian, he turns to Elli, pale, with a "disfigured face" and a "satanic smile," his eyes "glistening with dark malice."[61] After Elli confirms her love for Fabian, Lalli "with frenzy" throws the girl against the cliffs and then pushes her bloody corpse into the sea as well. The entire episode, full of gory details and demonic references, invokes the alternative discursive tradition of the bloodthirsty savage Finn, but it does so through the poetics of frenetic romanticism, which developed out of the Gothic genre.

The family drama is suddenly succeeded by the historical one, as the action of the story skips one year and moves to 1151 when the Swedish and Livonian crusaders appear on the shores of Finland. The pagan Finns resist the Swedish invader but in vain, as King Eric eventually conquers the land. Lalli kills Bishop Henry, whose mission was to convert the local population to Christianity peacefully; moreover, he mocks the dead by putting the bishop's miter on his own head and, attracted by the bishop's golden ring, cuts off his finger. The power of the Christian God is manifested immediately as Lalli's skull comes off together with the archbishop's miter, and Lalli dies a painful death eaten by wild beasts in the woods. The story's end returns to the ethnographic mode connecting the legend with the archbishop's miter and ring found on the coat of arms of Åbo's Spiritual Consistory.

Lalli's murder of the bishop is motivated in Derschau's story by Henry's foreignness as much as by his desire to defend his people's traditional belief system. Just as Fabian was more than a romantic rival but an ultimate other, the bishop embodies the foreign threat, as Lalli exclaims: "May the power of all the foreigners who had come to our cliffs die with you."[62]

Although modeled after a Gothic villain, Lalli is a somewhat ambivalent figure in the story's ideology. On the one hand, he represents the pagan, dark, and barbarous aspect of Finland that needs to be overcome through a conversion, which is presented as a bloody colonial conquest. The last section of the story, which describes the semi-mythical crusade of 1151, switches from a folkloric and supernatural mode to a historical one. In this section, the historical context is established by an exact date, as well as specific ethnonyms—"Swedes, Livonians, and Estonians," as opposed to the vague *zamorskie* (foreign, from across the sea) Swedes of the previous part. The crusade and colonization, thus, mark the transition of Finland into history and its inclusion into Western European civilization.

On the other hand, Lalli's hatred for foreigners links him to the "good Finn" of the story, patriotic old Jan, and presents him as almost a Romantic avenger and independence fighter. The violent aspect of the crusade stressed in the story (even though crusaders are characterized as "protected by God") undermines the narrator's seeming support of its mission. Later Russian accounts of these events often emphasize the bloody nature of the conquest and, more generally, injustices inflicted on Finland by Sweden to implicitly contrast it to the benefits of Russian rule—again, not unlike the emphasis on the cruelty of the Baltic German knights in the Livonian tales.[63]

The Russian annexation of Finland remains outside of the story's chronological span but, given its persistent theme of proud Finnish independence and Lalli's threat to "all the foreigners who appear on the cliffs of Finland," the connection is implied. It is reinforced by the publication of another work in the same issue of *The Finnish Herald*, which explicitly explores the takeover of Finland by Russia—Nestor Kukol'nik's short novel, titled *Egor Ivanovich Sil'vanovsky, or the Conquest of Finland under Peter the Great (Egor Ivanovich Sil'vanovskii, ili zavoevanie Finliandii pri Petre Velikom)*. Although less conventionally Gothic than "Lalli," this work is not devoid of Gothic flavor; it is set first in an "old" and "bellicose" castle on one of the islands near Åbo, and later in Åbo itself, depicted as a university town populated by superstitious professors and mystically inclined students.[64] As is typical for the Finnish theme in Russian literature, the historical context, the Romantic plot, and the Gothic setting come together as the novel unfolds against the background of the Great Northern War. The opening of the narrative introduces the castle owner—the Finnish baroness Otilia, whose husband was "far away with the invincible king of Sweden, the Northern Alexander; he demolished the Danes, the Poles, and us" (6). The reference to the "invincible" Swedish king Charles XII cannot but ring ironic in retrospect in a novel where the narrator explicitly identifies with the Swedes' opponents and future victors (referring to the Russians as "us"). Finns are introduced from the start as being on the wrong side of history, even though they are still blissfully unaware of it. This changes, at least for some of the Finnish characters, in the course of Kukol'nik's novel.

As in many other contemporary publications, Finland's nature, and especially the sea surrounding it, is closely linked to the Finnish national identity. As the baroness puts it, "Since childhood, I have been used to not being afraid of the sea. For the Finns, it is more a homeland than our granite rocks. It is as if we were born in the sea" (10). She boasts about her and her daughter Augusta's swimming skills, but after their sailboat is caught in a storm, both barely escape death, rescued by the novel's protagonist Erik and his friends, the sons of Finnish sailors. A brief glimpse into the Finnish folk imagination (a legend narrated to the boys by Erik's father following the rescue) presents a vision of the world surrounded by water up to its outer limit, a realm that only Finnish sorcerers can access.

Most of the novel's events take place seven years later, in 1709, the year of the Battle of Poltava, in which Peter I defeated the Swedish army—a victory that decided the outcome of the war in Russia's favor and ultimately changed the balance of power in Northern Europe. During these seven years, Erik has become a sailor and a merchant; it is he who brings the shocking news of Charles's defeat to the baroness's high society (which strikes him as inauthentic and alien and where only French and Swedish are spoken). He, by contrast, presents himself as a victim of Swedish rule who is sympathetic to Russia and admires Peter's recent victories. In the meantime, Augusta has grown up with a strong sense of her Finnish identity and is passionately attached to the sea: she "swam like a fish," "sang only Finnish songs and only those where the sea took a poetic part" (19), and called herself Halcyone, after the sea-nesting bird from Ovid's *Metamorphosis* (11:410–728). Predictably, Augusta and Erik fall in love; in this version of the national romantic competition, the Finn Erik wins over his Swedish rival, a baron pursuing Augusta's hand. Curiously, one of Erik's arguments in persuading the Swedish baron to abandon his pursuit of Augusta is the fact that "she is the daughter of Finland, while you're a Swede" (31). However, eliminating his Swedish rival is not sufficient to become Augusta's husband: because Erik is not of noble birth, his only option of becoming his beloved's equal is through education. Erik dedicates himself to learning with such success that soon he is admitted to a prestigious Swedish academy.

Augusta's parents assume that Erik has enchanted their daughter, and ultimately academy members formally accuse him of black magic and a pact with the devil.[65] Notably, one of the main arguments at Erik's trial is that he is a Finn, intrinsically prone to magic and the irrational. As one of the Swedish professors snaps at his Finnish colleague at the trial, "Let us not forget that Finns are very susceptible to black magic. It is necessary to use a strong example to cure this people of this sin. You, my honorable colleague, yourself believe in various apparitions, and only because even science did not destroy the elements of Finnish nature in you" (57).[66] The fears of a demonic intervention are fueled by the anxiety among the Swedish population caused by the advance of the Russian army; Finns, by contrast, complain about the injustices of the Swedish rule and welcome the "Russian cannons" that will now "speak for [them]" (45). At the Inquisition-style trial, Erik is condemned to being burned at the stake but is saved thanks to the victorious arrival of the Russian army. Terrified Swedes flee the Russians, while Prince Golitsyn addresses the ecstatic Finnish population of the city promising them law and order, lower taxes, and freedom of trade and faith.[67]

The Russians, in other words, come as a benevolent, modern, and rational force and rescue the innocent natural Finn from the evil manipulations and the backward, superstitious power of fanatical Swedes.[68] As Prince Golitsyn puts it when informed about Erik's predicament, "We are not afraid of the devil" (My nechistogo ne boimsia, 62). He declares his love for the "light of knowledge" and is concerned that "stupid fear" drove all the professors away and deprived students of their education opportunities (66). Golitsyn sends Erik to bring him the remaining academy students, to whom he gives passports and money to travel to Sweden and continue their education, asking them to "tell the Swedes that the Russians honor enlightenment" (72). He thus establishes Russia as an equal, or even superior, member of civilized Europe. Grateful Erik begins to serve the Russian state, learns Russian and takes on the name of Egor Ivanovich Sil'vanovsky—a fact that marks, as Guzairov observes, his new status as a loyal subject of the Russian Empire whose "national identity is inseparable from [his] new imperial identity."[69]

After Russia's decisive victory in the war, peace settles in the Finnish land, and Erik marries Augusta. The Finns wholeheartedly support this marriage as a "guarantee of kinship with the [Russian] neighbors whom geography and nature ordered to be brothers" (81). The Romantic tradition typically presents a tragic love narrative as mirroring, but also problematiz-ing, a violent imperial conquest (from Pushkin's *The Prisoner of the Caucasus* and Baratynsky's *Eda* to Lermontov's "Bela"). However, Kukol'nik's happy ending depicts Russia's annexation of Finland as a noncoercive, loving, and even naturally predetermined union.[70] His version of the "geopoliti-cal romance" has less in common with the Romantic tradition than with the allegorical representations of the Great Northern War in both Russian folklore and official propaganda art.[71] In one folk legend, a Swede and a Russian pursued a beauty who promised to marry the one who would be able to conquer her. The Swede initially prevails, with the help of a Finnish sorcerer, but the Russian eventually defeats him, drowns the sorcerer in the sea, and takes the girl (Finland).[72] What differentiates Kukol'nik's allegory is the fact that his successful romantic hero is not a Russian but a Russified Finn—thus, Finland not only happily unites with Russia but also quickly and effortlessly internalizes a modern Russian identity, as it leaves its dark Gothic past behind.[73]

Odoevsky's *The Salamander*: An Alternative Conversion Narrative

This story of successful assimilation and unification is particularly striking when contrasted with the much darker narrative of cultural conversion from a Finn to a Russian penned by Vladimir Odoevsky in the early 1840s. I am referring to his novella *The Salamander*, published as a diptych for the first time in 1844 in his *Sochineniia*.[74] Its two separate parts had appeared earlier: the second part, "Elsa," was published under the title of "Salamandra" in the first issue of *The Notes of the Fatherland* in 1841, but Odoevsky's plans for this story go back to 1838.[75] The first part, "The Southern Shore of Finland in the Beginning of the Eighteenth Century" ("Iuzhnyi bereg Finliandii v nachale XVIII stoletiia") was also published in 1841 and it was probably con-ceived of later than "Elsa," after the publication of Grot's articles on Finland in 1839 and 1840. In my analysis, I approach this novella as one text and dis-cuss its parts in the order in which they were published as a diptych.

"The Southern Shore of Finland in the Beginning of the Eighteenth Cen-tury" takes us 130 years back from the narrator's time, to Finland during the Great Northern War. The opening presents a picture of the untamed Finnish landscape, before the civilizing influence of Russia "turned the ter-rifying force of nature into entertainment" (143), referring to the banks of the Vuoksi River. The once wild riverside was transformed to appeal to

St. Petersburg tourists: "Now the banks of the Vuoksi are smoothed out, dec-
orated, a straight path with handrails runs through the cliffs; gazebos in the
tasteless English style, well whitewashed, are expecting leisurely travelers"
(142). The homogenizing effect of borrowed Western culture ("smooth,"
"straight," "tasteless English style") is immediately undermined by the reference to the horrifying sublimity of the river that resists time and historical
change: "But now, just as before, one is overcome by horror when he dares to
glance into the terrifying seething abyss" (142). The description of the landscape in the opening does not merely provide a backdrop for the main events
of the narrative. Instead, it sets up the tension between forces of progress
and culture and the persistent threat of the irrational and natural. This tension, dramatized as "wild" Finland's resistance to assimilation by Westernized Russia, constitutes the central conflict of the story.

The narrative then zooms in on a hut inhabited by a poor Finnish family:
an old man Rusi, his wife, their granddaughter Elsa, and the boy Jakko who
is raised by them. The boy wonders where Elsa's father is and, upon learning that he was taken to the war as a guide, inquires what war means. Old
Rusi's explanation is characteristic in that it puts Finland at the center of the
military conflict, presenting the country as an arena of competing imperial
interests: "The Swedes (rutsy) come from one side, the Russians (veineleisy)
from the other, and they argue who will get our land" (144). To clarify the
role of Finland as an object of foreign conquests, the old man narrates a
"Finnish legend" about Sampo—a magic object mentioned in *The Kalevala*
and described in the legend as a treasure that used to provide the Finns with
everything needed, guaranteeing them blissful paradisiac existence. It is
Sampo (which had since disappeared under the earth) that, according to the
legend, is at stake in the present Russian-Swedish conflict. This explanation
of the war illustrates the Finns' tendency to mythologize recent history or
even contemporary events, postulated by Odoevsky in his footnote to the
story, as does the legend's defamiliarized folkloric account of Peter I's rule,
including the construction of St. Petersburg.

As the old man concludes his story, the family hears the sounds of a can-
nonade; Elsa, in a prophetic vision, witnesses the death of her father; and
a Swedish officer enters the hut, as the boundaries between the supernatural and the real, myth and history collapse. The war, and with it history,
enters the narrative and destroys the Finnish idyll: the old man dies taking
revenge on the Swedes for killing his son; the old woman is murdered by
the Swedes, while Jakko takes the side of the Russians. The Russians bring
him to St. Petersburg, which Odoevsky describes as "risen from Finnish

swamps" (154). Elsa is left behind—a fact whose significance for the story will become clear.

In the first part of *The Salamander*, Jakko's story can be read, on the surface, as an optimistic narrative of Russia's benevolent civilizational mission.[76] Sent by Peter I to study foreign languages and physics in Holland, "the half-savage Finn" turns into an "educated European" (154).[77] Here again, Finland serves as an uncanny mirror to Russia's former "savagery." Just as Helsingfors, in Grot's description, appears as a "wilder," untamed version of St. Petersburg, here Jakko repeats Peter I's journey, which resulted in his Westernization of Russia. Jakko seems to be destined for a similarly transformative mission: appointed to oversee the printing press, the former poor Finnish orphan from the woods "was intended to become one of the tools of enlightenment in Russia" (156).

Throughout the story Odoevsky undermines this positive interpretation. After his return from the West, as we learn, the young Finn is caught between his newly acquired rationality and the mythological thinking he imbibed as a child in Finland. He still thinks of Russia as a "fairy-tale-like" (basnoslovnyi) world and perceives Peter as now a giant, now a wizard (volkhv) who is conquering the elements. Jakko's educated mind relies on reality to confirm the myths of his childhood, whereas his rational understanding of Peter's accomplishments is referred to as a "[superstitious/mythical] belief" (verovanie). The word "magic" or "miraculous" (chudnye) repeatedly occurs in the passage describing his impressions upon his return to Russia where "the reality is mixed in the Finn's soul with enchantment (ocharovanie)" (155).

Jakko's split between his Finnish and Russian identities (which, schematically put, represent the irrational/organic and rational/mechanistic principles respectively) manifests itself particularly vividly in the novella's romantic plot. As with many other narratives of the conquest of Finland, romantic rivalry here takes on ideological connotations and assumes a symbolic dimension. In 1722, we learn, Jakko travels to his native Finland to bring Elsa to St. Petersburg with him. Jakko is wearing a German dress and has almost forgotten the Finnish language. By contrast, Elsa, untouched by the course of history, is shown to be singing traditional folk songs about Sampo and dancing on the shores of Vuoksi, representing authentic Finnish culture. Elsa's confusion of the terms "Rutsi" (Swedes) and "russkie" (Russians) in her conversation with Jakko alludes to the evasive nature of Russianness in the novella; moreover, she challenges Jakko's new identity when she corrects him that his true homeland is here, not in Russia.[78] Jakko's nostalgia for

Finland (he kisses the land on his arrival) is clearly in conflict with his Russian self-identification made explicit in his comment, "*our* Russian carts are not at all appropriate for *your* mountains" (160). Similarly, on his arrival in St. Petersburg with Elsa, he is torn between two women who are competing for his affection: untamed Elsa who connects him to his Finnish childhood and the superficially Westernized Russian girl Mar'ia, the daughter of his benefactor Zverev. When, after the St. Petersburg flood, Elsa goes back to Finland, Jakko proposes to Mar'ia, thus fully embracing, it seems, his new Russian self. His last visit to Finland reinforces this shift, as the hero declares, "My land is alien to me. Farewell, Suomi, farewell forever. And greetings, Russia, my fatherland!" (183).

This assimilation narrative is problematized at several levels. First, the notion of Russianness proves elusive in the novella. Odoevsky's skepticism about Petrine Russia is particularly clear from his description of the Zverev family, which hosts Elsa during her stay in St. Petersburg. Unlike the Novgorodian Derzhikrai, whose virtues impressed the Estonian Nor in Kiukhel'beker's "Ado" so much that he was inspired to convert to Christianity, the Russian hosts here are portrayed in a far more critical light. The Zverev family, whose last name is derived from the Russian word for "beast" or "animal" and thus already undermines the idea of a refined civilization, serves as an illustration of the mechanical and superficial adaptation of Western ways. The "half-German, or, better to say, half-Dutch" Zverev keeps his house as a "wound machine" following a strict schedule meant to imitate the lifestyle he observed in Holland. His daughter becomes "Dutch" as needed when she puts on a corset and abandons her natural behavior on social occasions; only Zverev's wife sticks to her old ways. The "wild" and natural Finnish girl does not fit well into this family and, more broadly, into the new Russia undergoing rapid modernization. Elsa refuses to learn Russian, resists assimilation, continues to sing Finnish folk songs, and does not abandon her mythological worldview and her proclivity for magic. Elsa's otherness is quickly translated by Zverev's wife and servants into supernatural terms: they suspect her of being a witch who has enchanted Zverev. Elsa, in turn, links assimilation with sorcery when she observes to Jakko: "Oh, Jakko, how the *veineleises* [Russians] have enchanted you. Whatever they come up with seems right to you, and all our ways seem wrong" (170).

In linking Gothic-fantastic motifs to the notion of otherness and assimilation, Odoevsky establishes a peculiar reversed symmetry. The Russian characters in the novella repeatedly invoke, derogatorily, the stereotype of Finnish wizards and sorceresses, while the new Petrine Russia appears to the Finns as an uncanny semi-supernatural space.[79] The young boy Jakko's first experience of Russia is that of "objects unseen before," "unfamiliar people," and "unfamiliar food"—all of which nonetheless had an "enchanting" effect on the Finnish youth (153). St. Petersburg strikes Jakko as a "city of a strange appearance" with "astonishingly gigantic" buildings. When he returns to St. Petersburg after his studies abroad as the Russian subject Ivan Ivanovich Jakko, an eerie feeling envelopes him in his new homeland, which is just as strange and unknown to him as it had been when he was brought there as a half-savage orphan: "The Finn felt both terrified and happy (I strashno, i veselo bylo na dushe finna). Now, as before, he only knew Russia by hearsay; but even more so was he struck by its grandeur" (155). The narrator confirms the naive Finn's perspective when he seemingly admires Russia's newly acquired greatness: "Indeed, the Russian tsardom lived through wondrous moments at that time: The treaty of Nystad was signed; Russia celebrated its power and offered the tsar the title of the emperor and of the Great . . . Russia resembled a gigantic machine whose infinite power knew no bounds" (155). Notably, this transition from pre-Petrine and fairy-tale-like tsardom to modern empire is described as a quasi-miraculous transformation; however, the reference to the mechanistic nature of Russia's sublime grandeur undercuts the optimistic narrative of the country's modernization.

While Jakko is both awed and enchanted by new Russia, Elsa preserves a defamiliarized and mostly negative perspective, repeatedly referring to the fear this country and its inhabitants instill in her: "People are so scary (strashnye) here! They can't even speak but scream terrifyingly all the time"; "All of this seemed strange and terrifying (i chudno, i strashno) to Elsa" (161); "Whatever you say, but this is a scary land (strashnaia zemlia) and your *veineleisy* (Russians) are scary people (strashnye liudi)" (163). Observing the construction in the city, Elsa interprets the process as wizards punishing the earth, after she sees timber piles being driven into the ground. Jakko translates her vision into the modern language of civil engineering. But Elsa's compelling description of the violence done to nature in the construction of St. Petersburg casts a dark shadow on the Petrine project, as does her concern with the unstable soil on which the city is built: "And the earth doesn't hold here! Everything is not quite right here! It's terrifying, Jakko, terrifying! (Strashno, strashno, Jakko!)" (164).

The familiar elements of the St. Petersburg myth—the city's defiance of nature, its demonic aura, the flood motif—are introduced here through the perspective of a naive and "natural" Finn, an object of Russia's civilizational mission. In contrast to most other preceding texts describing the emergence of the new imperial capital, such as Pushkin's *The Moor of Peter the Great*

(*Arap Petra Velikogo*, 1827) and *The Bronze Horseman*, Odoevsky explicitly inscribes the construction of the city into the context of Russia's imperial expansion into its adjacent northern territories.[80] The Finnish focus of the story allows Odoevsky to inject the Gothic-fantastic elements into the narrative of imperial conquest and assimilation, drawing on the conventional perception of the Finns as magic-prone, ahistorical people. At the same time, Odoevsky reverses this convention and presents an uncanny portrayal of Petrine Russia, thus implicitly critiquing Peter's modernizing project.

The second part of the diptych abounds in more conventional Gothic-fantastic motifs: we find here a mysterious house, a haunted room, a transgressive, semi-incestuous passion, the theme of doubling, and an appearance by a mystical spirit. This part is set in Odoevsky's time, in Moscow of the late 1830s–early 1840s, and it opens by juxtaposing the rationalist nephew and his mystically inclined uncle (anticipating, in a reversed way, the Aduev pair from Ivan Goncharov's novel *An Ordinary Story* [1847]). To test his nephew's skepticism for things immaterial, the uncle tells him about a haunted room in a house that used to belong to his friend, a Russian prince. The uncle emphasizes specifically that this was a *boyar* Moscow house (referring to the pre-Petrine nobility) that symbolized family traditions and historical continuity, as opposed to the modern rented apartments. As is typical of a Gothic novel, a house here not merely functions as a setting for suspenseful and supernatural events but becomes a site where a transgressive past seeps into the present, revealing contemporary social and historical anxieties. We learn that the house has been recently sold to a merchant who is planning to convert it into a textile factory. The history of the house thus mirrors the degeneration of old Russian nobility and the advance of the commercial and industrial spirit, which Odoevsky criticizes throughout his oeuvre.[81]

After the nephew's attempts to scientifically explain the strange howling noises and screams in the room fail, the uncle narrates to him the history of this room that takes us back to Jakko and Elsa. The story of the poor Finn Westernized by the benevolent Russian state did not have a happy ending, as we learn. After the death of his benefactor, Peter I, Jakko falls into disfavor, loses his position, and cannot support his greedy wife, who bemoans her lot of being tied to a "cursed Finn (chukhna), a heretic, and a wizard." Desperate Jakko engages in alchemic activity under the guidance of an old and wealthy Russian count who hopes to find the philosophical stone and uses the Finn's modest lodging as a conveniently inconspicuous site for his alchemist pursuits. Disillusioned in his Russian life, as well as his Russian wife, Jakko nostalgically reminisces about his Finnish past and fondly invokes his beautiful and simple "sister" Elsa. Soon after this, Elsa appears, both as a mystical salamander in the fire during his experiments and as a "real" woman in a traditional Finnish dress who visits him in Moscow and stays. Her appearance brings ruin to Jakko and his family. Mar'ia dies consumed by some mysterious flames, while Elsa-salamander helps Jakko to turn lead into gold and to gain access to immortality. However, when Jakko—transformed into an old but not aging count—starts pursuing a young noble girl, Elsa takes revenge by destroying him with fire, while his old house with the laboratory also perishes in flames. The house bought by the prince, the uncle's friend, was built on the spot of Jakko's house, and the haunted room is located in the place of the old laboratory.

The Salamander was initially planned by Odoevsky to be part of a trilogy dedicated to man's contact with elemental spirits, the other two stories being "The Sylph" (1837) and "The Undine" (never written).[82] According to the Renaissance mystic and alchemist Paracelsus, such beings—peculiar hybrids of spirits, people, and beasts in their nature—lacked a soul and sought union with Adam's descendants to obtain salvation and immortality.[83] These creatures will come back to punish their unfaithful human lovers; as they are denied access to human legal institutions, they are justified in taking judgment into their hands. Each group of such beings (nymphs, sylphs, salamanders) inhabits its element, which Paracelsus calls "chaos," and cannot exist outside of it, just as humans cannot survive without air.[84]

Salamanders, the fire spirits, are not found in Finnish folklore.[85] This figure in Odoevsky's story is essentially a carryover from an earlier version of the narrative that did not include the Finnish setting. The early drafts of *The Salamander*, dating approximately to 1838, indicate that the story was supposed to be unfolding in sixteenth-century Italy and it centered on a young "adept" assisting an older alchemist. During the experiments, the salamander appears in the fire and offers the young man to reveal the secret of obtaining gold in exchange for his love. The young adept accepts the offer but, prosecuted by the Inquisition, he flees to Germany and then to France where he falls in love. The salamander strangles both her unfaithful lover and his new love object, and the house where it happens has since been haunted by strange screams and moaning. Odoevsky's manuscripts include a note on the margin, clearly a later addition, "to transfer the setting to Moscow (before to St. Petersburg)" and to move the screams in the house at night to the time of Peter I.[86]

Finland is not mentioned explicitly in the drafts but Odoevsky, as many before him, associated the Finnish theme with the creation of "new" Petrine Russia. Odoevsky's interest in Finland is well documented: the Russian writer was trying to learn the Finnish language, penned travel notes about

Finland, recorded twenty-five Finnish runes, and would eventually buy a dacha near Vyborg.[87] As both P. N. Sakulin and M. A. Tur'ian point out, the "discovery of Finland" by Grot was instrumental and it provided the writer with new material more appropriate for putting rationalism to test against a more intuitive and mystical approach to knowledge that Odoevsky associated with a naive (folk or child's) psyche.[88] The transfer of the plot to Finland/Russia, while preserving the main elements of the original "alchemist" plot—at the expense of ethnographic accuracy—allows Odoevsky to fuse traditional mystical motifs with a commentary on post-Petrine Russia's cultural and historical path.

It is significant that the first appearance of the salamander in Elsa's vision in part I is linked to the theme of identity and true homeland. Elsa describes the salamander as her sister (sestritsa) who warns her about the threat of assimilation posed by Russia: "'Flee this land,' my sister is telling me now, 'here they will distract you, separate you from me, extinguish you, you will forget our language! On the shores of Vuoksi people will not corrupt you, the pine trees and cliffs are speechless there, the moon is shining with its life-giving power and spiritualizes the crude body'" (174). Elsa insists that Jakko, too, should flee with her, that he belongs to the realm of the salamander: "You're one of us (nash), Jakko! You're mine and nothing will separate me from you!" (174). The salamander's monologue invokes the idea of the creature's true element, the "chaos" described by Paracelsus. Elsa is incapable of living outside of her Finnish element, and the move to a different environment—Russia—will prove fatal for Jakko as well.

It is curious that by linking his authentic Finnish heroine with the salamander, the fire spirit, Odoevsky breaks the traditional association of the Finns with water. Elsa, who wears a red dress during a St. Petersburg assembly and sees prophetic visions in flames, and her double, the salamander, inhabit the element of fire, while Russia is linked to water, an element inherently inimical to fire (note the salamander's warning that here "they will extinguish you"). Notably, the Neva flood ends part I, which is concluded with the ostensible triumph of new Russia over "archaic" Finland, while the second part is dominated by fire—the main element and tool of Elsa's revenge.[89] The association of Russia with water, the realm of chaos, undermines this triumph, especially as the flood scene features Peter I as a captain of a sinking boat.[90] The tension between the two elements complicates both the thematic and compositional organization of the diptych.

The mystical context of the salamander's monologue suggests that what is at stake in Odoevsky's novella is not only the issue of cultural or national identification but also a metaphysical problem of belonging and primordial unity. From the salamander's warning, Finland emerges as a realm of nature and the elements uncorrupted by speech and human civilization ("the pine trees and cliffs are speechless there"), the realm of a perfect union of the material and spiritual, invoking Schellingian philosophy of identity.[91] More than an actual geographical and political concept, Finland functions in the novella as a metaphor for a state of organic unity and nondifferentiation, as opposed to rationalism and mechanistic worldview embodied by the new Russia. Therefore Jakko's choice of Russia over Finland and of Mar'ia over Elsa does not merely indicate the abandonment of his cultural and ethnic roots—rather, it allegorizes the modern man's "fall" into the divided and mechanistic realm of Western modernity.[92]

As Sakulin shows in his monumental study of Odoevsky's art and thought, in the 1830s idealist philosophy and mysticism in Russia were entwined with the questions of West versus East and Russia's messianic historical role.[93] "The Russian Faust," as the writer was nicknamed by his contemporaries, was deeply engaged with these issues and even raised them in his conversation with Schelling.[94] Close to Slavophiles but more balanced in his evaluation of Western culture, Odoevsky was ambivalent about Peter's reforms and their consequences.[95] The final version of *The Salamander* illustrates the fusion of metaphysics, medieval mysticism, and philosophy of history described by Sakulin, as Odoevsky both inscribes a medieval mystical story about a human's contact with a spirit into a specific historical context of the creation of the Petrine empire and universalizes the story of the "poor Finn" as the metaphysical predicament of the Westernized subject.

Cynthia C. Ramsey argues that the true Gothic revelation of *The Salamander* is the crises of engendering—from the unclear origins of its protagonist Jakko and his unresolved quasi-incestuous relationship with his lover / sister Elsa, his transition from the Finnish family of Rusi to his Russian family of Zverev (as well as of his new "father," Peter I) to the complicated origins of the tale of Jakko and Elsa within the complex narrative structure of part II.[96] Attention to the historical and imperial context of the story shows that this crisis of engendering can be extended to Russia that is paying the price for its "new" origins, its interruption of organic development. In Odoevsky's novella these origins of the new Russia are inextricably linked to its conquest of the Finnish territory.

Elsa's return in part II is a manifestation of the imperial uncanny, "the return of the repressed." In other words, it is the return of the Finland that Jakko left behind and everything it symbolizes in the narrative of Russian modernity: nature, authenticity, intuitive knowledge, and the irrational.[97] Finland remains a troubling and inalienable part of Jakko's self, and in Odoevsky's parable it functions as Russia's imperial unconsciousness. Suppressed part of the new Russia built on "Finnish swamps," conquered and subjugated, both geographically and politically, it continues to haunt contemporary Russia, as the latter is moving increasingly in the direction of scientific rationalism and bourgeois pragmatism in Odoevsky's own time. The imperial conquest of Finland, recast in Gothic terms, proved, for Odoevsky, to be an apt historical precedent to address the discontents of Russia's modernity.

The ambivalence of Russian literary and ethnographic discourse on Finland that conceptualized it as simultaneously a historical part of Russia and an exotic, recently tamed northern land made it a particularly productive setting for the Russian imperial uncanny. Moreover, the persistent portrayal of the Finns as a magic-prone, semi-mythological people, surrounded by sublime, gloomy nature and destined by both history and geography to be ruled by others, produced specifically Gothic variations on some traditional colonial narratives: the plot of romantic rivalry as a national and imperial allegory, as well as accounts of cultural assimilation and conversion. Odoevsky's Gothic novella *The Salamander* stands in stark contrast to the optimistic interpretations of the annexation of Finland in both literary works (cf. Kukol'nik's novel) and journalistic publications. In this dark story of a failed conversion where "natural," intuitive, and irrational Finland resists the mechanistic spirit of Petrine Russia, Odoevsky inscribes Gothic motifs into the imperial context of Russia's northern expansion to critique both Russia's historical path and Western modernity more generally. Similar to its southern Gothic counterpart, Ukraine, "gloomy Finland" served as an uncanny space for the literary exploration of Russia's own imperial identity and historical destiny.

PART II

The South

CHAPTER 4

Ukraine

Russia's Uncanny Double

In his review of Nikolai Gogol's *Evenings on a Farm near Dikan'ka* (*Vechera na khutore bliz Dikan'ki*, 1831–32), Russian critic Nikolai Nadezhdin expressed his contemporaries' Romantic fascination with Ukraine, the setting of Gogol's colorful stories: "Who does not know, at least from hearsay, that our Ukraine has a great deal of the curious, interesting, and poetic in its physiognomy? Some silent consensus acknowledges it to be a Slavic Ausonia [Italy] and anticipates in it a rich harvest for one's inspiration. Our poets fly away to it in order to dream and feel; our storytellers are feeding off the crumbs of its legends and fantasies."[1] This quote captures the duality of Ukraine in the Russian Romantic, as well as the imperial, imagination. It is "our" Ukraine but is also "curious" and "interesting," and thus somewhat exotic; it is Slavic "Italy," a foreign land but at the same time the locus of origins and a source of poetic inspiration and folk culture. Indeed, to quote Polevoi again, it is "ours, but not us"—it is a culturally and geographically distinct place.

Fifteen years later, Nadezhdin, in a speech delivered at the annual assembly of the Russian Geographic Society on the "ethnographic study of the Russian nationality," would observe that Ukrainians living outside of the Russian Empire exhibit, paradoxically, more affinity with the "Great Russian" nation than "our Ukrainian Little Russians who have always lived next to us, Great Russians, and have almost always shared a common history with us." The language of the Hungarian Ruthenians, Nadezhdin would argue, is closer and more understandable to the Russians than "the dialect of the Ukrainian Little Russians."[2] In some travel accounts, Ukraine appeared markedly distinct, as in Ivan Sbitnev's *A Trip to Kharkiv* (*Poezdka v Khar'kov*, written in 1830, just a year before Nadezhdin's review of Gogol): "It is known to everybody that beyond the Seym river the fertile Ukraine begins, a land that differs from our parts in its dialect (narechie), traditions, clothing, and even the very appearance of people, their life, agriculture, and soil."[3]

Ukraine's complicated history of its integration into the Russian Empire justifies such a paradoxical perception.[4] The Russian Empire claimed Kievan Rus' as its historical predecessor; after the decline of Rus', however, most of the Ukrainian lands were ruled by Poland or Lithuania and after the two joined together, by the Polish-Lithuanian Commonwealth for over four centuries. Ukrainian territories, mostly east of the Dnipro River (Left-Bank Ukraine), were incorporated into the Russian Empire only in the middle of the seventeenth century, as a result of the Cossack uprisings against the Polish-Lithuanian rule. The Cossacks viewed themselves as defenders of Orthodox Christianity, threatened by the Polish-Lithuanian Catholic influence. This sense of threat intensified after the controversial Union of Brest (1596), which created a new church that allowed the Ukrainian and Bielorussian population of the Commonwealth to keep Orthodox rites and liturgy while submitting to the pope's authority. The Cossacks eventually sought the support of the Moscow tsar, and under the Treaty of Pereiaslav (1654), the Cossack hetman (commander) Bohdan Khmel'nyts'ky accepted the Russian tsar's sovereignty over Ukraine.[5] After Khmel'nyts'ky's death, the region experienced intense fighting, and in 1667 Russia and Poland divided Ukraine, with Russia receiving Left-Bank Ukraine with Kyiv and Poland keeping its control of Right-Bank Ukraine. The Ukrainian lands within the Russian Empire were divided into three self-governing Cossack territories with a certain degree of autonomy: the Hetmanate, the Zaporizhzhian Sich, and Sloboda Ukraine.

During the eighteenth century, this political autonomy was gradually dismantled. First, hetman Ivan Mazepa's siding with Sweden against Peter I during the Great Northern War led to a massacre of the entire population of Baturyn, the hetman's capital, and to measures that severely limited the Hetmanate's autonomy. The full abolition of the Hetmanate took place during the reign of Empress Catherine II, who was determined to centralize regional administrative structures.[6] With the elimination of the Hetmanate and the razing of the Zaporizhzhian Sich in 1775, Catherine destroyed any remnants of Ukrainian autonomy. In the meantime, because of three partitions of Poland in the late eighteenth century, Russia added more Right-Bank territories claiming about 90 percent of the Ukrainian population under its rule. Labeling Ukrainians as "Little Russians," the official imperial policy strove to deemphasize the linguistic and cultural difference between Russians and Ukrainians. The developments of the second half of the nineteenth century—the Valuev Circular (1863) and the Ems Decree (1876), which banned the use of the Ukrainian language in print with few exceptions—are beyond the chronological scope of this book, but they vividly demonstrate Russia's eventual, and rather extreme, encroachment on Ukrainian cultural autonomy.

Whereas the Finns' full assimilation remained a Russian imperial fantasy, promoted by Kukol'nik and questioned by Odoevsky, Ukraine's case was quite different. In exchange for the loss of autonomy, the Ukrainian elites were invited to participate in the political and cultural life of the Russian Empire through voluntary assimilation.[7] This fact of the Ukrainian elites' involvement in the Russian (and later Soviet) imperial project, along with a series of other factors, such as the ethnic and geographical proximity of Russians and Ukrainians, has provoked debates in contemporary scholarship regarding the status of Ukraine as a colony of Russia. I side with the view articulated by Yohanan Petrovsky-Shtern: although not a "classical" colony (distant, racially different, and militarily subjugated), Ukraine, at least in the eighteenth and the nineteenth centuries, was a colony (of both Poland and Russia)—a territory whose "resources . . . were exploited, people economically subjugated and socially oppressed, the elites successfully assimilated, the national-minded discourse shuffled or neutralized, and the culture and language considered uncivilized and scornful."[8] I use the terms "colony" and "colonial" to refer to Ukraine in this sense throughout the remaining chapters while being fully aware of the complexity of the issue from a historiographical point of view.[9]

Markedly "southern" and invariably "fertile," blessed by an advantageous geographical location (and its different status in the Russian Empire notwithstanding), Ukraine nonetheless enjoyed a reputation similar to that of Finland. It was also viewed as a repository of authenticity, untouched by external influences; a land whose child-like population preserved their archaic way of life.[10] The same imperial discourse, armed with the tropes of Romantic primitivism, blurred the North/South binary, presenting both imperial borderlands as antipodes of the imperial center and of modernity itself.

Unlike Finland, Ukraine was perceived as a repository of specifically Slavic authenticity and national culture. In his "Glance at the Making of Little Russia" ("Vzgliad na sostavlenie Malorossii," 1832), Gogol described "Southern Rus'" (Ukraine) at the time of the Tartar-Mongol yoke as the "true homeland of the Slavs, the land of . . . pure Slavic tribes, which, in Great Russia, began to mix with Finnish peoples, but here were preserved in their former integrity with all the pagan beliefs, childish superstitions, songs, folk tales, Slavic mythology, which they so naively mixed with Christianity."[11] Nadezhdin viewed Ukraine's unique location under "the southern sky," in the steppe, framed by the Don and Danube rivers, seas and mountains, as particularly favorable for the development of the free and poetic Slavic spirit. In the critic's words, Ukraine became "the Ark of the Covenant (zavetnym kovchegom), in which the liveliest features of the Slavic physiognomy and the best evocations of Slavic life are preserved."[12] This "Slavic physiognomy" was both familiar and intriguingly (or frighteningly) alien; the image of Ukraine in the Russian imperial discourse was constructed along a dual axis of "Polish alterity and Russian sameness."[13] The exoticism of Ukraine—especially its more recently annexed Right-Bank territories—paradoxically coexisted with its status as Russia's ultimate origin and the setting of the medieval Russian past, Kievan Rus'. That pastness of Ukraine, according to Shkandrij, could be perceived in an idealizing Sentimentalist-Romantic vein as the "Russian Arcadia" (or "Ausonia") or, more negatively, as a sign of its arrested development, backwardness, and historical irrelevance.[14]

Ukraine thus emerged as Russia's uncanny double, vacillating between its ideal pure past self and its dark twin, whose progress toward modernization and Enlightenment had been stalled. It is "doubly doubled"—both externally, as a double of Russia, and internally, with its split and conflicting images.[15] Ukraine's history, especially the Cossack era, could be romanticized as that of heroic battles and of a republican ideal (an article in a Russian journal went as far as to call Ukrainian history "the most poetic history of all known to us").[16] But it could also be perceived as a period of unruly anarchism and even barbarism. The latter image of the Cossacks was canonized by Voltaire in his *History of Charles XII, King of Sweden* (*Histoire de Charles XII, roi de Suède*, 1731) and then replicated throughout the Enlightenment era. In particular, this image dominated the political and historical thinking about Ukraine and its Cossackdom during Catherine II's rule.[17] As the Russian scholars Vitalii Kiselev and Tat'iana Vasil'eva argue, a doubling image of the Ukrainians as simultaneously dangerous and tame, unruly and submissive, the "strange . . . political throng" of the Cossacks and the simple-hearted ethnographic "singing and dancing people," was created in the late eighteenth century.[18] Yet another ambivalence can be discerned in the perception of Ukrainian folk culture in the Romantic era. Its rich folklore, replete with demonic creatures, fascinated the Romantic imagination and served as a source of poetic inspiration for Russian writers. Yet it also sealed the image of the Ukrainians as a superstitious quasi-barbarous people frozen in a semi-mythological past.

Kyiv, in particular, embodied the paradox of Ukraine as the origin of (supposedly Russian) history, the place where Orthodox Christianity was introduced to the East Slavs in tenth-century Rus', but also as a ghostly mythological realm. Mykhailo Maksymovych, the editor of the almanac *The Kievan* (Kievlianin), historian and folklorist, and the first rector of Kyiv University, describes the city as both the "cradle" and the "cemetery of Russian life."[19] In the same essay, Maksymovych explains how history and myth became entwined during the period of Kyiv's decline after the Tartar-Mongol invasion: while the city lay in ruins, its past glory and real history (e.g., the era of prince Vladimir) was compressed, exaggerated, and reimagined as folklore. Thus Kyiv emerged as a quintessentially ahistorical space—a setting of the largely fictionalized, legendary past and the dwelling of supernatural demonic creatures, like the witches who routinely gather on the city's Bald Mountain for their Sabbath. Another contributor to *The Kievan* lamented contemporary Kyiv's stifling banality, in contrast to the city's romanticized reputation as the ultimate origin: "You know, my dear readers, that I live in Kyiv—this primordial nursery of Russian Orthodoxy, Russian life, and Russian folk poetry. But what you don't know is how joyless life is here, how exhaustingly long the evenings, how torturously important the whist games, and how reasonable and bookish the conversations."[20] This demythologization of the city and its exposure as a trivial Russian provincial town reflected yet another aspect of Ukraine's status in the Russian Empire: having lost both its central historical role and its unique culture, Ukraine eventually became an indistinct imperial periphery.

These complexities made "fertile Ukraine" indeed a fertile ground for staging the Russian imperial uncanny where, as in the case of Finland, Russia's problematic origins are confronted. It is the ambiguity of Ukraine's colonial status within the Russian Empire that made the deployment of the Gothic mode in the Ukrainian setting so abundant and multivalent. As I demonstrate in the subsequent chapters, Gothic tropes used in Ukrainian-themed works reflected not just the widespread popularity of this literary form or the vogue for the Ukrainian setting in Russian Romanticism. More important, they served as symptoms of ambivalence, as the writers, whose identity was tied to Ukraine, attempted to negotiate their position in

the context of the empire, caught between the ideals of Romantic nationalism and the values of Enlightenment and "civilization" that the imperial
order seemed to embody.

Nikolai Gogol/Mykola Hohol is the most famous and best studied case of
such ambivalence.[21] My discussion focuses on two stories from his Dikan'ka
cycle—"A Terrible Vengeance" ("Strashnaia mest'," 1832) and "The Night
before Christmas" ("Noch' pered Rozhdestvom," 1832). The former is perhaps Gogol's most Gothic story, replete with the genre's traditional tropes,
such as the castle, the incest motif, the figure of a villain torturing a young
maiden, an original transgression, and the curse that is passed over generations. Set in seventeenth-century Ukraine, it focuses on the family of the
Cossack Danilo, his wife Katerina, and her father who turns out to be an
evil sorcerer living in an old castle on the "dark side" of the Dnipro River.[22]
The sorcerer (who murdered his wife) now controls the soul of his daughter,
whom he pursues with incestuous intentions. Most important, he conspires
with the Poles to "sell the Ukrainian people to the Catholics" (156) and thus
poses a mortal danger to Ukraine. Imprisoned by Danilo, but released from
the dungeon by Katerina, the sorcerer continues his evildoings, murdering
Danilo, Katerina, and their newborn son, but eventually finds his death at the
hand of a mysterious, majestic knight. At the end of the story, a blind bard
performs a song accompanying himself on the bandura, a traditional Ukrainian string folk instrument. The song sheds light on the origin of the evil
sorcerer: he descends from a fratricide cursed by his betrayed brother.[23] The
curse called for the extinction of the fratricide's clan, with the last descendant
being the worst villain the world has ever seen; upon his death, he would
be forever gnawed on by his dead ancestors. This fate indeed befalls the evil
sorcerer.

This story does not explicitly engage with the imperial context, but its
Gothic motifs are closely linked to the problematic aspects of Ukrainian history and identity. In particular, it is the sorcerer's disturbing otherness, his
non-Ukraineness that makes him an uncanny presence in "A Terrible Vengeance." The sorcerer's first appearance at the beginning of the story immediately marks him as an outsider: he attends a wedding in Kyiv disguised
as a Cossack, whose identity is not known to the rest of the guests. The
sorcerer is mainly defined through negation, as Katerina's father who has
not come to the wedding and as the Cossack whom "nobody knew" (140).[24]
Her father is both present and absent, a Cossack and an ultimate other
(the devilish sorcerer), an insider and outsider (svoi and chuzhoi). Once the
bridegroom's father brings the icons and reads a prayer, the sorcerer's true

nature is revealed, and, transformed into a monstrous old man, he disappears. As Robert Maguire characterizes his appearance at the wedding (a communal ritual), "what is alien is now present; a boundary has been crossed."[25]

After this incident, Katerina (who is as yet unaware that the evil sorcerer is her father) is haunted by the stories about the old man's evil deeds, especially when she sees the corpses rising from the earth in the vicinity of the sorcerer's castle. Her husband, however, is little concerned with the old man's infernal powers. "It's less terrifying (ne tak strashno) that he is a sorcerer than that he is an evil guest," Danilo states and elaborates by linking the appearance of the old man in Ukraine to the Poles' scheming to build a fortress to cut off this Cossack community from the Sich (142). The danger represented by the sorcerer, then, comes not so much from his supernatural destructive power as from his status as an outsider ("evil guest") and his potential association with the enemies of Ukraine.[26] In the same conversation, Danilo states, "A Cossack . . . fears neither the devils nor Polish priests (ksendzov)," thus linking the demonic supernatural to Ukraine's political woes (142). When the sorcerer is caught and chained by Danilo, the narrator specifies that "the sorcerer is put into the deep dungeon not because of his sorcery and ungodly deeds: may God judge them; he is imprisoned for his secret treason, for conspiring with the enemies of the Orthodox Rus' (Russkoi) land—to sell the Ukrainian people to the Catholics and to burn down Christian churches" (156).[27]

The Gothic villain of the story is above all a traitor and an other, which proves more critical to his villainy than his demonic nature.[28] Foreignness is continuously emphasized in the characterization of Katerina's father, even before he is revealed as the evil sorcerer.[29] The old man spent twenty-one years in "a foreign (chuzhoi) land" defined, again, through negation: there "everything is not the same (ne tak): and people are not the same (ne te), and there are no Christian churches" (139). Upon his return, he refuses to eat typical Ukrainian food, to drink mead or gorelka (Ukrainian vodka), and declares his distaste for pork, which immediately marks him as the other: "Only Turks and Jews do not eat pork," comments Danilo who previously observed that his father-in-law lacked a "Cossack heart" (150; 144).

Danilo's suspicions are confirmed when he notices the old man entering the sorcerer's castle—"itself a foreign object" in this area, to quote Maguire.[30] Danilo climbs a tree and, through the window, observes his father-in-law's transformation from a Cossack in a red zhupan into the same monstrous old man he had seen at the wedding—the evil sorcerer.[31] This supernatural metamorphosis is described as changing from a more familiar to a more exotic form of dress. First the "red zhupan" disappears, and the old man is wearing wide Turkish pants; then a hat appears on his head, "written all over by a script that is neither Russian nor Polish" (152). Thus, the old man goes through the degrees of ethnic / religious otherness before he leaves the human sphere altogether and becomes a supernatural demonic creature.

In her reading of the story, Bojanowska points out that the sorcerer is particularly dangerous precisely because of the evasive nature of his otherness that cannot be pinpointed or traced to Ukraine's traditional adversaries or allies; "he epitomizes pure foreignness, the absolute unfamiliar."[32] The weapons hung on the walls of his castle are not carried by "either Turks or Crimeans or Poles or Christians or the glorious Swedish people" (151–52). Bely argues that this negative characterization establishes the sorcerer as a Renaissance individuality (lichnost'), irreducible to a clan identity and that it ultimately redeems him.[33] Yet his "pure foreignness" is still described, albeit negatively, through a specific list of ethnic and religious attributes, just as the sorcerer's refusal to partake of Ukrainian food and drinks marks him as a Jew or a Muslim before his ultimate demonic alterity is revealed. As Bojanowska observes, "The sorcerer's presence threatens to transform Ukraine from a space bound by ethnic custom and natural borders into a confluence of various 'others.'"[34] His elusive otherness, then, is particular to the Ukrainian political, historical, and geographical situation.

Both Bojanowska and Ilieva make an important point about the doubleness of the sorcerer figure: for all his foreignness, he is also an insider, a traitor who attempts to infiltrate his community from within—both the Cossack community and his own family (hence the incest motif). As he is destroying his own family, the old man is also scheming to harm his nation. The demise of Ukraine, all the external enemies notwithstanding, comes from its internal strife. Shkandrij reaches a similar conclusion reading the fratricide legend as describing "a fundamentally divided society cursed by history, tragically torn between its Left and Right Banks, between Russia and Poland, and unable to form an independent entity. The suggestion is that Ukraine's ceaseless civil strife has permanently disabled it."[35]

These interpretations are valid, especially given Danilo's complaints about the internal disorder in his contemporary Ukraine, in contrast to the "golden time" of a not-so-distant past (160–61). I would argue that this dark and tragic story also redeems Ukraine by endowing it with a grand and sublime past, with both history and myth. And it does so, once again, through a negation. Conspicuously absent from the story's elaborate ethnography and geography is "the elephant in the room," Ukraine's northern neighbor—Russia (or Muscovy). Granted, the time setting of "A Terrible Vengeance" predates Ukraine's inclusion into Russia. Yet, it is curious that, for all the vertiginous variety of peoples, places, and religions mentioned in the text, from Uniates to Swedes, Turks, Jews, Poles, Wallachia, Transylvania, and Hungary, Muscovy is not invoked.[36] When the "unheard-of miracle" (chudo) occurs in the spatial organization of the narrative and suddenly the whole world becomes visible from Kyiv, Gogol mentions the south, now open to the unobstructed gaze all the way to the Black Sea, as well as Galicia and Carpathian mountains in the west. The northeast is not part of this grand picture, even though the Russian Symbolist Aleksandr Blok interprets this scene, in his 1909 article "Gogol's Child" ("Ditia Gogolia"), as Gogol's spiritual vision of future Russia (clearly an imperial reading of the story's geography). Similarly, when the disoriented sorcerer is frantically galloping across Ukraine trying to escape his fate, he is heading south but ends up in western Ukrainian lands, "Galich, a city even further away from Kyiv than Shumsk, and already not far from the Hungarians" (172). The imaginative geography of "A Terrible Vengeance" does not accommodate Russia/Muscovy, even as Gogol is writing his cycle primarily in the Russian language for the imperial audience.

I believe that this curious omission plays a strategic function: it disassociates Ukraine from Russian history and geography and establishes Ukraine as an autonomous entity with its own history, its own, however dark, Gothic past, and myth of origins: note that the curse originates in a liminal space, the Carpathian Mountains, which in the story marks the boundary between the Ukrainian world and the space of foreignness.[37] Ukraine, in the historical framework of the tale, is defined without any reference to Russia, which is excluded from the list of Ukraine's others (again, I do not read the adjective "russkii" in the text as referring to Russia proper). Ukraine's distinct national past might indeed be dead, as Bely observes referring to the corpses rising from the earth and later gnawing on the sinner: "Who are the corpses? In the texts they are 'ancestors.' There are too many of them: from the Carpathians, Kyiv, Galicia—isn't it the entire Ukrainian nation (narod ukrainskii)?"[38] At the same time, these corpses are not entirely dead: they do rise and are still shaking the earth as the blind bard reminds his audience in the final scene of the story. They are still haunting the present, both "the present" of the story and the imperial present of Gogol's time.

This final scene, set in modern time, is perhaps the only allusion to the Russian imperial present in the text. In terms of space, the setting is transferred from Kyiv, the majestic Dnipro, and the sublime Carpathian

Mountains to the town of Glukhov (now Hlukhiv), where the blind bard is singing to a crowd. The town's name is associated with deafness (*glu-khoi*) but also with provinciality, as in the Russian phrase *glukhaia provintsiia* (deep province); Maguire, for example, refers to this scene's setting as "the otherwise insignificant town of Glukhov."[39] However, this is not just any provincial Ukrainian town but a place rich with Ukrainian history. After the destruction of Mazepa's Baturyn in 1708, Hlukhiv became the capital of the Hetmanate, and Hetman Kyrylo Rozumovs'ky turned the town into a vibrant Europeanized cultural center.[40] Gogol does not mention the city's past glory but subtly alludes to it through the songs of the bandura player invoking the heroic times of Cossackdom which, in its heyday, "nobody dared to mock" (173). The transformation of the sophisticated Cossack capital into a provincial Russian town mirrors the descent of Ukraine from its glorious past to the insignificant present.

The bard eventually performs the song of fratricide and familial curse, which provides the readers with a background narrative for the sorcerer figure. Sandwiched between humorous tales from Russian and Ukrainian folklore, this song calls on its listeners to contrast their banal present to Ukraine's sublime past, with its larger-than-life apocalyptic horsemen-knights, its demonic villains, majestic mountains, and "terrible" (strashnye) transgressions and punishments. Nobody could mock the Cossacks at the time, the bard reminds his audience, and the Ukrainian "terrible" mythological past is no laughing matter, either.

In his analysis of the spatial organization of the story, Maguire observes that in the town of Glukhov/Hlukhiv, the space of the story bursts, after being extended over the entire universe open to the gaze from Kyiv; as typical of Gogol's fiction, it proceeds from "a small, well-enclosed space to any place, or no place at all."[41] But the town of Hlukhiv is a "no place" only in the context of the Russian imperial present; it epitomizes Ukraine's paradoxical image as an ahistorical land with a rich and heroic past. In the temporal plane, too, history explodes in this scene after being expanded from the seventeenth-century "present" of the story to the ultimate origin of the fratricide myth. It can intrude into the ahistorical present only as an uncanny force, *strashnoe delo* (a terrible affair), through the bard's song that makes such an impression on his contemporary audience (176).

Imperial Russia may be absent from "A Terrible Vengeance," but it is very much a presence in the preceding story of the cycle, "The Night before Christmas." In the story's memorable scene, the Ukrainian blacksmith Vakula, the son of a witch, travels on the devil's back to St. Petersburg to request the tsarina's shoes for his capricious beloved Oksana. The tsarina in question is none other than Catherine II, who happens to be receiving a delegation of Zaporizhzhian Cossacks—a delegation Vakula joins to gain access to the empress. The Cossacks have a completely different agenda: they are complaining to Catherine about increasing restrictions on the autonomy of the Sich. Their political speeches are unceremoniously interrupted by Vakula's request for the shoes—a request that pleases the tsarina because of the young man's *prostodushie* (naivete), and she grants it.

The story's protagonist is transferred from the Gothic-fantastic world of Dikan'ka, inhabited by witches and devils, into the historical present, Russian imperial modernity.[42] "The Night before Christmas" offers us the most explicit moment in the cycle where Ukraine and the Russian Empire come face-to-face, rather literally (in contrast to the rest of the Dikan'ka stories, set in a deliberately obscure and remote location and reaching out to the Russian imperial audience through a set of elaborate narrative techniques). This "Ukraine" is not homogenous: mythological Ukraine, the realm of demonology, folklore, and the supernatural appears next to its historical incarnation, as the Cossacks face real-life historical figures, Prince Potemkin and Catherine the Great, and refer to the actual historical moment of Catherine's attempts at eliminating the Sich. While Catherine is there to "meet her people (narod)," as she puts it, this *narod* is far from uniform. If the blacksmith represents the stereotypical "dancing and singing [or, in this case, "painting"] tribe," as Vakula is a renowned artist in his village, the more militant Cossacks epitomize Ukraine's problematic political image. As Bojanowska points out, Vakula embodies a more subdued, domestic Ukraine, which replaces, in the novella's concluding part, the independent Sich with its romantic aura of masculine Cossack heroism.[43] Furthermore, the "naive" Vakula appears next to "crafty" (khitrye) Cossacks, who are adjusting their manner of speaking to the imperial expectations of backward and provincial Ukraine. Not unlike the blind boy in Lermontov's Taman' (to be published only seven years later), who was switching to Ukrainian in his encounter with the imperial official, the Cossacks hide their ability to speak *gramotnyi iazyk* (proper Russian [133]). As Shkandrij observes, the Cossacks mimic and perform an act of auto-ethnography, reenacting an image of themselves created by the imperial center.[44]

In this episode, not only does Catherine look at Ukraine, but Ukraine also looks back at the empire. What it sees is the abundance of light: "'My God, what light!' the blacksmith thought, 'Back home we don't have that much light even during the day'" (129). The entire novella is built on the interplay between light and darkness. For a significant portion of the story Dikan'ka remains immersed in darkness, as the devil steals the moon, and the appearance/disappearance of light, linked directly to the demonic super-natural agent, propels a great part of the story's plot.

It is tempting to interpret the light/darkness opposition in Gothic terms as if dark backward Ukraine encounters the center of Russian enlighten-ment, St. Petersburg, and the mythological and historical past meets moder-nity. However, the St. Petersburg light is artificial and truly demonic, while Dikan'ka is newly illuminated by the stars, the moon, and the white snow.[45] Russian "light"/enlightenment proves deceitful—as is the *svetleishii* (bright-est) prince Potemkin in the hetman clothing, whose last name means dark-ness, or dusk.

The presence of the Russian satirist Denis Fonvizin in the St. Petersburg scene of the story is quite telling and deeply ambivalent. Catherine addresses him immediately after her comment on Vakula's "simple-heartedness" and offers him this scene as a subject "worthy of his witty pen" (132). The play-wright modestly dismisses his talent, saying that this subject calls for Lafon-taine, the renowned French fabulist. Peter Sawczak reads this moment as a comic legitimization of the Cossacks' and Gogol's minoritarian strategy—while Ukraine is being colonized in the military and political realm, the Ukrainian language in this scene (and in the Dikan'ka stories, more gen-erally) deterritorializes Russian, making the latter also a minor language.[46] Fonvizin's "modest refusal," Sawczak argues, "endows the author and the Dikan'ka narrators with an ironic creative status, as they succeed in fulfill-ing the task for which Fonvizin summons a talent from abroad."[47] Moreover, the reference to a French author as superior to a Russian one stresses the dependence of Russian culture on Western models and contributes to the minorization of Russian literature. The fact that the historical Fonvizin him-self was a harsh critic of Gallomania and Western civilization in his com-edy *The Brigadier* (*Brigadir*, 1769), as well as his letters from France, adds to the irony and ambiguity of the scene. Gogol's depiction of the encounter between Ukraine and imperial Russia undermines the latter's claim to the status of an enlightened center in relation to its colonized borderlands by exposing the borrowed nature of its civilizational mission.

"The Night before Christmas" and "A Terrible Vengeance" capture the fun-damental anxiety about Ukraine's submissive provincial present, its receding heroic past, its historicity and existence as a nation and, most important, the cost of its inclusion into the Russian Empire—a civilization whose own authenticity is viewed as problematic. The next two chapters examine how these concerns are addressed by two very different cultural figures—Gogol's older contemporary, Antonii Pogorel'sky; and his younger contemporary and first biographer, the Ukrainian writer and cultural activist Panteleimon Kulish. The two works analyzed in the remaining chapters do not explicitly deploy Gothic-fantastic elements, as do some of the Dikan'ka tales; nonetheless, they rely on the conventions and tropes of the Gothic genre and introduce Gothic/demonic motifs more indirectly. Ukraine's uncanny doubleness captured by Gogol is echoed in Pogorel'sky's complex portrayal of the Russian Empire's vicious cycle of colonial mimicry, as well as in Kulish's pursuit of the ghost of heroic Ukraine.

CHAPTER 5

On Mimicry and Ukrainians

Empire and the Gothic in Antonii Pogorel'sky's
The Convent Graduate

The narrator of Gogol's "Night before Christmas"—a story that epitomizes Ukraine's uncanny doubleness—exclaims: "How strangely (chudno) is our world made! Everything living in it strives to borrow from and mimic one another!"[1] The play of doubling and mimicry associated with Ukraine is extensively explored in the works of Gogol's older contemporary Antonii Pogorel'sky (the penname of Aleksei Perovsky). Widely regarded as the first Russian writer of the fantastic genre who creatively and ironically adapted the German Romantic tradition of the fantastic and supernatural, especially Tieck and Hoffmann, Pogorel'sky is also believed to be the first to use the Double as a character in Russian literature.[2] The writer himself embodied this doubleness by using a penname (based on his estate Pogorel'tsy in northern Ukraine) and playfully inserting his "Pogorel'sky" alter ego as both a narrator and a character into his novel *The Convent Graduate* (*Monastyrka*). Pogorel'sky's personal history, which included an illegitimate aristocratic birth and a rumored incestuous relationship with his sister, could itself be the subject of a Gothic novel.[3] He was the oldest of several illegitimate children of the Russian minister of education, Count Aleksei Razumovsky. The latter's father, Kirill Razumovsky (Kyrylo Rozumovs'ky in Ukrainian), was the last hetman of Ukraine, and his uncle, a Ukrainian Cossack Aleksei Razumovsky (born Oleksii Rozum), was Empress

Elizabeth's lover and most likely her secret husband. Although educated in St. Petersburg, Pogorel'sky knew Ukraine intimately, having lived there as a child and later at his estate Pogorel'tsy and at the hetman estate Krasnyi Rog in the then Chernihiv region, between 1822 and 1826.[4]

His first major work, a cycle of novellas titled *A Double, or My Evenings in Little Russia (Dvoinik, ili Moi Vechera v Malorossii*, published in 1828 but written a few years earlier and predating Gogol's Dikan'ka cycle) explicitly links Ukraine with the idea of doubling, both in its title and its framing narrative. The work opens with a description of the narrator's leisurely evening in northern Ukraine and his boredom, which he tries to dispel by building castles in the air, with the help of "the best of architects"—his lively imagination.[5] His fanciful dreams are interrupted by a stranger, whose sudden and inconspicuous entrance "made a bizarre and inexplicable impression" on the narrator. Moreover, the visitor's "gait, his tiniest motions and his entire appearance resembled something familiar, one could even say something closely related (rodnoe)" (9). The visitor, predictably, turns out to be none other than the narrator's Double, and on recognizing his alter ego, the narrator is enveloped in terror and breaks into a cold sweat (10). The Double assures the narrator of his best intentions and friendly disposition, and the two spend several evenings exchanging fascinating stories—the novellas that constitute the core of the cycle.

In this work, the uncanny effect of the Double's presence is quickly dispelled, and none of the inserted novellas unfold in Ukraine. The link between the "Little Russian" locale and the uncanny, albeit significant, remains only as a framing device in this work. However, Pogorel'sky would fully engage with the Ukrainian setting in his later novel, *The Convent Graduate (Monastyrka* 1830–33), which was welcomed by critics as the first successful *roman de moeurs* in Russian literature and enjoyed tremendous popularity throughout the nineteenth century.[6] Not a Gothic novel per se (the novel draws on various genres from the family and adventure novel to ethnographic sketches), *The Convent Graduate* nonetheless is indebted to the Gothic tradition. As Vatsuro points out, in Russian literature of the 1830s, Gothic motifs are most fully exploited not in the historical novel but in the novel of mores (*nravoopisatel'nyi roman*), and he specifically used Pogorels'ky's novel as an illustration of this tendency.[7] Vatsuro's discussion of the traditional Gothic tropes and their travesty in the novel nonetheless does not take into consideration the peculiarity of the work's setting and treats it as another novel set in the "Russian" provinces. By contrast, I demonstrate that the use of Gothic and uncanny elements in *The Convent Graduate* is directly related to

Pogorel'sky's construction of his heroes' identities as imperial subjects in the context of colonized Ukraine.

Ukraine as the Other

The novel's central narrative about its heroine's adventures is prefaced by an introductory section that focuses on the Ukrainian setting of the novel and its cultural distinctiveness. This section is narrated on behalf of a local land-owner who is traveling on the Chernihiv road in "Little Russia"; during his stay at an inn he discovers letters written by the heroine and later meets her and learns her entire story. In the first dialogue of the novel, the traveler's coachman replies to him in Ukrainian; bilingual exchanges continue as the traveler arrives at the post station where he is refused horses. Pogorel'sky transcribes the Ukrainian spoken by the locals into Russian and provides his translation in footnotes (anticipating thus Gogol's glossary in his Dikan'ka tales).[8] This technique firmly establishes the otherness of Ukraine, with its language different enough to require translation and its local details that call for explanations.

The typically colonial figure of the narrator—Pogorel'sky's alter ego, well familiar with the Ukrainian language, folk songs, and ways of life—serves as a mediator between his Russian audience and the Ukrainian ethnographic material.[9] Throughout the introductory section, the narrator flaunts his in-depth knowledge of Ukrainian life and culture, making generalizations, such as "In Little Russia I happened to stay at such inns in many small towns situ-ated by the main road; and almost everywhere I would find an old woman—the owner, her young daughter, and the guitar" (165); "In Little Russia not every post station has its official postmasters" (162); or revealing his intimate familiarity with Ukrainian folklore ("the sounds of my favorite Little Russian song 'Don't go, Hryts'"; 164). Despite his "insider" status, his class and educa-tion unmistakably identify him with the Russian imperial order, as becomes evident during a conflict that erupts between the traveler and the scribe at the post station. The narrator demands to see a book of records that would confirm that no horses indeed are available. The notebook that the Orien-talized scribe—a sluggish, "heavy, mustachioed Ukrainian," his head shaved around—presents to him is a barely readable hodgepodge of official records and the clerks' personal calligraphic exercises. The narrator's appeal to the authority of the law, "What do you mean, you don't have [another book] (Kak 'nema')? Aren't you required to always have a special clean book to record travel permits and the horses that are in use?" is met with the clerk's irreverent reply in Ukrainian, "Eh, sir, not everything is done that's required" (E! pane!

Ne vse to robytsa, shcho prykazuiut'; 162–63). The imperial bureaucratic order disintegrates in the provincial and colonial space of Ukraine, emblematized by the chaotic document presented to the traveler.[10]

As the conflict escalates and the frustrated traveler raises his voice at the scribe, the latter suddenly pretends to be deaf, thus comically literalizing the potential language barrier between the two. As in Lermontov's "Taman'," an encounter between the representative of the empire and that of the colony or periphery involves the latter's performance of a physical disability and facial immobility that renders him unreadable to the gaze of his visitor: "My threats did not change a single trait of the stubborn Ukrainian's immobile physiognomy" (163). That is the case until the traveler offers him a bribe and finally gets horses, which again demonstrates his competence in dealing with the locals (in contrast to Pechorin who does not know how to handle the Taman' smugglers and is easily manipulated by them).

This "ethnographic" chapter introduces to us not only the exotic low classes of Ukraine, not fully assimilated into the Russian imperial identity. As Pogorel'sky's narrator continues his journey across Little Russia, we also move up its social hierarchy, and this travel reveals a more problematic Ukrainian self. As the traveler approaches the inn where he will spend the night and discover the heroine's letters, he hears the sounds of "[his] favorite Little Russian song 'Don't go, Hryts'.'" At the inn he meets an old owner and her pretty daughter, who stops her singing when seeing a stranger. When introducing her daughter to the traveler, the old woman makes sure to inform him "in half-Russian and half-Ukrainian dialect" how much she has spent on her education. But it could not be otherwise: "You know yourself how it's done among us, noblemen" (nashe delo dvorianskoe; 164), she states, rhetorically obliterating the distance between her and her obviously more educated and sophisticated interlocutor. The narrator, with mild irony, observes to the reader (again, showing off his regional competence) how typical such an encounter is in Little Russia, including the usually questionable claim to noble origin by these small-town Ukrainian families.

This seemingly insignificant episode points to an essential development in relatively recent history—the abolition of the Hetmanate by Catherine II and the subsequent gradual incorporation of the "new" Little Russian gentry (shliakhta) into the Russian imperial nobility (dvorianstvo).[11] The narrator explicitly refers to the liquidation of the Hetmanate in chapter 3 of the novel when narrating the heroine's family history: "When, at the will of unforgettable Catherine, Little Russia received a new organization and the last hetman put the symbols (kleinody) of his status, *bunchuk* and *bulava*, into the family archive for the eternal memory of his posterity, many officials of

FIGURE 5.   Louis Tocqué, *Portrait of Count Kyrylo Rozumovskyi*, 1758. Oil. State Tretyakov Gallery, Moscow.

the previous government began to seek positions with the new authority" (174).[12] Here Pogorel'sky playfully inscribes himself and his family history into the novel, for this last hetman of Little Russia, whom Catherine forced to resign and whom she replaced with the governor-general Count Petr Rumiantsev, was no other than Kyrylo Rozumovs'ky, Pogorel'sky's grandfather. It is important to note that the Ukrainian geography of Pogorel'sky's novel—primarily Chernihiv and Poltava provinces—belongs to the territory of the former Hetmanate. Thus, this geographical setting is not just a tribute to the popularity of the Ukrainian locale in the Romantic era—it is fraught with personal, national, and imperial history.

Along with important economic, administrative, and other structural changes that accompanied Ukraine's integration into the Russian Empire, education of the young generation played a key role. Count Rumiantsev specifically negotiated the right for the children of the new Ukrainian gentry to study at privileged imperial schools for nobility, such as the Smolny Institute, in the hope of creating a new generation of Ukrainians loyal to the Russian Empire (earlier such a right had been denied to them, since the official view held that Ukraine had no nobility).[13] By stressing the linguistic and cultural hybridity of the local population and alluding to the problematic history of the region, the introductory chapter captures the uneasy process of the formation of the new imperial identity in Ukraine. This section provides an essential background to a fuller development of this theme in the Gothic vein throughout the central part of the novel.

The Convent Graduate offers us several competing models of education and the resulting cultural identification. At the center of the novel is Aniuta Orlenko, a descendant of an "ancient Little Russian family," whose grandfather refused, after the abolition of the Hetmanate, to serve the new government and retired to his estate (174). He, however, encouraged his son Trofim—Aniuta's father—to explore the new opportunities offered by the Russian imperial service but on one condition: as a Cossack, Trofim was to serve only in the cavalry. He even took Trofim to Baturyn, the residence of the last hetman of Ukraine, to introduce him to "field-marshal Razumovsky" (whom the old man still stubbornly addressed as "hetman"). Razumovsky/Rozumovs'ky gave a blessing to Trofim's service for the Russian imperial army as a hussar. Trofim valiantly fought in Russian imperial wars, retired at the rank of major, and married a neighbor's daughter with whom he enjoyed blissful marital happiness until her premature death from fever. Unable to cope with the loss of his beloved wife, Trofim died only four months later, leaving the five-year-old Aniuta an orphan. Trofim's biography seems to suggest a rather smooth transition of the Ukrainian elite to the Russian imperial service, sanctified by the last hetman of Ukraine who had himself made the transition. Aniuta's story, however, shows a more problematic aspect of the integration of the Ukrainian elite into Russian imperial culture.

After the early death of her parents, Aniuta was growing up on the Ukrainian estate of her loving aunt until her legal guardian Klim Diundik, whom she hardly knew, decided to send her to the prestigious Smolny Institute, also known as the Smolny "Convent," for education.[14] Her kind, simple-hearted aunt was devastated: "Oh! I lost my Halechka!" (186), she exclaims in Ukrainian. Indeed, her Halechka (derived from "Hanna," the Ukrainian for "Anna") does not come back: the refined and educated Aniuta who returns to her aunt's house several years later bears no traces of her "early upbringing," detests the Ukrainian version of her name, and has a faint recollection of her homeland: "The Smolny Convent . . . became her new motherland, as it were, a focus of all her thoughts, desires, and concerns" (186).[15] After spending her formative years at the institute and a few months in St. Petersburg after graduation, Aniuta fearfully envisions her return to Ukraine as a journey to "a different country,—to a different part of the world!" (188).

Aniuta's letters addressed to her institute friend picture Ukraine as a radically other space: "Oh, Masha, my sweet Masha! I've been living for an entire week at my dear aunt's in Little Russia, and I'm still not accustomed to it. What will happen to me in the future, I don't know; but for now I feel that I'll never get used to this life and these people! When sleeping and awake, I dream of St. Petersburg, the Neva, our convent, and you, my dear friend! And R*, and S*, and F*, and all of you, my sweet unforgettable friends!" (166–67). Aniuta's experiences in St. Petersburg heavily predetermined her perceptions, and she expects the provinces of the empire to be a replica of the imperial center: "During my entire trip from St. Petersburg to Barvenovo, while ceaselessly thinking about the convent, I indulged, at the same time, in picturing the impending encounter with my relatives . . . I imagined that my aunt would resemble A**, and I pictured my older cousin like N*. . ., and the younger one like you, my Masha, or at least like R**. How mistaken have I been in my expectations!" (167). Following the same logic, the heroine is disappointed that her aunt's village of Barvenovo is nothing like the suburbs of St. Petersburg (Tsarskoe Selo or "at least" the Kamennyi Island). Even her notions of ethnic and class diversity are based on the St. Petersburg model—the sight of the exotic Ukrainian peasant, with his shaved head and a forelock (khokhol), confuses the heroine, for he does not resemble a Petersburg coachman nor a *chukhonets* (Finn or Estonian) who sells butter there (interestingly, the St. Petersburg chukhonets is less frightening to her than her Ukrainian compatriot). Aniuta's comparisons continue throughout her three letters, with comments on her aunt's and cousins' old-fashioned dress, unpolished manners, and more generally the provincialism of the local beau monde. Her repeated assurance, "At least, they are *so kind!*" (167) appears to be a defense mechanism against the challenge of difference.

But nothing embodies the confusing otherness of Aniuta's forgotten homeland more poignantly than the Ukrainian language she hears around her: "Above all, I'm tired of the language which they use to communicate here. Will you believe me that I don't understand almost anything?" (169). She transcribes the Ukrainian phrases spoken by her relatives and translates them for her St. Petersburg addressee, just as the narrator does for his Russian audience in the introductory chapter (as Romanchuk observes, she begins to function as a kind of Pogorel'sky's double).[16] But she is also far less competent in the local language than the narrator, which leads to some comical misunderstandings. When hearing the word "barda," she associates it with the word "bard," familiar to her from the Russian Romantic poet Zhukovsky's works: "In my distraction, it appeared to me that the *barda* whom they are praising so much, should be the wife of some bard or a poet" (169). Aniuta wants to be introduced to this famous woman but instead learns that *barda* refers to wine sediment.

These examples make it clear that Aniuta's letters fulfill at least a double function. On the one hand, they offer an ethnographic account of the Ukrainian province through a defamiliarized perspective of a cultural outsider. On the other hand, this perspective is compromised: Aniuta, a product of refined St. Petersburg education, with her Gallicisms, mannerisms, and her blindness for diversity and difference, is as much an object of the author's satire as are Little Russian provincials. The reader soon learns that the young woman happily adjusted to her rural life and came to appreciate her simple-hearted and loving Ukrainian relatives. With cultural tensions resolved, the play of different narrative perspectives ends: the narrative switches to a conventional, third-person account of Aniuta's adventures, the satiric tone is abandoned, and the local color, with its linguistic tensions, is toned down. In one of her letters, Aniuta offers to Masha to present her aunt's language, "as if she speaks Russian" to spare her from the inconvenience of being exposed to obscure Ukrainian—and the narrator does the same, accommodating his implied audience (169). Romanchuk interprets this moment as the beginning of the process of vampiric recycling and incorporation of the Ukrainian by Russian in the novel (paralleled by Little Russian fiction being "swallowed" by imperial Great Russian literature and ultimately resulting from the colonial incorporation of Ukraine by the Russian Empire).[17]

At this point, Aniuta's perspective on Ukraine merges with that of the narrator who expresses admiration for the locals' simplicity, hospitality, and naturalness: "In Little Russia, in those homes where people haven't managed yet to exchange the traditional Russian hospitality for new society manners, one does not need a lot of time to get to know a family closely and be accepted as their own" (190). Aniuta's aunt and her daughters seem to represent this authentic, if naive and unpolished, side of Ukraine, the "good" double of the Russian imperial self, untouched by Western influence.

Once Ukraine is safely domesticated (or even "swallowed," to follow Romanchuk's line of interpretation) as an idealized Russian "past" self, the cultural distance and shock experienced by the heroine are eroded. At the local ball, Aniuta meets Blistovsky—a brilliant (as his name, derived from the Russian verb *blistat'* [to shine], suggests) officer from St. Petersburg, educated by a certain abbé Nicolas, and the owner of a neighboring estate in Little Russia. The heroine now knows that she has found her match in this imperial province. The young people who share educational background, St. Petersburg experience, taste in music, and polished manners become the novel's ideal couple. Their happy marriage, however, is delayed by the plots of the evil Diundik family, who had erroneously assumed that Blistovsky intended to marry one of their daughters. The Diundiks' intrigues aimed at separating the lovers occupy most of the second part of *The Convent Graduate*, where Gothic elements begin to accumulate.

The Novel's Gothic Threats, Real and Imaginary

At first glance, the novel's Gothic motifs revolve around the figure of the Gypsy Vasilii whom Blistovsky meets at the local fair and later befriends. With his exotic "Indian" look, "yellow" skin tone, an aquiline nose, curly black hair, and sparkling dark eyes (197–98), Vasilii could be easily taken for a demonic Gothic hero from the various southern settings of British Gothic fiction. But his potential as the Gothic villain is consistently undermined in the novel. For example, in a chapter titled "Murder" ("Smertoubiistvo"), Blistovsky finds himself lost in a forest at night, where he overhears a conversation between a man and his wife about a certain Vas'ka, whom the man confesses to murdering. When an alarmed Blistovsky attempts to flee, he is captured by "a man of a terrifying appearance" (220). The scene is set up to invoke the Gothic or "brigand" genre expectations.[18] But the "terrifying man" turns out to be Vasilii, who quickly recognizes Blistovsky and not only lets him go but also accompanies him to the station. During the trip, Vasilii explains that his unfortunate victim, Vas'ka, was a goat.

In other instances, the impression of a Gothic threat is deliberately created by Vasilii. Part 2 of the novel, in which Aniuta is abducted by the Diundiks, contains a series of Gothic motifs and pseudo-supernatural events; a contemporary reviewer criticized one scene from this part specifically for its "Radcliffism."[19] Among them are the appearance of a hairy monster in Aniuta's room, the hooting of an owl, a suspicious whistling outside meant to invoke the spirit of the legendary bandit Harkusha, and an invisible force that snatches Klim's hat.[20] As the reader finds out, all these events are orchestrated by Vasilii and his son, whose name, interestingly, is also Vasilii, as is the goat's—thus the uncanny doubling or even tripling continues even in the comic plotline.[21]

The Gypsies, villains-turned-helpers, control the Gothic threat and provide a misleading source for it. The superstitious Diundiks who believe in ghosts, werewolves, and witches easily fall prey to their pranks. The aunt's family embodies Ukraine's (and by extension, Russia's) more "authentic" and idealized, if provincial, image, whereas the Diundik family functions as its darker, truly backward, and superstitious Gothic incarnation. But their Gothic characteristics undergo a comical travesty in the novel: their unfinished house, which has an unoccupied section (a dark room used for punishment of female servants), is a caricature of the conventional Gothic castle; their evil scheme of separating an inexperienced girl, an orphan, from her protectors and imprisoning her in their house ("castle") reproduces, in a reduced form, the plot of Radcliffe's *The Mysteries of Udolpho* and some other Gothic novels.[22] It is tempting to conclude that in Pogorel'sky we find a self-conscious use of Gothic motifs with a satiric purpose. And this is certainly true. However, I maintain that the Gothic element in its serious, uncanny manifestation is present in the novel. Although the Diundiks are described with merciless mockery, this family embodies a real Gothic threat.

When Klim Diundik visits Aniuta's aunt to take the heroine away to his house, Aniuta feels inexplicable fear and trepidation (a feeling she later dismisses with her usual "He is so kind!" [251]). This effect of Klim's presence is not only a foreshadowing of his and his wife's mistreatment of Aniuta. The detailed description of Klim Diundik earlier in the novel, when he appears at the same fair as Blistovsky and Vasilii, suggests an uncanny void:

> This was a man of about sixty years old, with thin and completely gray hair. He was rather tall and stocky. His chubby and ruddy face showed not a single notable trait, or, one should rather say, all his facial features were equally insignificant. At the first glance, the expression of his physiognomy could appear kind . . .; but upon a careful observation, anybody could notice that his immobile and never changing smile, so to speak, had no meaning at all; just as his big bulging eyes, which could be compared to tin because of their indefinite color and immobility. His attire was nothing special, either. (199–200)

This indeterminacy, indistinctiveness, and mechanistic immobility of Klim's appearance (anticipating Gogol's "negative" description of Chichikov in *Dead Souls*) make him far eerier than the "Gothic" Gypsy. More important, a similar lack of any positive identity is reflected in his family's abandonment of their national and cultural roots and in the world of simulacra, which they inhabit.

The Diundiks are depicted as a symmetrical reversal of Aniuta's aunt's family: their daughters anxiously follow the latest fashion trends, read Moscow journals, and have a French tutor. In contrast to Aniuta's cousins who are emphatically not like N* and R* from the Smolny Institute, Vera and Sofia Diundik are brought up to imitate the imaginary refined and Europeanized Russian elite. Blistovsky, when visiting the Diundiks, is almost as lost culturally as Aniuta was at first at her aunt's: he also does not understand the language spoken around him—not because it is Ukrainian but because it is what they believe to be French. In their zealous desire to speak perfect French (the only condition to be considered fully Russian, to be accepted in St. Petersburg high society, according to their father), the Diundik sisters even translate Vera's name into French, referring to her as Foi (Faith). The translation of the name parallels their attempt at a full translation of identity, which leads to its complete disintegration.[23]

This situation offers us an interesting variant of colonial mimicry—a concept explored in Homi Bhabha's seminal essay "On Mimicry and Man" (1984). For Bhabha, mimicry is a key aspect of colonial discourse, which also reveals this discourse's profound ambivalence. The colonizing power (the British Empire, in Bhabha's example) strives to produce a mimic man, "Indian in blood and colour, but English in tastes, opinions, in morals, and in intellect."[24] At the same time, the colonized is prohibited (usually based on postulated racial difference) to be completely identical to the colonizer as this would undermine the colonizer's superiority and the civilizing mission underlying the colonial enterprise. "Colonial mimicry," Bhabha states, "is the desire for a reformed, recognizable Other, *as a subject of a difference that is almost the same, but not quite.*"[25] This discursive ambivalence becomes a menace to the colonial power because it subverts the very premise of its existence—reforming of less civilized nations in the spirit of Enlightenment universalism.

The Ukrainian situation differs from the one analyzed by Bhabha: because of the perceived unity of origin of the colonizers and colonized (an essential identity between Russians and Ukrainians), Ukrainian mimicry was supposed to faithfully reproduce the Russian imperial self. Unlike Bhabha's Anglicized Indian, who could not (and should not) become fully English ("almost the same, but not quite"), a properly Russified Ukrainian could become Russian, as did Aniuta and Blistovsky in Pogorel'sky's novel. Thus the Russian colonial strategy in Ukraine involved inclusion of the Ukrainian elite into the process of empire-building, typically accompanied by their moving to the capitals and adopting the Russian imperial identity.[26] But as I show below, the kind of mimicry described by Pogorel'sky in the case of Ukraine also proves threatening to the colonial order and destabilizes the imperial self by revealing its emptiness.

As Bhabha puts it, "mimicry conceals no presence or identity behind its mask."[27] The theme of absence and void is pervasive in the description of the Diundik family. Klim gains respect in the region by telling everybody a story about the nonexistent hospital he supposedly built where patients are treated for free; the location of this "hospital" vacillates between the Poltava and Chernihiv provinces depending on the region in which the conversation is taking place. Moreover, he shows an actual plan of the hospital, but there is no reality behind this "document" (as in the case of the fabricated "will" of Aniuta's father he presents to the heroine). His daughters are taught "French" by a tutor who is not a teacher and does not know French; their house is built by an architect who is not an architect but a German carpenter. Finally, the Diundiks believe in fantastic creatures that do not exist. This family does not just represent a world of "half-Enlightenment, of a superficially appropriated and distorted civilization," as Vatsuro put it; their world is that of phantoms, of a complete dissolution of the self.[28] Even their pro-Western orientation turns out to be a mask: after realizing that her daughters do not speak any recognizable French and fearing Aniuta's mockery, Marfa quickly resorts to the language of Russian nationalism, berates Aniuta's European education, and insists on speaking exclusively Russian in her house.

Marfa can call herself and her language Russian as much as she wants, but the narrator points out that "her dialect (narechie) smacked strongly of blessed Ukraine" (204). Assimilation into the Russian identity does not come easily to the Little Russian gentry, as was already suggested by the narrator's encounter with the inn owner who was speaking a mixture of Ukrainian and Russian. Unlike the Finnish Gothicized narratives, where assimilation is either fully embraced or resisted, Pogorel'sky's Ukrainian stories, with the notable exception of Blistovsky and Aniuta, tend to unfold along the more uncanny scenario of Bhabha's colonial mimicry. Such is the case of foppish and disgusting Pryzhko, Marfa's nephew. Educated in St. Petersburg, he, "following the example of many others," Russifies his last name by adding a "v" to the ending. The added letter, however, becomes an empty sign of a failed identity shift: Pryzhko(v) still speaks bad French and cannot get Aniuta, the refined product of Russian imperial education—just as superficially Russified/West-ernized Vera/Foi Diundik cannot win over Blistovsky's heart.

Their failure is made inevitable by the fact that their object of mimicry—Russianness—is itself a mask and an absence. Pogorel'sky alludes to this when he notes that Marfa Diundik, as a Ukrainian provincial, had to resort to wax when covering her missing teeth: "for due to the lack, in Little Russia, of Saucerottes and d'Espines, nobody could insert the latter" (203). In the imperial capital, a similar gap would be filled in by French dentists, just as the Russian cultural void is filled by French—and more broadly Western—cultural influence. Similarly, when the Diundiks' house is finished and proves to be an architectural disaster, Klim is only comforted after Sofronych—the same French tutor who taught his daughters nonexistent French and who also secured the false German architect—"swore that even in Moscow there are houses with drawbacks" (255). By imitating what they think to be the culture of Russian imperial centers, they mimic distortions and void. Characteristically, in the novel's epilogue we learn that Pryzhko(v) sells his Ukrainian estate and moves to Paris where, according to rumors, he hangs himself in Palais-Royale—the relay of mimicry thus ends in an ultimate self-annihilation.[29]

Alternatives to Mimicry

What makes *The Convent Graduate* particularly interesting and somewhat elu-sive is the fact that the positive characters are not spared uncanny cultural indeterminacy. The aunt and her daughters, as Aniuta disapprovingly notes in one of her letters, when receiving guests, do not sing "beautiful Little Russian [folk] songs," but instead perform, in distorted Russian, some senti-mental songs (romansy) imported from Kyiv. Perhaps as an intended paral-lel, in the introductory chapter, the daughter of the inn's owner interrupts her singing of the narrator's beloved Ukrainian folk song on his arrival. The supposedly more authentic Ukrainians seem to have just a closer object of mimicry—Kyiv, rather than Moscow and St. Petersburg, as is the case with the Diundiks. After all, the greatest authority for the aunt in her village is the German Klara Kashparovna (herself a product of colonization), "for she spoke German and has visited Kyiv Contract fairs more than once" (188).[30] Her experience with the "center," as well as her foreignness, qualify her to be sent to St. Petersburg when the time comes for Aniuta to return to Ukraine after her graduation.

Blistovsky and Aniuta seem to embody the novel's ideal of an enlightened couple and success of the Russian imperial project but their rootlessness is somewhat disturbing, as suggested by the author's ironic treatment of Aniuta's letters earlier in the novel. The two protagonists are so assimilated into an imperial culture that twentieth-century Polish scholar and the author of a monograph on Pogorel'sky, Jósef Smaga stated, contrary to the facts of the novel, that "main characters of the novel are not Ukrainians."[31] Aniuta's story is particularly striking because of her persistent mobility: she is taken from her parents' home to her aunt's; then to the Smolny Institute in St. Petersburg; then back to her aunt's estate in Ukraine; then to the Diundiks' house; then to their remote farm (khutor) from which she eventually escapes. This often-involuntary mobility mirrors her cultural homelessness. Her displacements are not only a legacy of the Gothic genre; they are also geographically specific to her situation as a representative of the new generation of the Ukrainian gentry in the Russian Empire. Once separated from her Ukrainian roots, she undergoes a cultural transformation in the imperial capital and receives a Russian education, which is based on Western models.

The title of the novel points precisely to the place of Aniuta's education—the Smolny Institute, or Smolny Convent (monastyr'), as it was typically referred to even after the convent was replaced by the institute in 1764. This title also sets up Gothic expectations—a convent, a monastery or an abbey were some of the favorite Gothic settings, associated with Catholic mysticism, superstition, and lack of Enlightenment. The problem of education, or Enlightenment, was critical for the Gothic genre, as it was for European imperialist and colonial practices. It held particular importance for Perovsky / Pogorel'sky who served as a trustee of the Kharkiv educational district and composed a note "On National Education in Russia" ("O narodnom prosveshchenii v Rossii") for Nicholas I in 1826. In this note Perovsky closely linked the educational system with the political order, arguing that Russian education should follow the Austrian imperial model (as opposed to the German one) and that teaching of "abstract" disciplines had to be centralized and unified across the empire, to avoid spreading of potentially subversive ideas.[32] The position of the writer Pogorel'sky, however, is more complex. The title of his novel refers to the locus of Enlightenment and refinement (the Smolny Institute founded by Catherine the Great), which is simultaneously the site of the formation of the new Russified Ukrainian elite. At the same time, the title preserves its Gothic "medieval" associations, reflecting the same ambivalence about imperial education and the absorption of the Ukrainian gentry into the empire as expressed in his characterization of the novel's heroes.

At the end of the novel, the protagonists refuse to take part in the imperial project. Blistovsky retires from military service, and the couple settles in the bucolic setting of "blessed Little Russia," not far from the narrator, who marries one of Aniuta's provincial plump, red-cheeked cousins. The final scene of the novel focuses on Gypsy Vasilii, who, liberated from serfdom by Blistovsky, starts his own horse-trading business and continues to visit his friends and benefactors. "Our children aren't afraid of him," observes the narrator, "especially my Antoshka; when the Gypsy picks him up, he plays with his black beard" (324). The Gypsy, who resists assimilation and Europeanization, is the novel's demonstratively pseudo-Gothic character, the one who seems threatening but is not to be feared. His function is to highlight the genuine Gothic threat of the work—"the menace of mimicry," to use Bhabha's expression.[33] Ukrainian mimicry mocks and exposes its very object, the Russian imperial self, as a simulacrum and thus seems to undermine the Russian colonial strategy of assimilation.

Yet the novel's idyllic finale reads like an artificial, if satisfying, ending, just as Aniuta's transformation from a sophisticated St. Petersburg convent girl to a happy Little Russian provincial remains perfectly unconvincing. The subtle resistance of the Ukrainian nobility to the Russian Empire's "invitation through assimilation" is no more than a fantasy. In 1825, after a few years of blissful solitude and tranquility at his Ukrainian estate, Aleksei Perovsky petitioned to Alexander I asking for a state appointment, returned to imperial service, and eventually moved to St. Petersburg—a turn of the plot denied to his fictional alter ego, the novel's narrator Antony Pogorel'sky.[34]

Inscribed in its proper imperial context, both geographical and historical, Pogorel'sky's *The Convent Graduate* emerges as a critical text in the tradition of the Russian imperial uncanny. Along with the surface layer of conventional Gothic tropes, mocked and parodied by Pogorel'sky, the novel gradually unveils its unique arsenal of Gothic horrors, from historical doubles and uncanny colonial mimicry to unsettling rootlessness as a cost of assimilation. Beneath the entertaining plot and comic elements of this once popular work lurk deep anxieties about the disappearance of Ukraine's cultural and political distinctiveness—its dissolution into the void of Russian imperial culture. This concern became even more pressing in the 1840s with the rise of Ukrainian Romantic nationalism, as evidenced in the works of Panteleimon Kulish who, through different literary means, confronts some of the same questions that haunted his older contemporaries.[35]

CHAPTER 6

'Tis Eighty Years Since

Panteleimon Kulish's Gothic Ukraine

In 1846, the St. Petersburg-based journal *The Finnish Herald* (*Finskii vestnik*) reviewed an obscure work titled *Hetman Ostrianytsia, or The Era of Troubles and Tribulations for Little Russia, A Historical Novel from the Seventeenth Century* by Vasilii Korenevsky. The review found no literary value in the novel, but it encouraged a further exploration of the material used by its author: "Not the book itself but its subject seems to us worthy of great attention. Little Russia (Malorossia) for Russia, in a literary sense, is the same as Scotland is for England; it is awaiting its Walter Scott, awaiting him with love and will be able to give him his due appreciation."[1] What the Russian reviewer was unaware of was that the "Ukrainian Walter Scott" had already entered the literary scene: the young Ukrainian writer Panteleimon Kulish (1819–97) was perceived by his contemporaries as an incarnation of the renowned Scottish novelist, especially after he published his first historical novel *Mikhailo Charnyshenko, or Little Russia Eighty Years Ago* (*Mikhailo Charnyshenko ili Malorossiia vosem'desiat let nazad*) in 1843. In his memoir about historian Nikolai Kostomarov, Kulish half-jokingly reminisced: "I perceived him as a future Tacitus, and he regarded me as a future Walter Scott. We both were far from the truth."[2] For the young

Kulish, this comparison nonetheless was fraught with both literary and ideological significance.

A Ukrainian Walter Scott

What exactly did it mean to be a Ukrainian Walter Scott at the time? The "Scottish sorcerer," as the novelist was often labeled by his contemporaries, succeeded in "domesticating" history, making it vivid, detailed, and familiar.[3] At the same time, he populated this intimate fictionalized world with exotic heroes, such as medieval knights or Scottish Highlanders, who either belonged to a distant era or preserved an archaic lifestyle and ethos in the recent past or present. This world spoke a familiar language occasionally colored by dialectisms and folkloric elements, and it felt authentic due to its degree of ethnographic detail—a result of the author's antiquarian activity. In this world, history and private life came together thanks to Scott's main novelistic innovation—the introduction of the so-called middling hero, a rather passive young man caught between two warring camps, who comes into direct contact with fictionalized historical characters, as well as the colorful representatives of a bygone era, and typically triumphs at the end, having chosen the rational world of contemporary civilization.[4]

This world is not devoid of Gothic elements, which is hardly surprising in a writer whose formative years coincided with the peak of this genre in Britain. It is to Scott's pernicious influence that the Russian critic Osip Senkovsky, in his 1834 article, ascribed the neo-Gothic extremes of the contemporary French "frenetic school": "It was he who introduced executioners, Gypsies, Jews onto the stage, under the cover of all the charms of his narrative talent; he opened up to the European public the disgusting poetry of gallows, scaffolds, executions, massacres, drunken revels, and wild passions."[5] Senkovsky's criticism notwithstanding, Scott's masterful blending of history, romance, ethnography, and the Gothic proved a powerful influence in Russia and beyond, comparable perhaps to that of only Byron.

The specific points of criticism leveled at the novel reviewed in *The Finnish Herald* help us understand what it meant to become a Ukrainian Walter Scott in the 1840s. *Hetman Ostrianytsia* lacked, according to the critic, "a general idea," "historical truth in its characters," "contemporary colors," knowledge "of the most common rituals" (the author sets, for example, Jewish Sabbath on a Saturday night) and "the spirit of the era," as well as stylistic mastery. A "true" Ukrainian Walter Scott would have potentially succeeded in bringing to life the heroic and colorful past of "Little Russia," reproducing its *Volksgeist* and the atmosphere of the time based on an in-depth knowledge of historical and ethnographic detail. When publishing his first historical novel, Kulish aspired to accomplish precisely such a task. He did it not only to apply Walter Scottian techniques to the Ukrainian material but also to pursue a more pressing ideological agenda.

The same year the plea for a Ukrainian Walter Scott appeared on the pages of *The Finnish Herald*, Kulish, who at the time lived and worked in St. Petersburg, wrote in a letter to Moscow-based historian, journalist and novelist Mikhail Pogodin: "My life is not too bad. However, I do miss Little Russia. I want to go there in the summer but everybody finds it extremely silly. I agree, but what, in this intelligent city, will replace for me my native language and the views of my home country? Walter Scott was not insincere (ne mutil) when he told Washington Irving, 'I'd die if I couldn't see Scotland for a long time.'"[6]

Kulish's self-fashioning as a Ukrainian Walter Scott writing nostalgically about his homeland from the imperial capital is more than a literary gesture. The anonymous reviewer's parallel between Ukraine and Scotland in their relationship to Russia and England, respectively, is not limited to the literary sphere, either, despite the critic's qualification ("in a literary sense"). The grounds for this comparison (apparently widespread at the time) derive from Ukraine's and Scotland's political situations: in both cases, we have a region absorbed by the neighboring state into a larger entity, ultimately an empire, and yet preserving its language, folklore, customs, costumes, and way of life. In the age of intense preoccupation with national uniqueness, both Scotland and Little Russia highlighted the relative absence of an avidly sought national character (narodnost') for the dominant imperial powers. One of the reviews of Gogol's Dikan'ka tales, for example, opposed the "distinct physiognomy" of Little Russians to the lack of discernable "elements of the Russian character proper."[7] Katie Trumpener observed a similar tendency for the British Empire: "To the degree that England becomes the center of the empire, its own internal sense of culture accordingly fails to develop. . . . The peripheries, in comparison, struggle with the contradiction of underdevelopment, yet they each retain their distinctive, national, and non-English character."[8] The label of a "Ukrainian Walter Scott" referred not just to a particular literary trend, but it also powerfully invoked the ambivalent status of Ukraine as a Russian imperial periphery.

Ukraine's position as both an exotic colony and a drab province of the nineteenth-century Russian Empire is a critical context in which I analyze the Gothic aspect of Kulish's *Mikhailo Charnyshenko, or Little Russia Eighty Years Ago*. A prominent Ukrainian writer, ethnographer, translator, historian, the first biographer of Gogol, and a leading if controversial figure in the

Ukrainian national revival, Kulish now occupies a firm place in the Ukrainian literary canon, after decades of neglect during the Soviet time because of his "bourgeois nationalist" views.[9] Literary studies of Kulish's legacy tend to focus on his later and more mature novel *The Black Council* (*Chorna Rada*, 1845–57), while his first venture into the historical novel genre, *Mikhailo Charnyshenko*, published in Russian (with considerable Ukrainian and Serbian linguistic components) in Kyiv in early 1843 and reviewed in most major Russian "thick" journals in the course of the year, typically receives only a passing mention.[10]

I find that *Mikhailo Charnyshenko*, while clearly not Kulish's strongest literary work, offers rich material for exploring the author's attempts to navigate between national mythology and modernity and to come to terms with Ukraine's loss of its political and cultural autonomy in the Russian Empire. Throughout his tumultuous life and career, Kulish tried to negotiate a place for Ukrainian culture and national identity in relation to its various political, spiritual, and cultural models and influences, focusing on Russia and Poland but also turning to Islam. Yet his position as a Ukrainian writer in the Russian Empire was of primary importance. In his biography of Kulish, Luckyj states, "It is this Russian-Ukrainian coexistence which proved to be the central dilemma of his life."[11] An important aspect of this dilemma was the conflict between Kulish's Romantic fascination with the Ukrainian heroic past and its rich folk tradition, on the one hand, and, on the other, his deeply held Enlightenment values and belief in high culture, which he associated with Russian (and at times Polish) influences.[12] He famously idealized the Ukrainian Cossack past at the early stage of his career but denounced Cossackdom as a brutal and destructive force in his later historical studies (albeit not consistently). At the level of ideology, this conundrum translated into a split between his ideals of Romantic nationalism and his alignment with the dominant imperial culture.

Although Kulish's disavowal of his Romantic nationalist views is typically associated with the later period in his career, I argue that his ambivalence about Ukraine's heroic past and its current status in the Russian Empire can be observed in his first novel. As other authors discussed in this book, Kulish deploys a range of conventional Gothic tropes in order to address these historical and ideological concerns. This chapter demonstrates that the interaction of various Gothic registers in *Mikhailo Charnyshenko*—the fantastic, the Walter Scottian "historical" Gothic, and the Gothicized ethnic others— creates a complex and ambivalent picture of the Ukrainian subdued colonial present haunted by the ghosts of its glorious autonomous past. I use the Walter Scottian aspect of *Mikhailo Charnyshenko* as a productive point of reference that brings together central themes of the novel's Gothic visions: history, temporality, empire, and national identity.

'Tis Eighty Years Since

Kulish's familiarity with and admiration for Scott is well documented, and the Scottish writer's noticeable influence on Kulish's historical novels has been a subject of several studies.[13] Scholars diverge, however, on the question to what extent *Mikhailo Charnyshenko* follows the Walter Scottian model of historical novel. Bahrij argues that *The Black Council* adheres more closely to the Scottian model structurally and thematically, whereas *Mikhailo Charnyshenko* qualifies as a "Romantic Gothic tale." Neiman sees in the novel a didactic and mystical component untypical of Walter Scott, probably influenced by Gogol and the German Romantic tradition; the Walter Scottian "presence" in the *Mikhailo Charnyshenko*, the critic observes, is more felt in Kulish's predilection for detailed descriptions and *couleur locale*. By contrast, Viktor Petrov notes that in *Mikhailo Charnyshenko* we find more of recognizably "Scottian" paraphernalia, such as Gothic ruins, mysterious towers, and noble "knights," compared with the more mature and reserved *Black Council*. Ievhen Nakhlik points out that the novel combines the Walter Scottian tradition of recreating a specific historical period with the subjective interpretation of history, typical of German Romantics (and Gogol), which draws a contrast between the dull, uninspiring present and the idealized heroic past.[14]

The degree of Kulish's engagement with Scott in his first novel can be subject to debate, but the very fact of this engagement is undeniable. Even the novel's title, *Mikhailo Charnyshenko, or Little Russia Eighty Years Ago*, invokes Scott's *Waverley, or 'Tis Sixty Years Since*—with its emphasis on the change between "then" and "now." More specifically, the title of Kulish's novel takes us back to 1762, the short reign of Russia's ill-fated emperor Peter III and his aborted campaign against Denmark, whose goal was to restore the Schleswig region to his German Holstein-Gottorp Duchy (the war plan did not materialize because of the coup that ended Peter's reign and life and brought Catherine II to the throne). As described in Kulish's primary source for the novel, the *History of the Rus' or Little Russia*, Peter formed a Ukrainian Cossack regiment for his army where young people were lured by the recently converted calculating Jew, colonel Kryzhanovsky.[15] The novel's protagonist, Mikhailo Charnyshenko, joins the Cossack recruits, despite his father's objections. The hero's disobedience of his father's ban on serving in the Russian army causes the latter's wrath, and when Mikhailo unintentionally burns down most of his father's house, the old Charnysh publicly denounces and curses his son. It is the father's curse that is responsible for the subsequent series of misfortunes occurring to the protagonist—his capture by bloodthirsty exotic Serbs, the tragic death of his beloved Katerina killed by Mikhailo's passionate new Serbian lover, and his own death, followed by his father's demise ten years later.

What exactly is at stake for Kulish in adopting the Walter Scottian temporality, the "eighty years ago"? Bahrij, who emphasizes the Gothic aspect of *Mikhailo Charnyshenko* over its Walter Scottian elements, claims that the historical setting in Kulish's novel is not significant per se; instead, the military campaign serves here as essentially a pretext for the hero's leaving the parental home and embarking on his adventures. I insist, however, that the historical context of the novel is far from being a purely formal device unrelated to the novel's problematics. Kulish's choice of this rather obscure historical episode is strategic. First, the irrelevance of this military campaign to the Ukrainian subjects of the empire enables Kulish to question his young protagonist's uncritical and ahistorical acceptance of the heroic ethos of the past. Second, it allows the writer to set his novel on the eve of Catherine II's rule, during which any vestiges of Ukrainian autonomy in the Russian Empire would be annihilated. The geographical setting of the novel, which opens in the town of Hlukhiv, then the capital of the Hetmanate and the venue of the final scene of Gogol's "A Terrible Vengeance," also invokes the last period of Ukraine's relative autonomy.

Scott's choice of the time setting for his first novel has a similar ideological motivation despite the narrator's playful disavowal in *Waverley's* introductory chapter:

> By fixing, then, the date of my story Sixty Years before this present 1st November, 1805, I would have my readers understand, that they will meet in the following pages neither a romance of chivalry nor a tale of modern manners; that my hero will neither have iron on his shoulders, as of yore, nor on the heels of his boots, as is the present fashion of Bond Street. . . . From this my choice of an era the understanding critic may farther presage that the object of my tale is more a description of men than manners. A tale of manners, to be interesting, must either refer to antiquity so great as to have become venerable, or it must bear a vivid reflection of those scenes which are passing daily before our eyes, and are interesting from their novelty.[16]

"Sixty Years Since" is supposed to be an "in-between" epoch, neither too distant to conjure up a romanticized medieval past nor close enough to call for a faithful depiction of contemporary mores. It is presented as a historically unmarked, almost random time period that seems to liberate the author from the constraints of history and allows him to focus on "the characters and passions of the actors."[17]

The text of the novel, as well as the author's historical ruminations in the concluding chapter, belie this declared disregard for historical specificity. *Waverley* is set in the tumultuous period of the Jacobite uprising in Scotland, and it offers a tantalizing picture of the then still vibrant Highland culture which, as the narrator reminds us at the end of the novel, is now all but extinct. If such a setting does liberate its author (and narrator) from history, it does so, paradoxically, because of its historical relevance. As James Buzard suggests in his study of English "autoethnographic fiction," this time setting—"a century removed from Scotland's formal unification with England and more than half a century after the paroxysms of the Jacobite rebellion of 1745–46"—places Scott's narrator (a Lowland Scott) "outside of [Scottish] history." This setting allows him to assume a semidetached perspective on its culture and to "export" it to the English audience: "For the Lowland Scott, the end of the Highlands as a distinct and viable society makes it possible to construct a Scottish culture associated mainly with the Highlands but claimable by the Lowlander as 'his,' such that he can assert an *auto*ethnographic . . . authority over it."[18]

In the concluding chapter of *Waverley*, Scott explains his motivation for writing this novel, undermining the ahistorical stance adopted in the introduction. It is Scotland's loss of its unique culture and autonomy in the aftermath of the suppression of the uprising described in *Waverley* that set him to "the task of tracing the evanescent manners of his own country."[19] As is made clear in the opening of *Mikhailo Charnyshenko*, Kulish pursues a similar goal of reconstructing a national life that has vanished, if not without a trace. It is above all the ideological subtext of *Waverley* and its relevance to the Ukrainian situation—the historical-political parallel between Scotland's absorption by England and Ukraine's dissolution in the Russian Empire—that attracts Kulish to the Scottian model, in addition to its Romantic and ethnographic appeal.

In the concluding chapter Scott discusses the disappearance of old Scotland in a rather neutral and analytical manner, citing "the destruction of the patriarchal power of the Highland chiefs,—the abolition of the heritable jurisdictions of the Lowland nobility and barons,—the total eradication of the Jacobite party," with its insistence on "maintaining ancient Scottish manners and customs," and "the gradual influx of wealth and extension of commerce." Kulish, by contrast, waxes lyrical and adopts a poetic, elegiac tone when evoking Little Russia of eighty years ago:

> Eighty or so years ago Little Russia still lived its own distinct life. Its memories, interests, customs, dress, way of life and poetry were purely national

(narodnye). People still remembered the Swedes and Mazepa, who has now become some kind of a dark myth for the common folk; they talked about hetman Doroshenko and even Bohdan Khmel'nyts'ky—names that have now lost their meaning and that sound without an echo in hearts in [our] historical songs, which are further dying away with each passing year. The Zaporizhzhian Sich still existed . . . Granted, the scope of the Cossack revelry was not as great as it used to be, for example, under our glorious hetman Bohdan of eternal memory or the "great warrior" Palii; and our nobility had long lost their national pride. But the people was still alive with its feeling of love for native things. . . . Not many years, it seems, have passed since the time of the last Hetmanate, and yet how Little Russia has changed! If you could transfer yourself to these times, an entirely different world would surround you.[20]

This "entirely different world" of the Ukrainian past includes the authentic clothing, contrasted with the contemporary Westernized dress, the pure Ukrainian language, as opposed to the current "barbarian" one (a mixture of Russian and Ukrainian), poetic folk songs, and its "magic" (divnaia) heroic history. This world, however, is presented as irrevocably lost: "You cannot help but ponder over the destiny of this extraordinary people (narod), which has appeared *in a miraculous way* like a lush flower among hostile elements, flashed with a remarkable blaze of glory, announced itself to the entire world; but it did not have enough energy for simmering life, and it bowed its head prematurely; it disappeared *like a supernatural apparition*, almost before our very eyes" (1:11–12; emphasis added). In other words, the "eighty years ago" refers to the last period of Ukraine's relative political autonomy and, most important, its cultural and national specificity before its often inept assimilation into Russian imperial culture. Essentially it is the moment before the death—or, as he puts it in more Gothic terms, the ghostly disappearance—of the nation. This ghost-like disappearance is closely linked to the *narod*'s elusive and phantasmagorical appearance. The nation's existence thus is so brief and fleeting that it acquires a quasi-supernatural quality. Kulish attempts to capture this ghost, to reconstruct this forever lost world through studying its folklore and ethnographic evidence. His novel is presented as "the last page from the history of such a magic (divnyi) phenomenon": "Let us see how this people lived and felt at the very end of its autonomous existence; let us take a look at the melancholy traces of its old-world life (byt), let us sing its songs, let us listen to its native legends—perhaps we will hear the echo of its ancient, mighty, and miraculous life . . . in these, already poor, remnants of its magnificent past" (1:1–12).

Kulish's antiquarian project of the restoration of the historical past is a recognizable anti-imperial nationalist strategy identified by scholars of the British Empire. Trumpener writes, in connection to Irish, Scottish, and Welsh nationalisms: "In their reconstruction of indigenous cultural forms and institutions suppressed after the English conquest, as in their arguments about the continuities of language and culture from ancient times to the present, the antiquaries demonstrated both the enormous cultural damage wrought by imperial occupations and the continuing strength of culture to oppose its homogenizing force."[21] The fictional storyline of *Mikhailo Charnyshenko* is accompanied by an impressive scholarly apparatus, with extensive ethnographic and historical notes and citations of documentary sources, aimed at the documentation and preservation of national culture. At the same time, Kulish persistently refers to the Ukrainian autonomous past as a ghostly, phantasmagorical bygone era—a feature not found in *Waverley* where ghosts are restricted to the Highlanders' superstitious imagination.

These two seemingly conflicting temporalities, "antiquarian/historic" and "fantastic," are expressed in the novel by two Gothic modes—what I term "the Walter Scottian Gothic" and the "supernatural Gothic." The former finds its expression in Kulish's fascination with ruins, towers, Gothic architecture, medieval allusions, and his propensity to draw parallels between the Ukrainian Cossacks and Western European knights. The analogy between the Zaporizhzhian Sich and knightly orders was not invented by Kulish. Rather, it was drawn by late eighteenth-century Western historians as part of their quest to "normalize" Cossackdom, previously perceived as barbarous, and became widespread in the Romantic period.[22] In his "Glance at the Making of Little Russia," Gogol views the emergence of Cossackdom within the context of the pan-European tendency toward creating brotherhoods and knightly orders.[23] In Russian and Ukrainian nineteenth-century historiography the idea that the Sich was a Ukrainian equivalent of Western knightly orders was popularized by the Russian imperial historian (a Ukrainian by origin) Apollon Skal'kovsky who published, in the early 1840s, his three-volume *History of The New Sich or the Last Zaporizhzhian Host*. Kulish cites this work in his polemics with Senkovsky over the latter's views on Ukrainian history: "I am referring him [Senkovsky] to Skal'kovsky's *History of the New Sich*: it proves with incontestable facts that Zaporizhzhia was a distinct brotherhood, which set as the only goal of its existence the eternal struggle with the enemies of Christianity."[24] In *Mikhailo Charnyshenko* these ideas are explicit as well: Kulish calls the Ukrainians' struggle with the Poles "crusades" meant to defend the Orthodox faith (1:87), and he mentions the strong bond of brotherly love characteristic of the Zaporizhzhian Cossacks as typical of "all the knightly orders" (3:75). In a sense, the writers engaged with the themes from Ukrainian history did not need to travel to Livonia in order to access the knightly Middle Ages—Ukraine had its own knights, the brave Cossacks.

In contrast to this more "historical" Gothic, the "fantastic" Gothic mode is introduced in the novel through the imagery of ghosts and apparitions, folkloric motifs and infernal forces. The seemingly paradoxical coexistence of the two modes can be related to the ambivalence inherent in the Gothic genre, as analyzed by Trumpener. The scholar describes the British Gothic novel, often relying on an antiquarian impulse as well (a found manuscript frame, for example, common in this genre), as "both historically expressive and historically evasive": while attempting to recapture the past, it is acutely aware of its status as "an artifact of its own moment."[25] The tension between the historicity of *Mikhailo Charnyshenko*'s antiquarian layer and the "evasion of history" in its Gothic-fantastic plane contributes to Kulish's complex portrayal of Ukraine, which seems gone. However, like a ghost, it is at the same time alive and dead, present and absent, historically specific and atemporally symbolic, belonging to the past and yet haunting the present.

Fathers, Sons, and Gothic Ruins

Differing attitudes toward the past are at the heart of the principal conflict of the novel between Mikhailo and his antiquarian father, the Cossack lieutenant (sotnik) Charnysh. Their past is even more removed from Kulish's time—it is the era of Cossack uprisings of the sixteenth and seventeenth century. The tension between the "antiquarian" and the "fantastic" perception of the past, which marks the narrator's temporality, is also observed at the characters' level. The elder Charnysh, retired from service after a series of injustices committed by the "Russian courtiers who were ruling Little Russia," dedicates himself to collecting Ukrainian songs, legends, chronicles, and other "remnants of antiquity." This semi-scientific project nonetheless bears a stamp of the supernatural:

> Lieutenant Charnysh dedicated himself to his study with some kind of a warm faith. The more he penetrated into the spirit of the traditions, songs, chronicles, and other various remnants of the old times, the greater the charm with which past ages and events appeared to him. Having focused all his talents on one point, he created for himself a

separate fantastic world, in which his soul found light and in which he found a substitute for the society he had forsaken forever. The brave knights of Ukraine, whose glory had resounded all over the world in days of yore, were alive in his imagination. (1:50–51)

For all his fascination with Ukraine's glorious past, old Charnysh is aware that "Little Russia has already lived its term (otzhila uzhe svoi vek)" (1:49–50) and is skeptical about transferring this heroic ethos into the contemporary historical setting. This is why he disapproves of military service in the corrupt imperial army and supports his son's civil career at the Little Russian Collegium, an imperial institution established by Peter I to oversee the Cossack self-governance of the Hetmanate. Old Charnysh, thus, acknowledges the irreversibility of time and "the otherness of his object of nostalgia from present life and [keeps] it at a safe distance"—a precondition for Romantic nostalgia, according to Svetlana Boym.[26] Mikhailo, by contrast, fails to acknowledge the otherness of the past, violates this distance, and attempts to reenact the heroic past of Ukraine in its imperial present.

The novel is often read as a religious-moral tale with a Gothic twist—a disobedient son castigated by his father's curse; yet the punishment the hero receives for his career choice seems a bit severe, even by the Gothic genre standards. Critics have interpreted Mikhailo's "guilt" in terms of a conflict of temporalities. Petrov points out that Kulish deliberately sets his novel after the era of heroic military battles to portray Mikhailo's Romantization of war and Cossacks as already outdated and even harmful. The critic sees here the kernel of Kulish's future disillusionment with Cossackdom, his critique of the Romantic fascination with Cossack heroism.[27] Nakhlik suggests that "from the point of view of Kulish the kul'turnyk (enlightened populist), Mikhailo's guilt and misfortune come from the fact that he did not understand the difference between the epochs: instead of the activity appropriate for modernity (governmental or 'antiquarian,' i.e., folkloric-ethnographic, in which old Charnysh indulges himself), he became fascinated by the old, military type of behavior."[28]

As Petrov reminds us, the didactic folkloric theme of disobedience to one's parents and abandonment of parental home had particular relevance in Kulish's time: the rise of the Ukrainian nationalist (narodnyts'ky) rebirth movement in the 1840s was accompanied by the rhetoric of going back "home," to the ancestors' culture, to one's fathers and roots. The scholar offers a rather extreme reading of this theme in the novel, interpreting Mikhailo's disobedience of his father as a manifestation of his rootlessness, a vain pursuit of glory and rank, regardless of its ethical and ideological implications, or even as a betrayal of Ukraine's national interests characteristic of the Ukrainian nobility of the second half of the eighteenth century.[29]

It is important to remember that it is not Mikhailo's disobedience alone but his (albeit unintentional) burning of his father's house that causes the fateful curse.[30] The house, where Mikhailo arrives in order to inform his father of his decision to enlist in the army and to collect his armor, in the manner of a typical Walter Scottian hero, becomes a locus of the novel's conflicting temporalities and nostalgic impulses. As we learn from a long narrative digression, this house was intended by Mikhailo's ancestors to be an exact replica of the house of Bohdan Khmel'nyts'ky in Subotiv, the hetman's residence and hypothetical birthplace. The project was successfully accomplished by Mikhailo's father, who happened to come across the draft of Khmel'nyts'ky's house. This more direct relation to history and origins is contrasted to the narrator's temporality, that of Ukraine "eighty years since." While contemplating the house, the narrator separates his perspective from that of the protagonist, noting that this building, full of historical meaning for him (a Ukrainian intellectual of the 1840s), does not hold nearly the same significance for the young hero from the 1760s who lacks the distance from and the reverence for this "antiquity" (starina). He also detaches the temporal plane of his narrative from Mikhailo's: while the narrator apologetically keeps his readers waiting by the gate, indulging in historical memories and associations, the hero, we learn, has already made his way through the house. "But," the narrator says, "we can't follow him so quickly: everything stops us in this house, a sample of the taste and a monument of the daily life (byt) of our ancestors. We want to prolong the sweet feeling aroused in us by these antiquities: more than history, more than chronicles and songs, they tell us about those miraculous ages which once were and can never be again" (1:86). Similarly to *Waverley*, the narrator here is placed "after the end" of the autonomous history of his native land. But despite his declarations of the irreversibility of this history and unlike Scott's narrator, he does not seem to fully acknowledge that end.[31]

The gate, leading to the house, is described through abundant Gothic references, invoking a medieval past of knightly battles. Even more important, the gate is presented as a fragment of a ruin, even before the house is destroyed by fire: "This gate, made out of oak and blackened with time, was so enormous and had so many roofs, grates, and carved wood decorations most enigmatic to an antiquarian that it seemed to be a fragment (oblomok) of a Gothic tower that had remained from some Gothic castle; the moss and wild grass covering it completed the resemblance" (1:57). Critics have interpreted Kulish's recurrent allusions to Gothic architecture as an influence of translated Western novels.[32] I contend that this description points to the symbolic function of the house *as a ruin* in its nineteenth-century sense, as discussed by Peter Fritzsche. In his *Stranded in the Present: Modern Time and the Melancholy of History*, Fritzsche argues that, while in the eighteenth century the ruins invoked the generic European cultural legacy, a universal set of meanings and continuity between the past and the present, in the nineteenth century they began to signal a temporal rupture between the imperial present and a unique but never fully accessible national past. Fritzsche theorizes ruins using the case of Germany in the wake of the French Revolution and during the Napoleonic Wars, but his conclusions aptly apply to Kulish's Ukraine under Russian dominance. The ruins in Kulish's novel are fraught with deeper and more tragic meaning than those in the Decembrists' Livonian tales discussed in chapter 2. The rift between the past and the present is particularly dramatic for Kulish, for Ukraine is portrayed in the novel as a ghost, a nation with a rich if fleeting past but no present. The burning of the house thus symbolically dramatizes the coming rupture and turns the building literally into a modern ruin, or even "the ruin of a ruin," "the hallmark of modernity."[33]

The notion of the ruin connects the two ostensibly separate temporalities and Gothic modes in the work. An antiquarian fragment of the historical past, a piece of material evidence about a bygone time, the Gothic ruin acquires ghostly, fantastic connotations because of the seemingly insurmountable gap between Ukraine's colorful autonomous past and its subdued provincial present. Paradoxically, because of the presence of the ruins (both literal and symbolic), this past does not fully recede—just as ghosts reappear to haunt the sites of national traumas. Fritzsche explicitly compares ruins to ghosts as "the residue of historical disaster," as well as "a testimonial power" to speak through history.[34]

Kulish appeals precisely to this testimonial power of ruins when describing an epic battle between militant Serbs and local Ukrainian lords and anticipating his reader's doubts about the possibility of these heroic—but also bloody and violent—events taking place in the relatively recent past:

> Perhaps some of my readers will call into question the veracity of such events in Ukraine; they will not believe that under Russian rule such violence could be happening with impunity only eighty years ago, and they will ascribe all of this to the play of my imagination. But . . . is it possible that all these redoubts, ruins (razvaliny), names, and legends have popped up by themselves like mushrooms after the rain? Is it possible that the folk imagination, out of nothing better to do, invented beliefs that are alien to the contemporary daily life (byt) of Ukrainian peasants? (3:166)

As typical of Romantic antiquarian practices, physical ruins' value as a histor-ical source here is comparable to that of folklore and ethnography (local top-onyms and legends but also Serbian epic songs that Kulish explicitly draws on in his portrayal of the battle). The boundary is thus elided between physi-cal and verbal evidence, the ethnographic and the imaginary, historical and mythological, "Walter Scottian" and "fantastic." The interrogatory form of the narrator's argument is not merely rhetorical. It betrays, despite his defen-sive position, the elusive and essentially imagined nature of the Ukrainian past of eighty years earlier, presented in the novel.

The grounds for potential doubts regarding the possibility of such feudal battles and the general chaos in the region is, as the narrator states, the pres-ence of "Russian rule" (the supposed guarantee of order) and the discrep-ancy between the "wild" mores of the time and the contemporary way of life in Little Russia. What happens in between, as he reminds his audience, is the unification of the administrative structure of the Russian Empire under Catherine II, the dissolution of the Sich, and the "correct organization of [the Russian government's] provinces" (3:168–69). It is the ultimate colonial moment—the full absorption of Ukraine into the Russian Empire—that con-stitutes the rupture between Kulish's present and the "eighty years ago" and makes the Ukrainian past open to an imaginative reconstruction.

The narrator's evaluation of this rupture is highly ambivalent. Kulish criticizes the peculiar mores of Ukraine of "eighty years ago" and partic-ularly its imposing, even violent, hospitality. He depicts these mores in a memorable scene where "pan Bardak" (whose name means "disorder" and "unruliness") tries to convince his guests, Mikhailo and his two fellow trav-elers, Cossacks Shcherbina and Sereda, to stay longer for a meal. When they refuse, he is ready to use weapons and fight to enforce his excessive hospi-tality. Kulish suggests that these violent outbursts have their roots in Ukraine's colonial status: the lack of external enemies and internal strife at this point of Ukrainian history left unfulfilled the heroic and combative ardor of the "Ukrainian heart, . . . which Russia, having drawn it closer thanks to broth-erly kinship, began to tame bit by bit by its European measures" (2:106–7). Despite this positive assessment of the "domestication" of wild Ukraine by civilized Russia, the commentary ends with an already familiar nostalgic—and quasi-Gothic—invocation of the last traces of Ukrainian administrative and legal autonomy, "the shadow of its earlier independence which was about to irrevocably vanish forever" (2:109).

The meandering evolution of Kulish's historical views on Cossackdom and Ukraine's absorption by Russia is discussed in detail by Nakhlik, who sums up Kulish's later position as follows: "Kulish in the 1870s and 80s strove to reconcile Ukrainian national interests with those of universal civilization and culture, which in practice meant justifying colonial efforts of the Russian monarchy and Polish nobility in Ukraine."[35] This contradictory agenda can be discerned in Kulish's first novel. But it is less the narrator's direct intrusions than the novel's artistic organization, and particularly its Gothic stratum, that yields a more nuanced insight into the author's complex position.

The Jew

The imperial "Golshtein" campaign, as well as Mikhailo's participation in it, is called into question from the start by the very fact that it is the novel's ultimate Gothic villain, as well as its cultural other—the converted Jew Kryzhanovsky—who forms the Cossack regiment in Little Russia. Local Cossacks describe the conscription process as an uncanny force that leads to severing family ties; the somewhat comical distortion of the terms "Golshtintsy" and "Peterburg" in their speech emphasizes their cultural, geographical, and linguistic distance from this imperial enterprise: "Everywhere one hears nothing but crying and screaming, for all the young men and boys are leaving their fathers and mothers and are going to some cursed 'Gostintsy.' It's even scary, I swear by God! . . . As if some evil (nechistaia) force is carrying them to that Petinburch" (1:155).[36] This description is influenced by the *History of the Rus'*, where we find a similarly worded narrative: "The local youth . . ., as if by a magic force, rose up and took off in a bird flight from the south to the north."[37] Notably, Kulish paraphrases what is described as a magic spell in the "chronicle" with more demonic terms. If in Gogol's "A Terrible Vengeance" the demonic character was misidentified as a cultural other, in Kulish's novel, a reverse mechanism is at play: the villain is not a supernatural figure; rather, it is his otherness that leads the characters to attribute to him infernal powers.

Katerina, Mikhailo's beloved, whom Kryzhanovsky also pursues, describes the inexplicable terror that envelopes her upon seeing him: "Once he looked at me for the first time, my heart began to ache and is still aching. I know that, like an infection, he won't depart from our house without leaving behind tears and grief" (1:139). She is positive that his supernatural demonic powers guarantee his control of Mikhailo's will and the latter's resulting filial disobedience. Katerina quickly convinces her father (who is at first doubtful that Kryzhanovsky can be "some kind of a vampire" or a "sorcerer") of the man's diabolical nature; during this short conversation, Kryzhanovsky is upgraded from "an ominous bird" and "a sinner" to nothing less than "Antichrist" and "the enemy of the Christian race" (1:142).

This conversation frames Kryzhanovsky as a traditional Gothic demonic figure, with a typical overlapping of Jewish/Judaist and vampiric motifs.[38] Critics have commented on the rather cliché character of Kulish's villain—a "ubiquitous," deus ex machina sorcerer figure.[39] I argue that this "ubiquitous character" in *Mikhailo Charnyshenko* has a specific cultural genealogy that goes back to the legendary Wandering Jew who made his most memorable Gothic appearance on the pages of Matthew Lewis's *The Monk* in the 1790s. The main source of the legend is the apocryphal story, which arose in the Near East and Eastern Mediterranean, of a Jerusalem resident who denied Christ a brief repose on the way to Golgotha, chasing him away from the steps of his house. The man was punished by incessant wandering until Christ's Second Coming.[40] The characterizations of Kryzhanovsky, cited above, as a "sinner" (and, later in the novel, "unrepentant sinner" [2:146]) and an "ominous bird" may implicitly invoke both the crime and the punishment of the "original" Jerusalem dweller. Later in the novel, we learn about his wandering around Eastern Europe and his elusive identity: introduced in the novel as a converted Jew Kryzhanovsky in the service of the Russian Empire in the Hetmanate, he is also the evil Jew Lutitsa who betrayed the novel's Serbian character, prince Radivoj, in his battle for the independence of Serbia from the Ottoman Empire. In addition, under the name of Kharlo, he had managed to ruin brave Cossack Shcherbina by betraying his friendship and destroying his family and his home.

Kryzhanovsky's characterization as an Antichrist also belongs to the classical arsenal of the Wandering Jew figure, as does his uncertain exotic ethnicity.[41] The latter trait of the Wandering Jew, with some variations, is ubiquitous in pre-Romantic and Romantic literature. It appears, for example, in Friedrich Schiller's *The Ghostseer*, published between 1786 and 1789, Lewis's *The Monk*, and Gogol's "The Portrait" ("Portret"), where the mysterious moneylender/Antichrist is believed to be a Greek, an Armenian, or a Moldovan in the 1835 version and Indian, Persian, or Greek in the 1842 one. Kulish faithfully follows the tradition. When pan Bardak who hosts Mikhailo and his fellow travelers finds out that the young recruits are headed to Gadiach where the regiment is being formed, he is concerned because of Kryzhanovsky's involvement. Explaining his apprehension, Bardak reports on Kryzhanovsky's unclear ethnic origins, along with his demonic association: "Some say he's a Jew; others claim he's a Montenegrin. There are some that call him directly the infidel Turk. It's impossible to know who is telling the truth. But one thing is sure—he is on familiar terms with the devil (on znaetsia s lukavym)" (2:82–83).

Establishing the provenance of Kulish's hero in the Wandering Jew tradition helps us elucidate his function in the novel, which proves far more complex than that of the structural deus ex machina or the stereotypical Gothic villain. As it has been suggested in the studies of the Wandering Jew character in British Gothic fiction, this transgressive figure is intimately linked to the deep-set anxieties of the post-Enlightenment era in Europe, ranging from "the nature and parameters of the European national identity" to the doubts and aspirations concerning the process of modernization, rationalism, secularism, and advance of capitalism.[42] One of the greatest nightmares of late nineteenth-century Britain that the recurrent figure of the Wandering Jew embodied was that of conversion, or "Judaizing England"—not literally but by threatening what were traditionally held as "English" values.[43] Both Kulish's novel and the "chronicle" emphasize the fact that Kryzhanovsky is a recent convert (svezhii perekrest) who is essentially concealing his demonic nature, evil intentions, and otherness under the mask of a fellow Christian. Unlike in the British Empire, with its anxiety over a metaphorical conversion, in Ukraine religious conversion could be perceived as a real threat, following the Union of Brest in 1596. Both *The History of the Rus'* and *Mikhailo Charnyshenko* (as well as Gogol's *Taras Bul'ba*) refer to the "uniia" in similar, most negative terms, associating it with the oppressive Polish rule and Jewish exploitation and stressing its destructive role in the history of Ukraine.[44] In *The History of the Rus'*, the Union is described as something that crept in "in a fox skin but with a wolf's throat"; the emphasis on its treacherous nature and deceptive appearance implicitly links it to the "freshly converted" Kryzhanovsky. In Kulish's novel, this connection is made explicit.[45] Upon hearing about Katerina's misfortunes caused by Kryzhanovsky, old Charnysh exclaims:

> What?! . . . Are the Jews and Poles (zhidy i liakhi) indeed back in Ukraine? So, did you, father Khmel'nyts'ky, fight in vain for ten years? Has the cursed Union indeed come back after the Nalivaikos, Pavliuks and Ostrianytsias? . . . I won't put up with Jews taxing Orthodox Christians for the use of their churches! I won't put up with the godless Polish priests traveling around the villages on the backs of the Orthodox priests! I won't put up with the bloodthirsty Polish beasts frying us in copper bulls and boiling Cossack children in cauldrons! (2:156–57)

Kryzhanovsky's appearance is perceived as a return of the Union and all the evils associated with it. Poles and Jews appear interchangeable in their detrimental impact on the Ukrainian Orthodox identity; in fact, Polish Catholics here acquire vampiric characteristics that are typically the prerogative of the Jews. The Polish origin of Kryzhanovsky's name (from *krzyż*, meaning cross) contributes to the conflation of the two ethnic and religious groups clearly presented in the novel as the enemies of the Orthodox faith and Little Russia more generally.

The fear of conversion is tied to the problem of identity that leads us to another symbolic aspect of Kryzhanovsky's character. The Wandering Jew of Kulish's novel appears not across various epochs but across space in multiple military conflicts; given the supernatural connotations of his characterization, he indeed transcends time. Homeless and rootless, he is the cause of other characters' displacements—he lures Mikhailo away from the parental house; he causes Katerina to flee from her relatives' home; he provokes the Serbian prince Radivoj's departure from his native land; and, finally, he is responsible for Cossack Shcherbina's losing his home and his family. The fundamental anxiety embodied by Kryzhanovsky, a protean character who changes names, religions, ethnicities, and loyalties, is also the one that dominates Mikhailo's plot—the fear of homelessness and a loss of identity. In a sense, Kryzhanovsky/Lutitsa/Kharlo can be seen as a dark and distorted doppelganger of the rootless Mikhailo.

Moreover, Mikhailo and Kryzhanovsky are romantic rivals in the novel, competing for Katerina who is portrayed, as Petrov observes, as the embodiment of the Ukrainian Volksgeist. Unspoiled by Western education, she expresses her soul in folk songs (1:30–31) and is associated with folkloric supernatural characters (2:149–50). A typical Gothic heroine—an innocent displaced maiden threatened by the novel's ultimate villain—Katerina is allegorized as the contested nation. Interestingly, both Mikhailo chasing the ghost of heroic Ukraine and Kryzhanovsky, the rootless Jew, pose danger to Katerina (Ukraine) who is threatened by the latter but eventually dies from the hand of Mikhailo's Serbian lover Roksanda.

Kryzhanovsky's attempts to seduce Katerina with his lavish gifts, which appear "as if by magic" (2:140), and his reputed supernatural power over women parallel his quasi-infernal luring of the Ukrainian youth into the imperial service. In other words, he poses the threat of devilish temptation to the entire Ukrainian nation. *The History of the Rus'* mentions that this historical moment highlighted each nation's most characteristic traits: "When extraordinary circumstances arise, typically the national characters or their dispositions reveal themselves, so, for example, with the Little Russians' enthusiasm for military service, the Jewish (Iudeiskaia) inclination for business deals has manifested itself."[46] In his recruiting effort, Kryzhanovsky capitalizes (literally) on the essence of the Ukrainian nation, its proclivity for military service.

As the personification of that uncanny force that makes young men leave their home, the recruiter Kryzhanovsky embodies the imperial center itself. Significantly, the author of *The History of the Rus'* emphasizes the direction of the recruits' movement "from the south to the north," from Ukraine to St. Petersburg. Ironically, this centripetal force is embodied by the novel's quintessentially homeless and nomadic character.[47] The empire's other also becomes the manifestation of its essence. The threat posed by the converted Wandering Jew in Kulish's novel thus is to turn young Ukrainians into eternal travelers, like himself—into uprooted and nomadic subjects of the Russian Empire.[48]

The Serbs

Kryzhanovsky looms large in Mikhailo's Gothic (and partly prophetic) nightmare that disturbs him during his visit to pan Bardak's house. In this dream sequence, Kryzhanovsky, unresponsive to the young man's plea for protection, pushes him into the abyss with demonic laughter (2:93–94).[49] Notably, Kryzhanovsky appears in the dream surrounded by the mysterious "red *zhupans*"— men in red jackets worn in Poland and Ukraine at the time—who also stayed at Bardak's house and aroused Mikhailo's anxiety. These red zhupans turn out to be Serbian fighters for independence who had to flee their native land in fear of persecution and secretly settle in Little Russia.[50] Soon they will attempt to capture Mikhailo and his fellow travelers, thus launching the "Serbian" subplot of the novel, which will dominate the narrative until the end. Mikhailo's nightmare associates the Serbs with the Jew and presents the novel's ethnic others as a threatening and demonic force. However, as in Kryzhanovsky's case, the boundaries between the national self and the demonic and exotic others prove unstable.

After the mysterious visitors precipitously leave pan Bardak's place, the latter comments on their elusive identity: "See, here you go: they came, ate and drank plenty, and left; but if you ask me who these guests were, I myself won't be able to tell you. Their dress is not like ours, they pronounce words in a strange way, and all their manners are completely not like ours. Only one thing I know is that they do cross themselves in a Christian way" (2:80–81). The Serbs are introduced in uncanny terms—not only because of their mysterious and alarming behavior but also because of their quality of being both exotic and foreign and yet somewhat recognizable and culturally relatable (note that the red zhupan again, as in Gogol's "A Terrible Vengeance," is associated with the confusion of the categories of self/other). Shcherbina is also alarmed by his inability to place the strangers—their itinerant lifestyle seems to suggest an affinity with the Zaporizhzhian Cossacks, "however, by their attire and manners, I can see they're not from Zaporizhzhia" (2:115). As with Kryzhanovsky, their otherness immediately suggests a demonic association, albeit rhetorically, and when the fight with the mysterious horsemen causes Mikhailo's fall into the river and his friends presume him dead, Shcherbina explodes with an angry tirade labeling them "cursed antichrists" (2:121).

The Serbs' dwelling is presented in Gothic terms as well: the captive Cossacks are led through a gloomy hilly landscape to a tower built out of the ruins of a former monastery, which kept locals away thanks to some superstitious legends associated with it. There they meet their leader who reveals the exotic/familiar dynamics: "His attire was also distinguished by particular luxury; however, it was not at all like the dress worn by Little Russian gentlemen. One could rather take him for a Turk, if the large golden cross hanging on his chest did not contradict this" (3:21–22).

This uncanny quality of the Serbs' presence in the novel is reinforced through the abundant use of the Serbian language which, as a related Slavic language, is somewhat understandable to the Russian and Ukrainian reader but not fully comprehensible. The title of the Serbian leader linguistically epitomizes the peculiar otherness this group of characters represents. The subordinates address him as *ban*, which means "kniaz'" (prince) in Russian (323). The Serbs themselves explain the title to perplexed Shcherbina: "Our *ban* is just the same *pan* [lord], that you have so many of in Ukraine" (3:54). "Ban" is indeed almost like a "pan"—just as the Serbs are both understandable and familiar and yet threateningly incomprehensible others.

To stress the Serbs' difference, Kulish heavily Orientalizes them.[51] Examples of such Orientalization abound, from Radivoj's Turkish and "semi-Asiatic" attire to his "Oriental" hospitality and his status as a tyrant who inspires fear and awe. "The king of beasts among his motley subjects" (3:43), Radivoj is repeatedly described as fierce like a lion, bloodthirsty and crude (3:71–72). His daughter Roksanda (who rescues Mikhailo after his fall in the stream and falls in love with him) wears "an Asiatic dress" and is surrounded by divans, which remind Shcherbina "of Crimea and Turkey," and by Oriental aromas (3:85–87). She is described as a typical wild, natural, and passionate Oriental beauty. In yet another Walter Scottian gesture, she is juxtaposed to the meek and somewhat bland "native" heroine Katerina whom she eventually kills in an "attack of horrible jealousy and Asiatic vengeance" (3:197).[52] Both heroines are closely associated with their native lands—namely, when falling in love with Roksanda, Mikhailo is ready to fight for "sweet Serbia"; while seeing Katerina at the end of the novel makes him realize not just his betrayal of his beloved but also his abandonment of his native Ukraine (3:196).

Mikhailo's temporary loyalty to Serbia is largely determined by his romantic infatuation with Roksanda, whereas the Cossack Shcherbina's affinity with the Serbs is more complex. With Radivoj and his people Shcherbina shares a condition of displacement, a common enemy (the Jew and ultimately an empire), Oriental characteristics, and above all the valorization of military courage. While Shcherbina observes the differences between the Serbian community and the Sich, including the latter's more democratic organization, he wonders whether he has not encountered "another Sich" (3:53) and later is described as a kind of "little *koshovoi*" (the leader of a Zaporizhzhian Cossack military unit) in this "new Sich" (3:71–72).

The most dramatic moment of Shcherbina's identification with the Serbs comes when he listens to Roksanda singing a folk song and accompanying herself on a traditional Serbian instrument. First skeptical and even derisive about the one-stringed instrument (gusle), he becomes deeply moved by her song, whose melody he describes as "somewhat familiar" even though he had not heard it before: "The Zaporizhzhian Cossack, whose musical taste was formed to the tune of Little Russian *dumas* (epic folk songs), solemn and at the same time meditative, felt some kinship (chto-to rodnoe) in Roksanda's song. Even though he did not understand its content fully, those emotional sensations that a warrior experiences in his bloody, torturous and yet sweet revel, found an echo in him" (3:96).

Nakhlik suggests that this affinity reflects the author's views on the solidarity of the Ukrainian and South Slavic peoples in their struggle for independence.[53] This aspect of identification certainly exists but it cannot solely explain the persistent theme of uncanny recognition. It is important to bear in mind that this closeness to the Serbs is attributed specifically to Shcherbina, the Zaporizhzhian Cossack who represents the nomadic, militant, and masculine ethos in the novel. This contrasts with his fellow traveler Cossack Sereda who is connected with his family and traditional values and returns home at the end of the novel. The most artistically successful character in the novel, as the critics have unanimously agreed, the colorful, witty, and courageous Shcherbina nonetheless embodies a questionable set of values, from the point of view of Kulish-"kul'turnyk"—military prowess, anarchic love for absolute freedom, and disregard for family ties. More important, Serbs are also portrayed ambivalently in the novel: the narrator is often disturbed by their purported cruelty, militarism, irrationality, "Asiatic despotism," sacralization of revenge, and the lack of body politic and legal institutions in their society. Rather than emphasizing the "solidarity" between Serbs and Ukrainians, Kulish portrays the Serbs as the Cossacks' dark twin, using their subplot as a cautionary tale of the danger of excessive valorization of militant heroism. Yet the Western, "knightly," and democratic Cossacks are different enough from their Orientalized Slavic "brothers" to preclude a complete identification of the two and to preserve the ambivalence in portraying the Cossack heroic past as simultaneously a lost national ideal and a chaotic and destructive period of Ukrainian history.[54]

The Chalice

Final episodes of the novels bring together its various Gothic subplots—the evil demonic Jew is beheaded by Radivoj, meek Katerina is murdered by passionate Oriental Roksanda, and Mikhailo's dead body is accepted by the earth only after his father prays to God for his forgiveness.[55] The final scene of the novel emphatically focuses not on the remaining characters' destinies but on the fate of an artifact. "I would much rather find out," the narrator states provocatively, "who now owns famous Doroshenko's cup (Doroshenkova charka; 3:202)." This magnificent (and even "supernatural") cup appears earlier in the novel during Mikhailo and his friends' stay at pan Bardak's house. Inspired by the golden bear-shaped goblet of the house of Bradwardine in Scott's *Waverley* (where the host notes that it was "supposed . . . to be invested with certain properties of a mystical and supernatural quality" "in old and Catholic times," that is in the era of dark superstition), the "supernatural" cup in Kulish is also heavily laden with history.[56] The goblet was supposedly a gift from Petro Doroshenko, the hetman of Right-Bank Ukraine in the 1660s and 1670s—a turbulent period of Ukrainian history after Khmel'nyts'ky's death, known as "Ruina" (the ruin). The novel ends with a "lost and found" ad—the narrator playfully invites the readers, in case one of them may own the precious artifact, to send him its drawing. To facilitate the recognition of the sought object, the narrator provides a detailed list of the inscriptions found on the cup. But he also considers the possibility that "this invaluable wine goblet has already been forged into some silly sugar bowl or a useless coffee pot. Perhaps, I myself, unaware of this, own an item made out of silver that used to be part of Doroshenko's chalice" (3:202–3).

The moralistic and tragic ending of Mikhailo's plot is undermined by the playful tone of the final scene, just as the supposed triumph of modernity over Mikhailo's anachronistic heroism is called into question by the "reappearance" of the missing chalice. "Doroshenkova charka" acquires symbolic connotations beyond its significance as an antiquarian object. It figures as a fragment (or a ruin) of a heroic history, which has been trivialized by Ukraine's embrace of modernity, with its emphasis on consumerism. The refined civilization that Ukraine entered through its absorption into the Russian Empire at the cost of losing its national authenticity is now presented with a great deal of skepticism: "Given the lamentable dissemination of false education, antiquity, in the eyes of the descendants, is negligible compared to a fashion or an accessory shop" (3:202). Metonymically, the lost chalice represents that inaccessible and irrevocable Ukrainian past, the Holy Grail that the knights of the novel sought in vain.[57] But this past is tantalizingly revived in the final line of the novel that cites "the most interesting inscription on the edges of the goblet: 'He who will drink this cup at once to the end, is worthy of standing under Doroshenko's *bunchuk*'" (3:203). The seeming finality of the ending that seals up the protagonists' destinies in their semi-mystical quest for lost Ukraine is contradicted by the open-endedness of the chalice episode.

Kulish's use of the Scottian "cup" motif highlights the difference between the two writers' treatments of the past. In stark contrast to the tragic yet open ending of *Mikhailo Charnyshenko*, with the chalice that may or may not be lost forever, the "Blessed Bear of Bradwardine" is duly recovered at the end of *Waverley*, having been salvaged from the devastation of the civil war, and thus provides a safe closure, along with the hero's happy marriage and his abandonment of the cause of the rebellious Highlanders. The Scottian "end-of-our-history" perspective, however, is not sustained in Kulish's novel where the ghost of heroic Ukraine continues to haunt its colonial present. The Ukrainian author's extensive reliance on Gothic tropes produces a fictional world where the past and the present are simultaneously alive and where the empire acts as both a benevolent agent of civilization and a demonic homogenizing force.

The Russian Critics

Kulish's first novel was reviewed in prominent Russian journals—a fact that by itself testifies to an acute interest on the part of the educated Russian public in the Ukrainian themes and the developments in Ukrainian literature. The reviews reveal various preconceptions about Ukrainian culture, "national character," and the place of Ukrainian history in the Russian imperial narrative. The reaction of the Russian critics to a Ukrainian historical-Gothic novel, written in Russian with an admixture of other Slavic languages, epitomizes the Russian imperial discourse on Ukraine, which has proven remarkably persistent.

Most reviewers evaluated the novel positively, with the notable exception of Senkovsky's *Library for Reading*. The Slavophile journal *The Muscovite* (*Moskvitianin*) edited by Pogodin, with whom Kulish maintained personal and professional correspondence, was particularly sympathetic to the young

Ukrainian writer's first attempt at a historical novel in the Romantic vein. Stepan Shevyrev, who reviewed *Mikhailo Charnyshenko*, noted with satisfaction a recent explosion of talent from Little Russia, hailing Kulish as a worthy heir of Gogol and Kvitka-Osnov'ianenko.[58]

Shevyrev quickly identifies Kulish's novel as a product of the "Walter Scottian historical school" and praises the author for a masterful reconstruction of the time period portrayed in the novel. The dominant idea of Kulish's novel, according to Shevyrev, is that of "ancient" Little Russia, whose "historical time" is left behind in the past. The critic's characterization of this period is quite revealing of his imperial attitude: he describes it as a "transition from the military and half-nomadic way of life (byt) to the civic and state one, which awaited [Little Russia] in its new unification with Russia."[59] The novel's protagonist, Mikhailo Charnyshenko, is, in Shevyrev's interpretation, a typical representative of this transition—a hero in whom obedience to the wise elders' advice to take up civic service clashed with the desire to seek military glory, a desire instigated both by "instinct" and the national tradition. This assessment of the Ukrainian historical development, for all the benevolent tone of the review, is guided by the logic of Russia's civilizational superiority.

Another ostensibly positive review appeared in *The Son of the Fatherland* (*Syn Otechestva*), edited at the time by Konstantin Masal'sky. The anonymous review offers a highly romanticized characterization of Ukraine of the past that mixes idyllic and medieval Romantic tropes. Ukraine is described as a poetic land under the bright sky and blessed with a benevolent climate and nature; but it is also the land of chivalry (with reference to their review of Skal'kovsky's *History of the New Sich*), where landowners lived "like German knights in their castles."[60] The reviewer's characterization of the period portrayed in *Mikhailo Charnyshenko* reveals the same ambiguity present in Shevyrev's account: it was "the epoch when Great Russia, fulfilling Peter the Great's idea, according to the brotherly kinship, was bringing the Little Russian region closer and closer." This region, the author states, was separated from "us" by the hostile policies of Poland and Lithuania but also by the "South Russian" people's free-loving spirit. The reviewer's sympathy for the imperial project is paradoxically combined with his Romantic admiration for the Ukrainians' pursuit of national independence. As the critic nostalgically echoes Kulish's narrator, "that was the last era of Little Russian distinct life" (samobytnosti). What the reviewer finds irritating is Kulish's extensive use of Serbian, as well as Ukrainian, which makes some passages of the work incomprehensible and turns the novel's language into a "bizarre mix."[61] One can argue whether the use of Serbian and Ukrainian is indeed unjustifiably excessive, but it is clear that his argument—followed by a detailed analysis of grammatical errors (usually Ukrainianisms) in Kulish's Russian—is made from the perspective of a "superior" normative culture and language. Indeed, the language of the novel had an uncanny quality, being familiar Russian and yet "tainted" by the foreign elements, which clearly unsettled the novel's Russian imperial critics.

Senkovsky's *Library for Reading* offered the most negative and sarcastic evaluation of the novel, along with the most unapologetically colonial assessment of Ukrainian history.[62] The reviewer (most likely Senkovsky himself) mocks the idea that Shevyrev finds to be the central theme of the novel— "sobstvennaia zhizn' Malorossii," Little Russia's unique life. He narrates his version of this "imaginary unique life" as essentially a degeneration of the once great princedom (Kievan Rus') which, after the Tartar-Mongol invasion, turns into a desert or a steppe. This desert eventually becomes a colony of Lithuania, comparable to Haiti, then its province, and is ultimately reduced to the status of a hetman's estate. Cossacks, whose etymology he mockingly traces to "wild geese" (gusaki), emerge not as noble Ukrainian knights fighting for the Orthodox faith and not as Romantic free-spirited rebels, but as gangsters ravaging the land. This gang is finally brought to enlightenment, civil society, and order by Peter the Great who de facto ended the Hetmanate autonomy and liberated Little Russia "from the yoke of the wild army."[63]

Along with this unsympathetic view of both the author's overall project and Ukrainian history more generally, Senkovsky ruthlessly criticizes Kulish's predilection for Romantic clichés, including Gothic tropes. The critic mockingly describes the Serbs' dwelling as "the Radcliffian cave of Ukraine." He interprets their presence in the novel—and in Ukraine—as yet another proof of the chaos and disorder characteristic of Ukraine before its full incorporation into the Russian Empire: "Such was Little Russia's unique life—whoever wanted could settle there and acted as if he was the master of the house." Far from a Romantic or Slavophile admiration of Ukrainian "poetic history," Senkovsky's vision of the imaginary Gothic Ukraine of the past presents it as a dark realm of chaos, statelessness, and barbarism; it is a shapeless land without a clear institutional and geographical structure, a desert roamed by criminals, a house without a master. No less chaotic, according to Senkovsky, is the language of the novel: "Without respect for the language in which he is writing, the author peppers his style with Little Russian and Serbian conversations, which makes the reading for a Russian both uninteresting and difficult."[64] Long after Gogol's Dikan'ka tales, an insertion of Ukrainian (and Serbian) terms into the fabric of the Russian narrative is viewed as a nuisance that pollutes the purity of the Russian language, prevents full comprehension, and requires a special effort on the part of the Russian reader—rather than, say, an introduction of couleur locale or a diversity of Slavic voices. Clearly troubled by Kulish's Gothic Ukraine, Senkovsky creates an alternative narrative of the Russian Empire as the true master that is able to give its chaotic neighbor shape and order—a narrative that still keeps hold on the Russian historical imagination.

The analysis of Kulish's novel and its reception in Russian criticism highlights Ukraine's dilemmas of its past and present, both opposed to and entwined with its new "home," the Russian Empire. It also shows just how disturbing the "Gothic Ukraine" reconstructed by Kulish appeared to the Russian imperial imagination. The forces of cultural memory invoking a unique national past proved to be hard to contain by the Romantic discourse of exoticism or primitivism, by the condescending colonial logic of the civilizational mission or by the empire's homogenizing effort. Even as the writers discussed in this part of the book participated in all these discourses and, more literally, in the imperial enterprise itself, they did not fully reconcile themselves to Ukraine's loss of its autonomy and its integration into the Russian Empire. Untamed Ukraine still broke through in these Gothic narratives, which created literary spaces of ambiguity and subtle resistance.

Afterword

In 1836, Petr Chaadaev published his famous first "Philosophical Letter" (written circa 1828–29) where he defines Russia in almost exclusively negative terms as lacking identity, history, any contribution to civilization, and even a definite facial expression: "I find that even in our gaze there is something strangely vague, cold, uncertain, which resembles somewhat the facial appearance [physionomie] of the peoples who are placed at the very bottom of the social ladder. In foreign countries, especially in the South, where the features [physionomies] are so animated and expressive, so many times, when I compared the faces of my compatriots with those of the locals, I was struck by the muteness of our faces."[1]

This lack of a clearly defined expression in the Russian people's faces is a literal counterpart to Russia's absence of a national "physiognomy"— a concern that pervaded Russian literary criticism of the time and found its manifestation in such uncanny fictional characters as Klim Diundik in Pogorel'sky's *The Convent Graduate*, with his markedly indistinct appearance. Significantly, Chaadaev associates the coldness of expression and the lack of animation in the Russians' faces specifically with Russia's Northern identity. Moreover, just as he was struck by the facial "muteness" (l'air muet) of his compatriots, he is amazed by the void of Russia's "social existence."[2] Chaadaev interprets Russia's imperial expansion (this time along the East/West axis) as a compensation, or even a "cover-up," for this void, for the lack of identity and historical significance. "In order to make ourselves noticeable," he states somewhat sarcastically, "we had to stretch ourselves from the Bering Strait to the Oder." Russia's early history fares no better, described in quasi-Gothic terms as the era of "brutal barbarism, crude superstition," and cruel foreign rule. The "sad story of our youth," for Chaadaev, is a story of a "dull and gloomy (sombre) existence, animated only by heinous crime and softened only by servitude."[3] With its history of darkness, violence, and isolation, Russia becomes a Gothic trope, a "maiden in a dungeon," as well as an uncanny space of emptiness.

Chaadaev was unique for the shocking directness with which he expressed his verdict. However, his concerns about Russia's historical development, the originality and authenticity of Russian culture, the implications of its geographical location, and the relation of its imperial expansion to national identity were shared by his contemporaries. This book has argued that these anxieties underlay several literary works of the time that deployed, seriously or subversively (and often both), popular Gothic tropes. The Gothic conventions served not exclusively as purely literary techniques intended to create a mysterious and suspenseful atmosphere in the work, to provoke certain emotions in the reader, or, in some cases, to mock a fashionable literary form. When *domesticated* in the Russian imperial context, these Western literary conventions found themselves in a different *dom* (home)—in a vast amorphous empire, whose problematic history, geography, and identity they unexpectedly and uncannily bespoke.

The tradition of the Russian imperial uncanny that I traced in this book begins in the North, with Karamzin's interrogation of Russia's alternative past in the Gothic mode in his "The Island of Bornholm" and with the Decembrist writers' obsessive Gothicizing of medieval Livonia—a region both accessible and irrevocably distant, Russian and not, in their own time; a repository of the heroic and Romantic Middle Ages but also of bloodthirsty feudal cruelty. But in its most spectacular form in Russia's "Northern" Gothic, the imperial uncanny unfolds in literary and ethnographic works dedicated to Finland, the land of wizards and gloomy desolate cliffs. An old neighbor/relative and a new exotic colony, the docile imperial subject and a dangerous and destructive irrational force, uncanny Finland is most vividly represented by Odoevsky in his novella *The Salamander*. In the meantime, in the imperial "South," Gogol and Pogorel'sky almost simultaneously create uncanny representations of Ukraine as both a threatening alternative to Russian imperial identity and an idealized double of Russia's lost authentic self. Both writers deploy Gothic tropes to question Russia's imperial dominance over Ukraine, which Pogorel'sky exposes particularly powerfully through his portrayal of a complex play of colonial mimicry. The imperial uncanny of the Russian Southern borderlands culminates in the liminal space of Lermontov's "Taman'," with its disorienting anthropology and geography. Finally, Kulish's Walter Scottian novel offers an ambivalent and nostalgic Gothic vision of the heroic Ukraine of the past, which pays a heavy price for its inclusion into the Russian imperial order.

As I was working on this book, something genuinely uncanny happened, as Russia annexed Crimea in the aftermath of the Maidan Revolution and started a hybrid war in Eastern Ukraine. For many, a twentieth-first century war between Russia and Ukraine, given their shared history, had connotations of a Gothic nightmare. In September 2014, the Russian oppositional politician Boris Nemtsov, who would be murdered less than a year later, described the conflict as a "most nightmarish, bloodiest scenario of a fratricidal war" and directly linked it to Russia's "imperial hysteria."[4] The prominent Ukrainian writer and public intellectual Oksana Zabuzhko argues that a more dangerous war is waged by Russia at the information level. She paints a gruesome apocalyptic picture of the future "mass madness" and "mass suicide" of entire countries as a result of the technological manipulation of minds.[5] The Russian progovernment press has revived the discourse of barbarous and superstitious Ukraine "sinking into chaos," familiar to us from nineteenth-century characterizations of Ukrainian Cossackdom.[6] Ukrainian media, in turn, invoked nineteenth-century spectral rhetoric with such headlines as "A Specter Is Haunting Russia," referring to Russia's fear of its own revolution.[7] The events in Ukraine had their repercussions in what used to be the Russian (and later Soviet) imperial North, as the Baltic states began to fear Russia's intervention under the pretext of protecting native Russian speakers in the region—fears the Russian press dismissed, characteristically, as mere "horror stories" (strashnye skazki).[8]

In the concluding chapters of his book *Warped Mourning: Stories of the Undead in the Land of the Unburied*, Alexander Etkind shows how post-Soviet culture is haunted by the horrors of its totalitarian past, particularly Stalinist purges, whose victims, not having received proper mourning, are returning as the undead. Hence the neo-Gothic and "magical historicist" turn in contemporary Russian literature and film, full of monsters, vampires, and werewolves.[9]

The memory of the Gulag—and the return of its repressed terrors—is epitomized, for Etkind, by the uncanny *triton* (typically translated into English as "salamander"), described in the opening of Aleksandr Solzhenitsyn's *The Gulag Archipelago* (*Arkhipelag Gulag*, 1958–68): a frozen prehistorical creature, preserved so well in ice that it was immediately eaten by the starving Gulag convicts (zeks). Etkind reads the triton as "an all-encompassing symbol of terror," a totem for the zeks' "tribe," and a monstrous remnant of the past, paradoxically destroyed and yet immortal.[10] I would add that another salamander has made its return since 2014, the salamander depicted by Odoevsky and, less literally, by other writers examined in this book—the Russian imperial uncanny. How contemporary Russian and Ukrainian cultures are processing this historical experience is a subject for a different project. Mine started as an exploration of the past, which in a true Gothic manner has made its way into the present.

Notes

Introduction: From the Island of Bornholm to Taman'

1. Mikhail Lermontov, *A Hero of Our Time*, trans. Paul Foote, rev. ed. (London: Penguin Books, 2001), 58. I have slightly modified the translation to render the original more accurately and indicated what part of the conversation is rendered in Ukrainian in the original text of the novel.

2. The narrator refers to Taman' as "the most disgusting little town of all the coastal towns in Russia" (samyi skvernyi gorodishko iz vsekh primorskikh gorodov Rossii). M. Iu. Lermontov, *Sobranie sochinenii*, 4 vols. (Moscow: Izdatel'stvo Akademii Nauk SSSR, 1961–62), 4:340.

3. See Valeria Sobol, "The Uncanny Frontier of Russian Identity: Travel, Ethnography, and Empire in Lermontov's 'Taman',"" *Russian Review* 70 (January 2011): 65–79. Myroslav Shkandrij discusses Taman' as "colonized Ukraine" and links the locals' liminality and problematic identities to the imperial situation described in the novella. See Myroslav Shkandrij, *Russia and Ukraine: Literature and the Discourse of Empire from Napoleonic to Postcolonial Times* (Montreal: McGill-Queen's University Press, 2001), 53–55. For a broader analysis of liminality in "Taman'," see Joe Andrew, "'The Blind Will See': Narrative and Gender in 'Taman,'" *Russian Literature* 31 (1992): 449–76.

4. Mary Douglas, *Purity and Danger: An Analysis of Concepts of Pollution and Taboo* (New York: Frederick A. Praeger, 1966), 2.

5. The following summary of the genre's development is based on several seminal studies of the Gothic, such as David Punter, *The Literature of Terror: A History of Gothic Fictions from 1765 to the Present Day* (London: Longman, 1980); Fred Botting, *Gothic: The New Critical Idiom*, 2nd ed. (London: Routledge, 2014); and Vadim Vatsuro, *Goticheskii roman v Rossii* (Moscow: Novoe literaturnoe obozrenie, 2002).

6. For a more detailed list of conventional Gothic tropes, see Eve Kosofsky Sedgwick, *The Coherence of Gothic Conventions* (New York: Methuen, 1986), 9–10.

7. Punter, *The Literature of Terror*, 6.

8. The distinction between "terror" and "horror," based on Edmund Burke's concept of the sublime, was elaborated by Ann Radcliffe, the most famous Gothic novelist of the time. See Botting, *Gothic*, 65–69. Vatsuro distinguishes between "sentimental" and "frenetic" varieties of Gothic fiction (*Goticheskii roman v Rossii*).

9. The exact date of *The Monk's* publication is debated by scholars. See L. F. Peck, *A Life of Matthew G. Lewis* (Cambridge: Harvard University Press, 1961), 19–42.

10. Punter, *The Literature of Terror*, 73.

11. See Botting, *Gothic*, chaps. 8 and 9.

12. Vatsuro, *Goticheskii roman v Rossii*, 210.

13. See Alessandra Tosi, *Waiting for Pushkin: Russian Fiction in the Reign of Alexander I (1801–1825)* (Amsterdam: Rodopi, 2006), 84–85.

14. For an example of the latter approach, see M. P. Alekseev, "Ch. R. Met'iurin i russkaia literatura," in *Ot romantizma k realizmu: Iz istorii mezhdunarodnykh sviazei russkoi literatury* (Leningrad: Nauka, 1978), 3–55. Most Soviet-era histories of Russian literature tend to avoid the term "Gothic," referring instead to this tradition as "fantastic" or more generically "Romantic" (although the 4-volume *History of Russian Literature* does mention the connection between Karamzin's "The Island of Bornholm" and the Gothic novel: *Istoriia russkoi literatury v 4 t.* [Leningrad: Nauka, 1980–83], 1: 760). See also *Istoriia russkoi literatury v 10 t.* (Moscow; Izd-vo AN SSSR, 1941–56). Vatsuro's articles, which appeared in Soviet scholarly journals and collections before the posthumous publication of his *Goticheskii roman v Rossii* as a monograph, are a notable exception to this tendency.

15. See Mark S. Simpson, *The Russian Gothic Novel and Its British Antecedents* (Columbus, OH: Slavica, 1986) and Neil Cornwell, ed., *The Gothic-Fantastic in Nineteenth-Century Russian Literature* (Amsterdam: Rodopi, 1999). Both Simpson and Cornwell lamented the lack of scholarly attention to the Russian Gothic. As Simpson puts it, "the topic of Russian Gothicism is not a scholarly field sufficiently plowed yet to reap a proper harvest of favourful digression" (*The Russian Gothic Novel,* 7). Neil Cornwell echoed this sentiment: "Russian Gothic as a term has not until recently enjoyed a great deal of currency in critical studies of Russian literature" (*The Gothic-Fantastic in Nineteenth-Century Russian Literature,* 3).

16. Scholarship on the Gothic is so vast that a separate bibliographical publication has been warranted. See F. S. Frank, *Guide to the Gothic: An Annotated Bibliography of Criticism* (Metuchen, NJ: Scarecrow Press, 2004). For an example of a psychoanalytical and feminist approach to the Gothic, see Anne Williams, *The Art of Darkness: A Poetics of Gothic* (Chicago: University of Chicago Press, 1995). Postcolonial readings of Gothic fiction are included in Andrew Smith, William Hughes, ed., *Empire and the Gothic: The Politics of Genre* (Basingstoke: Palgrave Macmillan, 2003).

17. Avril Horner, ed., *European Gothic: A Spirited Exchange 1760–1960* (Manchester: Manchester University Press, 2002). This volume includes an article on the Russian literary reception of the European Gothic by one of the pioneers of the study of the Russian Gothic in the West: Neil Cornwell, "European Gothic and Nineteenth-Century Russian Literature," 104–27. See also Avril Horner and Sue Zlosnik, ed., *Le Gothic: Influences and Appropriations in Europe and America* (Basingstoke: Palgrave Macmillan, 2008).

18. See Andrew Smith and William Hughes, "Introduction: The Enlightenment Gothic and Postcolonialism," in *Empire and the Gothic,* 1–12.

19. N. D. Tamarchenko, ed., *Goticheskaia traditsiia v russkoi literature* (Moscow: RGGU, 2008).

20. Alessandra Tosi, *Waiting for Pushkin*; Robin Feuer Miller, *Dostoevsky's Unfinished Journey* (New Haven: Yale University Press, 2007); Katherine A. Bowers, "Shadows of the Gothic: Adapted Terror in Russian Fiction, 1792–1905" (PhD diss., Northwestern University, 2011); "The City through a Glass, Darkly: Use of the Gothic in Early Russian Realism," *Modern Language Review* 108, no. 4 (2013): 1199–215; "The Fall of the House: Gothic Narrative and the Decline of the Russian Family," in

Russian Writers and the Fin de Siècle: The Twilight of Realism, ed. Katherine Bowers and Ani Kokobobo (Cambridge: Cambridge University Press, 2015), 145–61.

21. Muireann Maguire, *Stalin's Ghosts: Gothic Themes in Early Soviet Literature* (Berne: Peter Lang, 2012); Eric Naiman, *Sex in Public: The Incarnation of Early Soviet Ideology* (Princeton: Princeton University Press, 1997), chap. 4.

22. Dina Khapaeva, *Nightmare: From Literary Experiments to Cultural Project*, trans. Rosie Tweddly (Leiden: Brill, 2013); *Koshmar: Literatura i zhizn'* (Moscow: Text, 2010); *Goticheskoe obshchestvo: Morfologiia koshmara* (Moscow: Novoe literaturnoe obozrenie, 2007). Khapaeva has also contributed to the cluster of articles on the Russian Gothic published by *Russian Literature* in 2019. The cluster focuses on the twentieth and twenty-first centuries. See Kevin M. F. Platt, Caryl Emerson, and Dina Khapaeva, "Introduction: The Russian Gothic," *Russian Literature* 106 (2019): 1–9.

23. Svitlana Krys, "The Gothic in Ukrainian Romanticism: An Uncharted Genre" (PhD diss., University of Alberta, 2011); "Between Comedy and Horror: The Gothic in Hryhorii Kvitka-Osnovianenko's 'Dead Man's Easter' [1834]," *Slavic and East European Journal* 55 (2011): 341–58; "Intertextual Parallels between Gogol' and Hoffmann: A Case Study of *Vii* and *The Devil's Elixirs*," *Canadian-American Slavic Studies* 47 (2013): 1–20. Forum "Rethinking the Gothic in Ukraine," *Slavic and East European Journal* 62, no. 2 (2018): 247–317. The forum includes Valeria Sobol, "Introduction," 247–54; Roman Koropeckyj, "Towards a Cossack Gothic in Slavic Romanticism," 255–71; Robert Romanchuk, "Mother Tongue: Gogol''s *Pannochka*, Pogorel'skii's *Monastyrka*, and the Economy of Russian in the Little Russian Gothic," 272–92; and Svitlana (Lana) Krys, "All-Time Sinner or National Hero? Language and Politics in Oleksa Storozhenko's Ukrainian Gothic," 293–317.

24. The Russian scholars V. Ia. Malkina and A. A. Poliakova offer specific criteria for determining whether literary works qualify as part of the Gothic tradition, in which case they have to exhibit the "invariant" characteristics of the genre as defined by these scholars. See V. Ia. Malkina and A. A. Poliakova "'Kanon goticheskogo romana' i ego raznovidnosti," in *Goticheskaia traditsiia v russkoi literature*, ed. Tamarchenko, 15–32. Vatsuro argues that a description of a Gothic castle, for example, does not automatically make it a Gothic motif. "In order to be such, the castle has to be a metaphor and has to possess a suggestive principle (suggestivnoe nachalo)," rather than being a "purely formal compositional element" (*Goticheskii roman v Rossii*, 360). However, I contend that in the examples used by Vatsuro from the Livonian tales (see chapter 2), the castle almost always preserves a metaphoric character, serving as a silent witness to the past horrors and a remnant of the region's bloody history.

25. Alfred Tresidder Sheppard, *The Art and Practice of Historical Fiction* (London: H. Toulmin, 1930), 39.

26. On the relationship between Walter Scott's novels and the Gothic tradition, see Fiona Robertson, *Legitimate Histories: Scott, Gothic, and the Authorities of Fiction* (Oxford: Oxford University Press, 1994) and Robert Ignatius Letellier, *Sir Walter Scott and the Gothic Novel* (Lewiston, NY: Edwin Mellen Press, 1994). For an earlier study in Russian that acknowledges Scott's indebtedness to the Gothic novel, see B. G. Reizov, "Val'ter Skott," in Val'ter Skott, *Sobranie sochinenii*, 20 vols. (Moscow: Gos. Izdatel'stvo khudozhestvennoi literatury, 1960–65), 1:5–44. Vatsuro also admits the

influence of the Gothic mode on Walter Scott and his Russian followers who, their ostensible contempt for the "novels à la Radcliffe" notwithstanding, borrowed multiple literary motifs and techniques from this tradition "almost with fateful inevitability" (*Goticheskii roman v Rossii*, 368).

27. Punter, *The Literature of Terror*, 52.

28. Michael Holquist, ed., *The Dialogic Imagination. Four Essays by M. M. Bakhtin*, trans. Caryl Emerson and Michael Holquist (Austin: University of Texas Press, 1981), 245–46.

29. Kosofsky Sedgwick suggests that in Gothic fiction the self is "spatialized" in a particular way, and this spatialization ("the position of the self to be massively blocked off from something to which it ought normally have access") includes a temporal aspect, such as the self's past or family history (*The Coherence of Gothic Conventions*), 12.

30. Robert Mighall, *A Geography of Victorian Gothic Fiction: Mapping History's Nightmares* (Oxford: Oxford University Press, 2003), xiv.

31. The term "Livonia" typically refers to the region that corresponds for the most part to modern-day Latvia and Estonia. Livonian Wars were fought by tsarist Muscovy against various coalitions over the control of these territories. See chapter 2 for a more detailed discussion. The battle of Poltava (a city in today's Ukraine) was the decisive battle of the Great Northern War, in which Peter I of Russia defeated the army of the Swedish emperor Charles XII.

32. James Macpherson's "Poems of Ossian" (1760–65), supposedly a translation from a third-century Gaelic bard, introduced a new landscape in literature, which one scholar has called "a revelation for Europe": it was a vaguely northern scenery, sublime, bare, wild, and uncultivated, with rocks and turbulent sea, unspecific enough that many European readers could find an affinity with it. See Howard Gaskill, "Introduction: Genuine Poetry . . . Like Gold," in *The Reception of Ossian in Europe*, ed. Howard Gaskill (London: Thoemmes Continuum, 2004), 1–20, esp. 5–6. For the reception of Ossian in Russia, see Peter France, "Fingal in Russia," in Gaskill, *The Reception of Ossian in Europe*, 259–73.

33. In her otherwise insightful study of Panteleimon Kulish's *Black Council* and Gogol"s *Taras Bul'ba*, Romana Bahrij follows Sheppard's view of the relative irrelevance of the historical setting in Gothic works. Romana Bahrij, *Shliakh sera Val'tera Skotta na Ukrainu ("Taras Bul'ba" M. Hoholia i "Chorna Rada" P. Kulisha v svitli istorychnoï romanistyky Val'tera Skotta)* (Kyiv: Vsesvit, 1993), 13. Tosi repeatedly mentions the purely auxiliary role of the setting in the Gothic tradition (*Waiting for Pushkin*, 332, 358).

34. Scholarship on the Russian Empire is quite extensive. Because empire studies constitute only one aspect of my approach, I do not provide a full overview of literature here and only cite the works that directly informed this book's argument. For studies of Russian literature and empire, key works include Susan Layton, *Russian Literature and Empire: Conquest of the Caucasus from Pushkin to Tolstoy* (Cambridge: Cambridge University Press, 1994); Monika Greenleaf, *Pushkin and Romantic Fashion: Fragment, Elegy, Orient, Irony* (Stanford: Stanford University Press, 1994); Ewa M. Thompson: *Imperial Knowledge: Russian Literature and Colonialism* (Westport, CT: Greenwood Press, 2000); Shkandrij, *Russia and Ukraine*; Harsha Ram, *The Imperial Sublime: A Russian Poetics of Empire* (Madison: University of Wisconsin Press,

2003); Edyta Bojanowska, *Nikolai Gogol: Between Ukrainian and Russian Nationalism* (Cambridge, MA: Harvard University Press, 2007); Katya Hokanson, *Writing at Russia's Border* (Toronto: University of Toronto Press, 2008); Olga Maiorova, *From the Shadow of Empire: Defining the Russian Nation through Cultural Mythology, 1855–1870* (Madison: University of Wisconsin Press, 2010); and *Tam, vnutri. Praktiki vnutrennei kolonizatsii v kul'turnoi zhizni Rossii: Sb. statei,* ed. A. Etkind, D. Uffel'mann, and I. Kukulin (Moscow: Novoe literaturnoe obozrenie, 2011).

35. These parallels are addressed in chapter 6.

36. Ronald G. Suny, "The Empire Strikes Out" in *A State of Nations: Empire and Nation-Building in the Age of Lenin and Stalin,* ed. Ronald Grigor Suny and Terry Martin (Oxford: Oxford University Press, 2001), 43–44.

37. See Geoffrey Hosking, *Russia: People and Empire, 1552–1917* (London: HarperCollins, 1997); David G. Rowley, "Imperial versus National Discourse: The Case of Russia," *Nations and Nationalism* 6, no. 1 (2000): 23–42; Suny, "The Empire Strikes Out"; Vera Tolz, *Russia (Inventing the Nation)* (London: Arnold, 2001). For useful overviews of the works on Russian nationalism, see Bojanowska, *Nikolai Gogol,* chap. 1, and Tolz, *Russia,* introduction.

38. Mark Bassin, *Imperial Visions: Nationalist Imagination and Geographical Expansion in the Russian Far East, 1840–1865* (Cambridge: Cambridge University Press, 1999), 13.

39. Maiorova, *From the Shadow of Empire,* 5.

40. Bassin, *Imperial Visions,* 14.

41. Franco Moretti, *Atlas of the European Novel, 1800–1900* (London: Verso, 1999), 15.

42. Suny, "The Empire Strikes Out," 25.

43. Mikhail Epshtein, *Bog detalei: Narodnaia dusha i chastnaia zhizn' v Rossii na iskhode imperii. Esseistika 1977–1988* (Moscow: Izdanie R. Elinina, 1998), 24.

44. Anne Lounsbery, *Life Is Elsewhere: Symbolic Geography in the Russian Provinces, 1800–1917* (Ithaca: Cornell University Press, 2019), 11.

45. Hokanson, *Writing at Russia's Border,* 7.

46. Anne Lounsbery, "'No, this is not the provinces!' Provincialism, Authenticity, and Russianness in Gogol's Day," *Russian Review* 64, no. 2 (2005): 260.

47. Hokanson, *Writing at Russia's Border,* 7.

48. See, for example, Jane Burbank and Frederick Cooper, *Empires in World History: Power and the Politics of Difference* (Princeton: Princeton University Press, 2010), 271–76; Suny, "The Empire Strikes Out," 37–38.

49. Hosking, *Russia: People and Empire,* 40.

50. Tolz, *Russia,* 2.

51. "Recent studies of nineteenth- and twentieth-century colonial empires have emphasized that empire-builders—explorers, missionaries, and scientists, as well as political and military leaders—strove to make 'we/they,' 'self/other' distinctions between colonizing and colonized populations. From this perspective, maintaining or creating difference, including racialized difference, was not natural; it took work" (Burbank and Cooper, *Empires in World History,* 12).

52. N. M. Karamzin, *Izbrannye sochineniia v dvukh tomakh* (Moscow: Khudozhestvennaia literatura, 1964), 1:87. For a more detailed discussion of the motif of border-crossing in Karamzin's *Letters* (including this episode), see Ingrid Kleespies, *A Nation*

Astray: Nomadism and National Identity in Russian Literature (DeKalb: Northern Illinois University Press, 2012), 23–36, as well as her earlier article "Caught at the Border: Travel, Nomadism, and Russian National Identity in Karamzin's *Letters of a Russian Traveler* and Dostoevsky's *Winter Notes on Summer Impressions*," *Slavic and East European Journal* 50, no. 2 (2006): 234–41.

53. "Contiguous empires . . . did not have hard borders within the empire, and therefore migration created a mixed population, a highly integrated economy, and shared historical experiences and cultural features" (Suny, "The Empire Strikes Out," 33). I would add a qualification: these "shared historical experiences and cultural features" were, in many cases, constructed with the help of dominant cultural myths and tendentious historical narratives. See, for example, Bojanowska's summary of the narratives of the Russo-Ukrainian kinship in her *Nikolai Gogol*, 28–30, and Tolz, *Russia*, chap. 7.

54. Aleksandr Etkind, "Russkaia literatura, XIX vek: Roman vnutrennei kolonizatsii," *Novoe literaturnoe obozrenie* 59 (2003): 110. Starting with nineteenth-century Russian historians, such as Sergei Solov'ev, several scholars defined Russia's expansion as "self-colonization" or "internal colonization," suggesting that, as a result of a cultural and social distance between the ruling and intellectual elites, on the one hand, and the rest of the population, on the other, the main object of colonization and orientalization in Russia was its people. See Alexander Etkind, *Internal Colonization: Russian Imperial Experience* (Cambridge: Polity Press, 2011). This concept implies the relationship along the social-cultural axis, but one can also use it to describe the Russian Empire's geographical expansion into contiguous territories. For an updated sociological analysis of internal colonialism in the context of the British Empire, see the new edition of Michael Hechter's classical 1975 work, *Internal Colonialism: The Celtic Fringe in British National Development* (New York: Routledge, 2017).

55. See Sigmund Freud, *The Standard Edition of Complete Psychological Works*, trans. James Strachey (London: Hogarth Press, 1953–74), 17:219–52.

56. Julia Kristeva, *Strangers to Ourselves*, trans. Leon S. Roudiez (New York: Columbia University Press, 1991), 181.

57. Homi K. Bhabha, *The Location of Culture* (London: Routledge, 1994), 13.

58. David Huddart, *Homi K. Bhabha*, Routledge Critical Thinkers (London: Routledge, 2006), 60.

59. Laurie Johnson stresses the key role of literature for the study of the uncanny: "While psychology and psychiatry as well as philosophy are continually preoccupied with the problem of the uncanny, it is in literary texts that the dynamic tension between concepts such as illness and health, self and other, power and powerlessness, regress and progress . . . is most fully revealed." Laurie Ruth Johnson, *Aesthetic Anxiety: Uncanny Symptoms in German Literature and Culture* (Amsterdam: Rodopi, 2010), 31.

60. Mighall, *A Geography of Victorian Gothic Fiction*, 18.

61. Moretti, *Atlas of the European Novel*, 38.

62. Moretti summarizes the geography of the European Gothic tales (based on the sample of nearly sixty texts produced between 1770 and 1840) as follows: "In general, Gothic stories were initially set in Italy and France, moved north, to Germany, around 1800; and then north again, to Scotland, after 1820" (16). Despite its shifting geography, the North/South axis still prevails. William Beckford's *Vathek* (published

in French in 1782 and translated into English in 1786) has an exotic Eastern setting, but its status as a Gothic novel is problematic. See Botting, *Gothic*, pp. 54–55.

63. Matthew G. Lewis, *The Monk* (New York: Grove Press, 1993), 35. In Russian literature, this trope is extensively developed in Nikolai Gnedich's Gothic novel *Don Corrado de Herrera* (1803). See Tosi, *Waiting for Pushkin*, 332–33.

64. See, for example, Larry Wolff, *Inventing Eastern Europe: The Map of Civilization on the Mind of the Enlightenment* (Stanford: Stanford University Press, 1994); Maria Todorova, *Imagining the Balkans* (Oxford: Oxford University Press, 1997); Adeeb Khalid, Nathaniel Knight, and Maria Todorova, "Ex Tempore: Orientalism and Russia," *Kritika* 1, no. 4 (2000): 691–728; the discussion in *Ab Imperio* 1 (2002): Aleksandr Etkind, "Bremia britogo cheloveka, ili Vnutrenniaia kolonizatsiia Rossii"; David Schimmelpenninck van der Oye, "Orientalizm—delo tonkoe"; Nathaniel Knight, "Was Russia Its Own Orient? Reflections on the Contributions of Etkind and Schimmelpenninck to the Debate on Orientalism"; and Elena Kempbell, "K voprosu ob orientalizme v Rossii (vo vtoroi polovine XIX veka–nachale XX veka)." See also Vladimir Kantor, *Sankt-Peterburg: Rossiiskaia imperiia protiv rossiiskogo khaosa: K probleme imperskogo soznaniia v Rossii* (Moscow: ROSSPEN, 2009), as well as the works cited in note 34.

65. As Greenleaf puts it, "what was east to Europe was south from the vantage point of St. Petersburg" (*Pushkin and Romantic Fashion*, 108). See also Layton, *Russian Literature and Empire*; Ram, *The Imperial Sublime*, especially chapters 3 and 4; and Hokanson, *Writing at Russia's Border*.

66. Larry Wolff, *Inventing Eastern Europe*, 4–5.

67. In the Western cultural imagination, Russia was associated with the North beyond the eighteenth century. The opening of Mary Shelley's *Frankenstein* is set in northern Russia, described as a land of ice and snow, from whence the narrator departs for the North Pole.

68. Edith Clowes, *Russia on the Edge: Imagined Geographies and Post-Soviet Identity* (Ithaca: Cornell University Press, 2011), 6.

69. Otto Boele, *The North in Russian Romantic Literature* (Amsterdam: Rodopi, 1996), ch. 2. As Boele shows, the East/West dichotomy regains its prominence with the beginning of the Slavophiles/Westernizers debate in the 1830s.

70. W. Gareth Jones, "Catherine the Great's Understanding of the 'Gothic,'" in *Reflections on Russia in the Eighteenth Century*, ed. Joachim Klein, Simon Dixon, and Maarten Fraanje (Cologne: Böhlau Verlag, 2001), 237.

71. For example, while in Switzerland, the Russian traveler, offended by the Swiss' indifference to current Russian military campaigns, exclaims, "But the Geneva dweller does not deign to pay attention to you, poor North!" Karamzin, *Izbrannye sochineniia*, 1:291. When visiting the renowned Swiss scientist and philosopher Charles Bonnet in a company of Danes, the Russian traveler observes, "Now you are surrounded by the North," to which Bonnet replies: "We owe a great deal to your part of the world—this is where the new dawn of the sciences has risen; I am referring to England, which is also a Northern land; and Linnaeus was your neighbor." Karamzin, *Izbrannye sochineniia*, 1:323.

72. Karamzin, *Izbrannye sochineniia*, 1:679.

73. See Boele, *The North in Russian Romantic Literature*, 30–36 passim. Boele's work offers an excellent comprehensive discussion of the image of the North in eighteenth- and early nineteenth-century Russian literature and criticism.

74. A. S. Pushkin, *Sobranie sochinenii*, 10 vols. (Moscow: Izdatel'stvo Akademii Nauk SSSR, 1962–66), 2:68. For a detailed analysis of this poem in the context of the theme of exile, see Stephanie Sandler, *Alexander Pushkin and the Writing of Exile* (Stanford: Stanford University Press, 1989), 39–56.

75. Lermontov, *Sobranie sochinenii*, 4:347.

76. V. G. Belinskii, *Polnoe sobranie sochinenii* (Moscow: Izdatel'stvo AN SSSR, 1953–59), 5:125. I am indebted to Shkandrij's book *Russia and Ukraine* for this reference.

77. Richard S. Wortman, *Scenarios of Power: Myth and Ceremony in Russian Monarchy*, 2 vols. (Princeton: Princeton University Press, 1995), 1:22–41.

78. For a summary of the debate, see A. A. Khlevov, *Normanskaia problema v otechestvennoi istoricheskoi nauke* (St.-Petersburg: Izdatel'stvo St.-Peterburgskogo universiteta, 1997), 6–14; and P. N. Miliukov, *Glavnyia techeniia russkoi istoricheskoi mysli* (Moscow: Tipolitografiia Vysochaishe utverzhd. T-va I. N. Kushnerev i Ko, 1898), 1:13–113. Maiorova demonstrates that this foundation narrative was used in the nineteenth century strategically to construct the Russian national character as "naturally" submissive to authority and to promote the image of the Russian Empire as historically benevolent and peaceful (*From the Shadow of Empire*, chap. 2). For an analysis of literary treatments of the "Varangian" theme in the late eighteenth century, see Valeria Sobol, "'Komu ot chuzhikh, a nam ot svoikh': Variazhskoe prizvanie v russkoi literature kontsa XVIII veka," in *Tam, vnutri*, ed. Etkind, Uffel'mann, and Kukulin, 186–216.

79. See chapter 2 of this book, as well as Karsten Brüggemann, "The Baltic Provinces and Russian Perceptions in Late Imperial Russia," in *Russland an der Ostsee: imperiale Strategien der Macht und kulturelle Wahrnehmungsmuster (16. bis 20. Jahrhundert)*, ed. Karsten Brüggemann and Bradley D. Woodworth / *Russia on the Baltic: Imperial Strategies of Power and Cultural Patterns of Perception (16th–20th centuries)* (Vienna: Böhlau Wien, 2012), 111–41.

80. Literary depictions of the Caucasus are not immune to certain ambiguity as well. It is both the space to which Russian Romantics projected their yearning for freedom and which they at the same time often saw as a legitimate object of Russia's imperial conquest; and it is a radically other space, which "raised restive issues of Russia's own semi-Asiatic identity," to quote Layton (*Russian Literature and Empire*, 10). The Caucasus, however, was not as intimately associated with Russia's sense of selfhood as the regions examined in this book.

81. This is how fifteenth-century Ukraine is labeled in the 1842 version of Nikolai Gogol's *Taras Bul'ba*). N. V. Gogol', *Sobranie sochinenii*, 7 vols. (Moscow: Khudozhestvennaia literatura, 1976–79), 2:34. Vladimir Izmailov's narrative of his travel to Ukraine is titled, characteristically, *A Journey to Southern Russia* (*Puteshestvie v poludennuiu Rossiiu*, 1800–1802). For the terminology used in nineteenth-century historiography, see, for example, Gogol', "Glance at the Making of Little Russia" ("Vzgliad na sostavlenie Malorossii," 1832) where he refers to Ukraine as "Southern Russia"; Panteleimon Kulish's historical and ethnographic work *Notes on Southern Rus'* ("Zapiski o Iuzhnoi Rusi," 1856–57); or Nikolai Kostomarov's historical study *Southern Rus' at the End of the Sixteenth Century* ("Iuzhnaia Rus' v kontse XVI veka," 1867). In the nineteenth century, the territory of what is now independent Ukraine was divided between Russian and Austro-Hungarian empires and, in the former context, its various parts were called "Little Russia," "Southern Rus'," or "[Sloboda] Ukraina."

However, I refer to these territories as "Ukraine" throughout this book (unless I cite or allude to the alternative appellations used by the cultural figures of the time). For a brief overview of the terminology applied to various regions of today's Ukraine, see Aleksei Miller, *Ukrainskii vopros v Rossiiskoi imperii* (Kyiv: Laurus, 2013), 46.

82. For a more detailed discussion of the critical status of Ukraine in the Russian national identity and Russia's various national myths associated with Ukraine, see Tolz, *Russia,* chap. 7.

83. Much has been written about the status of Ukraine in the Russian cultural imagination in the Romantic era, especially in connection to Gogol. See, for example, Simon Karlinsky, *The Sexual Labyrinth of Nikolai Gogol* (Cambridge, MA: Harvard University Press, 1976), 30–31; and George S. N. Luckyj, *Between Gogol' and Ševčenko: Polarity in the Literary Ukraine, 1798–1847* (Munich: Wilhelm Fink Verlag, 1971), 75–87. For nuanced theoretical discussions of Ukraine's ambivalent status in the Russian Empire, see Shkandrij, *Russia and Ukraine,* chap. 1, and Bojanowska, *Nikolai Gogol,* 27–34.

84. I address the current scholarly debates on Ukraine's status as a colony (or not) within the Russian Empire in chapter 4.

85. Roman Koropeckyj and Robert Romanchuk have developed a concept of "Little Russian literature" (a term used by nineteenth-century Russian literary critics) as distinct from both Ukrainian and "Great" Russian literature, drawing on the Deleusian concept of "minor literature." See Roman Koropeckyj and Robert Romanchuk, "Harkusha the Noble Bandit and the 'Minority' of Little Russian Literature," *Russian Review* 76 (2017): 294–310.

86. For a discussion of Finnish Gothic literature (written in Swedish, the primary language of the educated elites for most of the nineteenth century), see Kati Launis, "From Italy to the Finnish Woods: The Rise of Gothic Fiction in Finland," in *Gothic Topographies: Languages, Nation Building and "Race,"* ed. P. M. Mehtonen and Matti Savolainen (Farnham: Ashgate, 2013), 169–86.

87. Brüggemann, "The Baltic Provinces and Russian Perceptions in Late Imperial Russia," 125.

88. Brüggemann, "The Baltic Provinces," 126–27. For the role of "manifest destiny" in Russia's expansion into the Far East, see Bassin, *Imperial Visions.*

89. See Wortman, *Scenarios of Power,* 1:299.

90. Nikolai Polevoi, "Malorossiia, ee obitateli i istoriia," *Moskovskii telegraf* 17 (1830): 85–86.

Chapter 1. A Gothic Prelude

1. Karamzin, *Izbrannye sochineniia,* 2:663. Hereafter the text of the story is cited from this edition and volume with page numbers in parentheses.

2. Most likely the illicit passion alluded to in the Dane's song and later is incest, one of the key tropes of Gothic literature. Soviet scholar N. D. Kochetkova discovered a previously unknown redaction of the story where the hero's beloved is referred to directly as his sister. See Vatsuro, *Goticheskii roman v Rossii,* 90. See also H. Riggenbach, "Inzest und Gefangenschaft in N. M. Karamzins 'Insel Bornholm,'" *Vortrage und Abhandlungen zur Slavistik* 9 (1987): 65–97. Nora Buhks offers an interesting analysis of various versions of the novella's incestuous plot in "Le Voyage à l'île

de la mort de Nikolaj Karamzin," *Le Sentimentalisme Russe*, Special Issue, edited by Jean Breuillard, *Revue des Études Slaves* 74, no. 4 (2002–3): 719–28.

3. Several scholars commented on the proximity between the narrators of "The Island of Bornholm" and *Letters of a Russian Traveler*. See Vatsuro, "Literaturno-filosofskaia problematika povesti Karamzina 'Ostrov Borngol'm,'" *XVIII vek* 8 (1969): 196, and Derek Offord, "Karamzin's Gothic Tale: 'The Island of Bornholm,'" in *The Gothic-Fantastic in Nineteenth-Century Russian Literature*, ed. Neil Cornwell (Amsterdam: Rodopi, 1999), 49. I use the qualifier "quasi-autobiographical," as some disagreement exists among scholars over the issue to what extent Karamzin's *Letters*—published after the writer's return from his journey to Western Europe—can be considered an autobiographical work. Iu. M. Lotman and B. A. Uspenskii argued for a heavily fictionalized nature of the *Letters* and traced a discrepancy between Karamzin's actual itinerary and the one suggested by the *Letters*. See their "'Pis'ma russkogo puteshestvennika' Karamzina i ikh mesto v razvitii russ-koi kul'tury," in *Pis'ma russkogo puteshestvennika* (Leningrad: Nauka, 1984), 525–606. Gerda S. Panofsky contests this interpretation in *Nikolai Mikhailovich Karamzin in Germany: Fiction as Facts* (Wiesbaden: Harrassowitz, 2010). See also Svetlana Geller-man, "Karamzine à Genève: Notes sur quelques documents d'archives concernant les *Lettres d'un Voyageur russe*," in *Fakten und Fabeln: Schweizerisch-slavische Rei-sebegegnung vom 18. bis zum 20. Jahrhundert*, ed. Monika Bankowski et al. (Basel: Helbing & Lichtenhahn, 1991), 71–90. Rodolphe Baudin concluded that Karamzin's account of his stay in Strasbourg reflects Karamzin's reliance on existing literary and documentary sources rather than his experience in the city. Rodolphe Baudin, *Nikolaï Karamzine à Strasbourg. Un écrivain-voyageur russe dans l'Alsace révolution-naire (1789)* (Strasbourg: Presses Universitaires de Strasbourg, 2011) and "Karamzin et la cathédrale de Strasbourg," in *Nikolaï Karamzin en France: l'image de la France dans les* Lettres d'un voyageur russe, ed. Rodolphe Baudin (Paris: Institut d'Etudes slaves, 2014), 75–98. For my analysis, the factual accuracy of the *Letters* is not relevant, while the constructed, literary nature of the narrator's persona is undeniable.

4. As Offord reminds us in his analysis of "The Island of Bornholm" (and as I argue in the introduction), "the relationship between Russia and the West was not, in Karamzin's time, being structured exclusively in terms of the antithesis between East and West . . .; it was also [I would say primarily] being conceived in terms of an opposition, inherent in Preromantic literature more generally and Gothic literature in particular, between North and South (It is the 'North' that the traveller in the *Let-ters of a Russian Traveller* sees himself as representing)" (Offord, "Karamzin's Gothic Tale," 58). For a discussion of various philosophical, political, and aesthetic problems in the travelogue, see Lotman and Uspenskii, "'Pis'ma russkogo puteshestvennika' Karamzina"; Andrew Kahn, "Karamzin's Discourses of Enlightenment," in Nikolai Karamzin, *Letters of a Russian Traveller* (Oxford: Voltaire Foundation: 2003), 459–551.

5. Victor Terras, *A History of Russian Literature* (New Haven: Yale University Press, 1991), 158–59.

6. Vatsuro, "Literaturno-filosofskaia problematika," 190–209.

7. Vatsuro, "Literaturno-filosofskaia problematika," 209.

8. Offord also points out this feature of the narrative and its role in establish-ing an "ethnic, cultural, and religious distance" between the narrator and the world

of Bornholm, although he does not consider its possible elimination ("Karamzin's Gothic Tale," 57).

9. For a detailed discussion of the imagery of the sublime in the story, see Offord, "Karamzin's Gothic Tale," 54–55.

10. For a detailed analysis of the story's Gothic elements against the background of the Western Gothic tradition, see Vatsuro, "Literaturno-filosofskaia problematika," 196–203.

11. Along with the elements that mark the novella as unmistakably belonging to the Gothic tradition, Vatsuro also points out Karamzin's story's weakened "narrative" element, unlike a typical plot-driven Gothic novel. The critic argues that the text functions as an "elegiac fragment" where the focus is less on the events than on the narrator's subjective perception of and reaction to them ("Literaturno-filosofskaia problematika," 195–96). I would add that this dialogue also slows down the plot progression and thus highlights the importance of the historical background to the story's events.

12. The song continues with an invocation of nature:

> "Sacred nature!
> Your tender friend and son
> Is innocent before you,
> You gave me a heart" (663).

13. Vatsuro, "Literaturno-filosofskaia problematika," 208.

14. Offord, "Karamzin's Gothic Tale," 58.

15. *Russkaia starina* 10 (1898): 36. Cited in Vatsuro, *Goticheskii roman v Rossii*, 95.

16. See the introduction to this book.

17. "Riugen," *Entsiklopedicheskii slovar' Brokgauza i Efrona* (St. Petersburg: Semenovskaia tipo-litografiia, 1899), 54: 502–3.

18. Khlevov, *Normanskaia problema*, 12.

19. The ethnicity of the "Varangians" was a subject of great controversy and held far-reaching ideological implications. Consider, for example, the Decembrist Mikhail Orlov's reaction in 1818 to Karamzin's *History*: "I was reading Karamzin. The first volume wasn't to my liking. . . . Why does he want to be an impartial cosmopolite rather than a citizen? . . . Why does he say that Riurik was a foreigner? That Varangians were not Slavs? What does he find praiseworthy in the invitation of a foreigner to the Novgorodian throne?" Letter to N. Turgenev, May 4, 1818, cited in Mariia Maiofis, *Vozzvanie k Evrope: Literaturnoe obshchestvo "Arzamas" i russkii modernizatsionnyi proekt 1815–1818 godov* (Moscow: Novoe literaturnoe obozrenie, 2008), 344. For a discussion of the ideological role of the Varangian theory in the nineteenth century, see Maiorova, *From the Shadow of Empire*, chap. 2.

20. In this regard, it is important that the mystery of the island of Bornholm is most likely illicit incestuous love. Incest, in addition to its moral and anthropological implications, can function as a powerful metaphor of a social and political crisis. See, for example, Richard A. McCabe, *Incest, Drama and Nature's Law, 1550–1700* (Cambridge: Cambridge University Press, 1993) and especially Lynn Avery Hunt, *The Family Romance of the French Revolution* (Berkeley: University of California Press, 1992). Gothic literature's obsession with incest reflected the social sentiment of the 1790s and particularly the growing anxiety about moral degeneration and the collapse of social structures. In this context the invitations of the Varangians in eighteenth-century

Russian literature were often presented as a family affair, whether literally (as in Catherine II's play *From the Life of Riurik* [*Iz zhizni Riurika*, 1786] where Riurik is the grandson of the legendary Novgorodian prince Gostomysl) or more symbolically, as in Ia. Kniazhnin's tragedy *Vadim of Novgorod* (*Vadim Novgorodskii*, 1788–89). See my "Komu ot chuzhikh, a nam ot svoikh."

21. I thank Ilya Vinitsky for this suggestion.

Chapter 2. In Search of the Russian Middle Ages

1. A. P. Bochkov, "Monastyr' sv. Brigitty (Otryvok iz puteshestviia po Estliandii)," *Kalendar' muz* (1827): 124. Cited in S. G. Isakov, "O livonskoi teme v russkoi literature 1820–1830-kh godov," *Uchenye zapiski Tartuskogo gosudarvstvennogo universiteta* 98 (1960): 155. The reference to the "Scottish bard," Walter Scott, alludes to the complex relationship between the Gothic literary tradition and the Walter Scottian historical novel (see introduction to this book, as well as chapter 6).

2. This section offers a schematic historical outline based on Kevin O'Connor's study, *The History of the Baltic States* (Westport, CT: Greenwood Press, 2003), particularly chaps. 1 and 2.

3. See Edward C. Thaden, ed., *Russification in the Baltic Provinces and Finland, 1855–1914* (Princeton: Princeton University Press, 1981), 5.

4. O'Connor, *The History of the Baltic States*, 14.

5. O'Connor, *The History of the Baltic States*, 27.

6. The incorporation of Ingria and Karelia is addressed in chapter 3 of this book, dedicated to Finland as the setting of the imperial uncanny.

7. See Karsten Brüggemann and Bradley D. Woodworth, "Entangled Pasts—Russia and the Baltic Region," in *Russland an der Ostsee*, 3–26. The references to the "most treasured possession" and the "balcony" come from Konstantin Arsen'ev's *Statistical Essays on Russia* (*Statisticheskie ocherki Rossii*, St. Petersburg: Tip. Imperatorskoi Akademii Nauk, 1848), 4. Cited in Brüggemann and Woodworth, "Entangled Pasts," 10. The idea of the Baltic region as a source of German enlightenment, thanks to the German-language Dorpat (Tartu) University in today's Estonia, belongs to Faddei Bulgarin (Arsen'ev, *Statistical Essays*, 10–11). For Bulgarin's contradictory views on the region, see Liubov' Kiseleva, "Istoriia Livonii pod perom F. V. Bulgarina," *Studia Russica Helsingiensia et Tartuensia X: "Vek nyneshnii i vek minuvshii": Kul'turnaia refleksiia proshedshei epokhi*, 2 pts. (Tartu: Tartu Ülikooli Kirjastus, 2006), 1:114–27.

8. For a detailed analysis of this process, see Brüggemann, "The Baltic Provinces and Russian Perceptions in Late Imperial Russia" and Thaden, ed., *Russification in the Baltic Provinces and Finland*. Although some Russophile sentiments emerged throughout the nineteenth century, both among Baltic peasants and the intelligentsia, Russification policies ultimately cemented the Baltic people's national identities. O'Connor, *The History of the Baltic States*, 53–56.

9. Belinskii, *Polnoe sobranie sochinenii*, 7:221. For a more detailed discussion on his view of the Middle Ages in connection to Romanticism in Russia and specifically the Decembrists' contradictory perception of this period, see Isakov, "O livonskoi teme v russkoi literature," 150–54.

10. For a detailed and illuminating discussion of the Livonian theme in Russian Romanticism, with a focus on less-studied writers, see Isakov, "O livonskoi teme,"

and his "Russkie pisateli i Estoniia," in *Estoniia v proizvedeniiakh russkikh pisatelei XVIII–nachala XX veka. Antologiia*, ed. S. G. Isakov (Tallinn: KPD, 2001), 3–38. Isakov addresses the role of Bestuzhev's travelogue in both articles; see especially "O livonskoi teme," 167–68.

11. The term "Russian" is anachronistic in this context as no "Russia" existed in the medieval period represented in most Livonian tales. I use "Russian" in this chapter to refer to the East Slavic population of the time, more properly described as the Rus', for simplicity's sake.

12. Bestuzhev's indebtedness to Karamzin's *Letters of a Russian Traveler* has been pointed out by several scholars. For one of the earliest assessments, see N. A. Kovarskii, "Rannii Marlinskii," in *Russkaia proza XIX veka*, ed. B. M. Eikhenbaum and Iu. N. Tynianov (Leningrad, 1926; repr. The Hague: Moutin & Co, 1963, 135–58). Citations refer to the Moutin & Co edition. Kovarskii mentions that later in life Bestuzhev criticized Karamzin as a historian. In his analysis of *A Journey to Revel*, Andreas Schönle argues that Bestuzhev polemicizes with Karamzin's conception of historiography. Andreas Schönle, *Authenticity and Fiction in the Russian Literary Journey, 1790–1840* (Cambridge: Harvard University Press, 2000), 141–44.

13. Lauren Leighton observes that, while Bestuzhev's "castle tales adhere to the Romantic tradition of the Gothic revival," they are more intent on recreating history than evoking a mysterious and terrifying atmosphere. In that sense, the critic argues, they "are more properly historical, rather than Gothic." See his *Alexander Bestuzhev-Marlinsky* (Boston: Twayne Publishers, 1975), 75. One of my goals here is to challenge the Gothic/historical binary, showing instead the productive symbiosis of the two modes.

14. A. Bestuzhev, *Poezdka v Revel'* (St. Petersburg: Tipografiia Aleksandra Pliushara, 1821), 19, 23–26, 74.

15. Bestuzhev, *Poezdka v Revel'*, 75–76. Incidentally, this convent would become quite a popular setting for Livonian stories in Russian literature—both A. P. Bochkov and V. P. Titov published stories with the identical title, "St. Brigitta Monastery," in 1827 and 1830, respectively. See Isakov, "O livonskoi teme v russkoi literature." Bestuzhev makes another ironic allusion to the Gothic tradition in his story "Another Page from a Guard Officer's Journal" ("Eshche listok iz dnevnika gvardeiskogo ofitsera," 1821), where the narrator comments on the typically "Radcliffian" setting for his journey. See Kovarskii, "Rannii Marlinskii" (153). Again, as Vatsuro and others show, an awareness and derision of Gothic clichés did not stop the writers from deploying them.

16. Bestuzhev, *Poezdka v Revel'*, 19–20.

17. Bestuzhev, *Poezdka v Revel'*, 120.

18. Schönle argues that the contrast between the irony of history and the utopia of the present in the travelogue has to do with Bestuzhev's overarching goal, which was not to objectively narrate history but to rhetorically suggest to the reader that "vital, meaningful change is possible *sub specie temporis*" (*Authenticity and Fiction*, 139–40).

19. Bestuzhev, *Poezdka v Revel'*, 26, 28, 51.

20. Schönle claims that Bestuzhev depicts historical events, including the Russians' victories and failures, in an ironic light, and this reflects his view of military (as opposed to social) history as inherently chaotic and meaningless (*Authenticity and*

Fiction, 132 ff.). This might be true at a micro-level of individual battles and events, but I perceive in these descriptions an overarching sense of inevitability in his historical account that ends with the Russians' "reclaiming" what they see as their original territories.

21. Bestuzhev, *Poezdka v Revel'*, 54. See O'Connor, *The History of the Baltic States*, 13.

22. Bestuzhev, *Poezdka v Revel'*, 58, 62, 67–70, 116–17.

23. Bestuzhev, *Poezdka v Revel'*, 53, 66.

24. Bestuzhev, *Poezdka v Revel'*, 73–74.

25. See Isakov, "O livonskoi teme v russkoi literature," and his "O 'livonskikh povestiakh' dekabristov (K voprosu o stanovlenii dekabristskogo istorizma)," *Uchenye zapiski Tartuskogo gosudarstvennogo universiteta* 167 (1965): 33–80. Scholars disagree over the question to what extent the Livonian theme reflects the Decembrists' political ideas (for the Soviet scholars' stance in favor of the connection, expressed particularly strongly by V. Bazanov, see Isakov's summary in his "O livonskoi teme v russkoi literature," 146).

26. See O'Connor, *The History of the Baltic States*, 41.

27. Isakov, "O livonskoi teme v russkoi literature," 147–48.

28. Schönle, *Authenticity and Fiction*, 132.

29. Bestuzhev, *Poezdka v Revel'*, 20–21. Many Soviet scholars tried to make a case for the Decembrist writers' sincere sympathy with the cause of the Estonian peasants. Bestuzhev pays particular attention to class dynamics in Livonia and often comments on the suffering of the local population under the despotic rule of the Livonian knights. As Schönle comments, Bestuzhev's narrative of social history shows the historical process not as chaotic but as rigidly deterministic: "Regardless of the military situation, the peasants are the perpetual losers of history" (*Authenticity and Fiction*, 136). At the same time, both in his travelogue and in his Livonian tales, Bestuzhev gives a somewhat negative portrait of Estonian peasants as uncivilized and culturally inferior.

30. For a discussion of the Decembrists' imperial attitudes toward the Caucasus, see Ram, *The Imperial Sublime*, chap. 3.

31. Bestuzhev, *Poezdka v Revel'*, 52, 85–86. Bestuzhev's portrayal of German knights was not exclusively negative. See Isakov, "O 'livonskikh povestiakh' dekabristov," 53–54, for a more nuanced discussion of this issue. The persistent theme of bloodthirsty and savage Livonian knights in Decembrist literature complicates the trajectory outlined by Brüggemann ("The Baltic Provinces and Russian Perceptions in Late Imperial Russia"), according to which Baltic Germans, viewed initially as paragons of Enlightenment and civilization, begin to be vilified as barbarian invaders only later in the century, with the rise of Russian ethnic nationalism. Similarly, the symbolic Russification explored by the scholar (e.g., the building of the Alexander Nevsky cathedral in Revel/Tallinn in the 1880s) starts as early as in the Gothic Livonian texts of the 1820s, which claim Livonia for Russia.

32. Bestuzhev's references to Estonia as a "gate" and "a boulevard" for foreign attacks on Russia anticipate the latter's portrayals of its geopolitical position as threatened by external invasions; the need for various "buffer zones" then serves as a justification for imperial expansion. I am indebted to Edyta Bojanowska for this observation.

33. Bestuzhev, *Poezdka v Revel'*, 114–15; emphasis added.

34. Peter Fritzsche, *Stranded in the Present: Modern Time and the Melancholy of History* (Cambridge: Harvard University Press, 2004), 104. I address his theory of ruins in greater detail in chapter 6. For an enlightening discussion of the aesthetic and political significance of ruins in the Romantic era in Russia, see Schönle, *Architecture of Oblivion: Ruins and Historical Consciousness in Modern Russia* (DeKalb: Northern Illinois University Press, 2011), chap. 3. Although Schönle does not include a discussion of Bestuzhev in his book on ruins, in his analysis of *A Journey to Revel*, he stresses the importance of the past in this work, a past that "keeps haunting him, imposing unwanted memories at the most inopportune moments" (*Authenticity and Fiction*, 138). Malkina argues that, compared to the traditional Gothic novel, Bestuzhev's tales engage more emphatically with the problems of time, history, and memory ("Povesti A. A. Bestuzheva [Marlinskogo]").

35. The primary historical sources for Aleksandr Bestuzhev were Balthasar Russow's 1578 *Chronica der Provinz Lyfflandt*; Christian Kelch's *Liefländische Historia, oder kurtze Beschreibung der Denkwürdigsten Kriegs- und Friedens-Geschichte Esth- Lief- und Lettlandes* (1695); and François Gabriel de Bray, *Essai critique sur l'histoire de la Livonie, suivi d'un tableau de l'état actuel de cette province* (1817). V. Bazanov, *Ocherki dekabristskoi literatury. Publitsistika. Proza. Kritika* (Moscow: Gos. Izdatel'stvo khudozhestevennoi literatury, 1953), 293–96.

36. Malkina comments on the reasons Livonia was such an appropriate setting for Gothic Romantic novellas: "[Livonia] satisfied all the requirements: it offered a plethora of castles and old terrifying legends; it was a part of Russia and yet a strange and unfamiliar country for the majority of the readers." V. Ia. Malkina, "Povesti A. A. Bestuzheva (Marlinskogo)," in N. D. Tamarchenko, ed., *Goticheskaia traditsiia v russkoi literature*, 38.

37. Nikolai Bestuzhev, "Gugo fon Brakht," in *Russkaia istoricheskaia povest' v 2 tt.* (Moscow: Khudozhestvennaia literatura, 1988), 1:134.

38. Bestuzhev, "Gugo fon Brakht," 140, 145.

39. Bestuzhev, "Gugo fon Brakht," 134. Hugo's control over the sea is described in the terms invoking the absence of the law: "Even though no law confirmed his realm, it spreads as far as the eye can see from the castle's observation tower."

40. Bestuzhev, "Gugo fon Brakht," 136.

41. Bestuzhev, "Gugo fon Brakht," 145.

42. A. A. Bestuzhev-Marlinskii, *Sochineniia*, 2 vols. (Moscow: Gos. Izdatel'stvo khudozhestvennoi literatury, 1958), 1:38–39. Hereafter A. Bestuzhev's stories are cited from this edition and this volume with the page number indicated in the parentheses in the main text.

43. Mark S. Simpson praises Bestuzhev's later tale, "The Cuirassier" ("Latnik," 1832), for the author's masterful adaptation of the Gothic mode to a Russian setting (the tale unfolds during the Napoleonic Wars in the Russian hussar milieu). See his *The Russian Gothic Novel and Its British Antecedents,* chap. 3. I would add that most of Bestuzhev's seemingly foreign, Livonian tales are also intimately connected to Russian historical problematics and are set in geographical proximity to what would become Russia.

44. The story, originally titled "Blood for Blood," came out in 1825 but, because of the Decembrist uprising, the almanac in which it had been published was seized by the government. The story appeared in 1827 in a different publication, under the

title "The Castle Eisen." For a summary of the story's publication history, see Bagby, *Alexander Bestuzhev-Marlinsky*, 128–29.

45. Isakov, "O livonskoi teme v russkoi literature," 155.

46. In Malkina's view, "The Castle Neuhausen" exhibits the most striking similarity with Gothic novels ("Povesti A. A. Bestuzheva [Marlinskogo]," 39). Vatsuro makes the case for "The Castle Eisen" as the most "Gothic" of Bestuzhev's Livonian tales, where the Gothic legacy is undermined by the narrative device of *skaz* (*Goticheskii roman v Rossii*, 365–68). The question of how Gothic Bestuzhev's tales are was a controversial subject, mainly because associating a Decembrist writer with the Gothic mode was ideologically problematic in Soviet scholarship. Most scholars have agreed that the influence of the Gothic tradition on Bestuzhev's tales is undeniable, but the extent and the nature of the writer's adaptation of the Gothic mode can be debated. For useful summaries, see Malkina, "Povesti A. A. Bestuzheva (Marlinskogo)," 36; and especially Vatsuro, *Goticheskii roman v Rossii*, 352–55. Vatsuro concludes that Bestuzhev's "tales about Livonia emerge . . . in the field of attraction and repulsion created by two poles—W. Scott and the historical novel predating him, including chivalric and Gothic novels" (358).

47. In "The Castle Eisen," too, the border location is invoked: "It wasn't hard back then to find enemies—just go out the gate: there were plenty of neighbors and even more reasons to drag them into a quarrel. Besides, Narva was only 30 versts away, and beyond that the Russian field opened up. . . . As soon as [the baron] would get bored of sitting around all day with his flagon, he'd hie off to the Russian borders" (153).

48. Moreover, von Mey is doubly other: he is not a typical Livonian German but a Maltese knight (originally from Westphalia) who is explicitly orientalized in the story. As Vseslav describes him, "His soul combined all the sultry passions of the East with an unrestrained will that wished everything and was able to accomplish everything" (83).

49. Again, as in N. Bestuzhev's novella, the Gothic villain is associated with the institution of the Secret Court regarded as a tool of dark ignorance and superstition, "that bogey of the Middle Ages," as A. Bestuzhev describes it (76).

50. As Vatsuro points out, his death is modeled after those of Ambrosio in Lewis's *The Monk* and Melmoth in Maturin's *Melmoth the Wanderer* (*Goticheskii roman v Rossii*, 365). John Mersereau also points the novella's indebtedness to *The Monk* (John Mersereau, Jr., *Russian Romantic Fiction* [Ann Arbor, MI: Ardis, 1983], 56).

51. As Malkina observes, by removing the spatial distance between his authorial persona and his narrative in the conclusion, Bestuzhev stresses the temporal gap instead ("Povesti A. A. Bestuzheva [Marlinskogo]," 41).

52. Bagby, *Alexander Bestuzhev-Marlinskii*, 122–23.

53. Mark Al'tshuller argues that this story was Kiukhel'beker's experiment in creating a prose work that would fully adhere to Admiral Shishkov's principles of the elevated archaic style. Interestingly, in a later version of "Ado," written in Siberia, Kiukhel'beker modernizes the language somewhat, purging it of excessively archaic elements. Mark Al'tshuller, "Neopublikovannaia redaktsiia povesti V. K. Kiukhel'bekera 'Ado,'" *Russkii iazyk* 46, no. 153/155 (1992): 185–225. John Mersereau comments that the ethnographic details of the novella are "largely fabricated" (*Russian Romantic Fiction*, 64).

54. V. Kiukhel′beker, "Ado: Estonskaia povest′," in *Mnemozina, sobranie sochinenii v stikakh i proze* 1 (1824); I–IV, Hildesheim: Georg Olms, 1986: 119–67; 129, 132. Citations refer to the Georg Olms edition.

55. Kiukhel′beker, "Ado," 134.

56. Kiukhel′beker, "Ado," 154.

57. During their stay in Novgorod, Yurii, who knew some Russian before, becomes fluent, and Maia learns some Russian as well.

58. The infernal connotations of the protagonist's name become obvious in the possessive form, for example, "Adova doch′" ("Ado's daughter," which sounds like "the daughter of the inferno"). Al′tshuller cites this example to illustrate what he calls Kiukhel′beker's "linguistic deafness," which he also credits as the basis for the writer's stylistic innovation ("Neopublikovannaia redaktsiia povesti V. K. Kiukhel′bekera 'Ado,'" 187). I would add that this particular linguistic play certainly reinforces the theme of the hero's spiritual transformation (his conversion from paganism to Christianity). Timur Guzairov comments on the Russification of names as a literary device in the plots of a Finn's conversion and mentions "Ado" as a prototype. See his "Pragmatika obraza 'vernopoddannogo finna' v ideologicheskikh tekstakh 1809–1854 gg.," in *Studia Russica Helsingiensia et Tartuensia XII: Mifologiia kul′turnogo prostranstva* (Tartu: Tartu Ülikooli Kirjastus, 2011), 157–58.

Chapter 3. "Gloomy Finland" and Russian Gothic Tales of Assimilation

1. "It is known that the east and north of present-day Russia have been, since ancient times, for the most part populated by the Chud′—which perhaps received their name from the Russians because they were completely strange (chuzhoiu) to them." N. I. Nadezhdin, "Ob etnograficheskom izuchenii narodnosti russkoi," *Zapiski russkogo geograficheskogo obshchestva* 2 (1847): 80. The actual etymology of the term "chud′" is somewhat problematic; the most established theory links both "Chud′" and "chuzhoi" to the Goth term "Þiuda" (narod). On "Chud′," see M. Fasmer, *Etimologicheskii slovar′ russkogo iazyka,* trans. O. N. Trubachev, 4 vols. (Moscow: Progress, 1964–73), 4:378. On "chuzhoi," see M. Fasmer, *Etimologicheskii slovar′,* 4:379.

2. "Chud′ i Rus′," *Finskii vestnik* 5 (1845): 30 [Materialy severnoi istorii]. Each section of the journal had its own pagination; therefore, I include the name of the section after providing page numbers of the citation.

3. N. I. Nadezhdin, "Ob etnograficheskom izuchenii narodnosti russkoi," 80.

4. Liubim Tarasenko-Atreshkov, "Pomor′e. Territoriia byvshego udel′nogo kniazhestva Polotskogo, sopredel′nogo emu Pskovskogo, i Velikogo Novgoroda," *Finskii vestnik* 24, no. 12 (1847): 2 [Materialy severnoi istorii]. In 1847, the previously bimonthly *Finskii vestnik* came out every month. Some other publications, even by the same *The Finnish Herald*, paint a less rosy picture and admit that, while formally converted to Christianity, various "Finnish tribes" in Russia gravitate toward paganism or schism. See *Finskii vestnik* 1 (1845): 34 [Raznyia raznosti] and D. Uspenskii, "Ingry, Vaty, Iagriamia, Savolaksy," *Finskii vestnik* 2 (1845): 1–19 [Etnografiia].

5. "Sever Evropeiskoi Rossii," *Finskii vestnik* 4 (1845): 86 [Materialy severnoi istorii].

6. This overview is based on Jason Edward Lavery, *The History of Finland* (Westport, CT: Greenwood Press, 2006), 44–45 and 51–52, as well as Nicholas V.

Riasanovsky and Mark D. Steinberg, eds., *A History of Russia*, 9th ed. (New York: Oxford University Press, 2018), 196. For a nuanced discussion of the Russian cultural perception of "Old Finland" as opposed to "New Finland," see Nathanaëlle Minard-Törmänen, *An Imperial Idyll: Finland in Russian Travelogues (1810–1860)* (Helsinki: Helsingfors Societas Scientiarum Fennica, 2016), chap. 7.

7. Finland's autonomy within the Russian Empire had its limitations, even though it was a welcome development for the Finnish elites. As Lavery reminds us, the "new autonomous state institutions were the products of Russian imperial power, not the popular will of the Finnish people. The new order was anything but democratic. The new state institutions gave bureaucrats unprecedented power over the people" (*The History of Finland*, 54).

8. See Lavery, *The History of Finland*, chap. 5, and Thaden, ed., *Russification in the Baltic Provinces and Finland*, chap. 5.

9. Pushkin, *Sobranie sochinenii*, 4:381.

10. See Lomonosov's "Ode to the Arrival of Empress Elisaveta Petrovna from Moscow to St. Petersburg in 1742 after Her Coronation" (1742). See also Boele's discussion of the portrayal of the Finn as a war victim in Russian literature. Boele, *The North in Russian Romantic Literature*, 225–28.

11. For a detailed analysis of the pastoral image of Finland in the Russian travel narratives, see Minard-Törmänen, *An Imperial Idyll: Finland in Russian Travelogues (1810–1860)*.

12. Boele, *The North in Russian Romantic Literature*, 225. In addition, Minard-Törmänen observes a paradoxical portrayal of the Finn in nineteenth-century Russian travelogues: an admirable "noble savage," a hard-working and simple-hearted "child of nature," on the one hand; and a lazy, slow, and unrefined barbarian, on the other (*An Imperial Idyll*, especially 208–12).

13. N.M. Karamzin, *Istoriia gosudarstva Rossiiskogo*, vol. 1 (Moscow: Nauka, 1989), 50–51. Immediately after this characterization, Karamzin states that Russian Finns were more civilized than one might believe based on the Roman historian's description.

14. Ia. K. Grot, "O finnakh i ikh narodnoi poezii," in *Trudy Ia. K. Grota*, vol. 1: *Iz Skandinavskago i Finskago mira, 1839–1881* (St. Petersburg, 1898), 109–10. The article was originally published in *Sovremennik* 19 (1840): 5–101.

15. This idea seems to be a part of the Russian discourse on Finland as it formed in the first half of the nineteenth century. See, for example, V. Mikhailov's comment about the Finns' indifference to their interest—a trait derived, among other things, from the fact that "The Finns have from the start been a conquered nation." V. Mikhailov, "Imatra," *Biblioteka dlia chteniia* 13 (1835): 46 [Russkaia slovesnost']. Cited in Valentina Naumenko, *"Zdes', na kontse Rossii ispolinskoi . . .": Finliandiia v tvorcheskom nasledii russkikh puteshestvennikov XVIII–nachala XX veka* (Iaroslavl': Remder, 2010), 487.

16. "Listki iz skandinavskogo mira," *Sovremennik* 29 (1843): 107.

17. K. M. Ber, "Ob etnograficheskikh issledovaniiakh voobshche i v Rossii v osobennosti," *Zapiski russkogo geograficheskogo obshchestva* 1 (1846): 107.

18. Minard-Törmänen, *An Imperial Idyll*, 213.

19. On the latter, see Minard-Törmänen, *An Imperial Idyll*, 212–19.

20. Hirvasaho's dissertation traces literary sources for Batiushkov's construction of an "Ossianic" Finland in this work, including descriptions of North American

landscapes (Iida Katariina Hirvasaho, "A Stepchild of the Empire: Finland in Russian Colonial Discourse" [PhD diss., UCLA, 1997], 35–63).

21. Jacob Emery, "Repetition and Exchange in Legitimizing Empire: Konstantin Batiushkov's Scandinavian Corpus," *Russian Review* 66 (2007): 603–4.

22. Emery, "Repetition and Exchange," 604.

23. Alina Bodrova, "Rhetoric and Mythology of the 1808–1809 Finnish War in Baratynsky's Poem *Eda*," in *Studia Russica Helsingiensia et Tartuensia XIV: Russian National Myth in Transition* (Tartu: Tartu Ülikooli Kirjastus, 2014), 70–71; see also Inna Bulkina, "Russian Warrior at a *Rendez-Vous*. The Sources and Reception of Evgeny Baratynsky's Finnish Poem," in *Studia Russica Helsingiensia et Tartuensia XIV*, 83–84.

24. See Guzairov, "Pragmatika obraza 'vernopoddannogo finna'"; Bodrova, "Rhetoric and Mythology of the 1808–1809 Finnish War in Baratynsky's Poem *Eda*"; and Bulkina, "Russian Warrior at a *Rendez-Vous*."

25. E. A. Baratynskii, *Stikhotvoreniia. Poemy* (Moscow: Nauka, 1982), 179–80. The epilogue was written for the fourth volume of the almanac *Mnemozine* (where Davydov's *Notes* on the Finnish war appeared) but did not pass censorship; Baratynsky sent it to the Decembrist almanac *Little Star* (*Zvezdochka*) where it was scheduled for publication in early 1826. The volume did not materialize because of the Decembrist uprising on December 14, 1825. Bulkina, "Russian Warrior at a *Rendez-Vous*," 80. For a colonial reading of *Eda*, see Neil Cornwell, "Pushkin and Odoevsky: the 'Afro-Finnish' Theme in Russian Gothic," in *Empire and the Gothic: The Politics of Genre*, ed. Andrew Smith and William Hughes (Basingstoke: Palgrave Macmillan, 2003), 74–75.

26. Guzairov, "Pragmatika obraza 'vernopoddannogo finna,'" 353–55.

27. For an overview of the representation of Finland in Russian travel narratives and literary works from the late eighteenth to the early twentieth centuries, see Naumenko, "Zdes', na kontse Rossii ispolinskoi . . ." For a discussion of "sublime Finland," see Minard-Törmänen, *An Imperial Idyll*, chap. 2.

28. "Dva slova o Gel'singforse," *Finskii vestnik* 11 (1846): 27 [Smes'].

29. For recent insightful studies on Baratynsky's treatment of the Finnish theme, see Elena Pedigo Clark, "'Many Lands Have I Left Behind Me': E. A. Baratynskii's Quest for Happiness in Finland, Italy, and the Homeland," *Poljarnyj Vestnik: Norwegian Journal of Slavic Studies* 17 (2014): 1–18; and her "'There Like Vast Waters Have Come Together Sea and Sky': 'Finland' and Finland in the Poetry of E. A. Baratynsky," *Slavic and East European Journal* 59, no. 1 (2015): 47–69. In the second article, Clark argues that Finland, a recently conquered territory, was, for Baratynsky, an empty space that he could fill with meaning relevant for his poetic and personal quest. At the same time, "real" Finland, with its unstable identity, destabilized Baratynsky's binary poetic world (including the North / South opposition) and allowed him to escape dualism through a creative act ("'Finland' and Finland in the Poetry of E. A. Baratynsky," 66–68). For an analysis of the representation of Finland and Estonia in Russian modernist poetry, see Katja Wiebe, "Die Perspektive der russischen Literatur des späten Zarenreichs auf den 'Norden' (Estland und Finnland)," in Brüggemann and Woodworth, ed., *Russland an der Ostsee*, 289–305.

30. S. Sh., "Utrenniaia Zaria, Al'manakh na 1841 god, izdannyi V. Vladislavlevym. Tretii god. S. Peterburg 1841," *Moskvitianin* 1, no. 2 (1841): 569.

31. Letter of June 14, 1847; *Perepiska Ia. K. Grota s P. A. Pletnevym*, 3 vols. (St. Petersburg: Tipografiia Ministerstva Putei Soobshcheniia, 1896), 3:88. Hereafter referred to as *Perepiska*.

32. For a detailed analysis of Russian colonial discourse on Finland, see Iida Katariina Hirvasaho, "A Stepchild of Empire."

33. Letter of September 27th, 1840. *Perepiska*, 1:70.

34. Letter of April 21, 1841. *Perepiska*, 1:329. As Guzairov points out, Russia's ideological battle against Swedish cultural influence in Finland and the Finns' identification with their former conquerors continued well after the military campaign of 1808–9. Guzairov cites a telling report made by Faddei Bulgarin to the Third Department in 1838, commenting on the close historical ties between Sweden and Finland that are hard to eradicate in only 30 years. Guzairov, "Pragmatika obraza 'vernopoddannogo finna,'" 353.

35. See Letter of October 8, 1840. *Perepiska*, 1:83.

36. Letter of April 18, 1841. *Perepiska*, 1:323.

37. Letter of October 15, 1840. *Perepiska* 1:96–97.

38. For more information on *History of the Rus'*, see chapter 6.

39. Guzairov, "Pragmatika obraza 'vernopoddannogo finna,'" 356. Guzairov cites M. M. Borodkin, *Istoriia Finliandii. Vremia imperatora Nikolaia I* (1915), 532. Derschau, the journal's editor, was the son of Karl Derschau, the Russian general of Baltic German origin who was the head (komendant) of the Åbo garrison between 1835 and 1862. See Minard-Törmänen, *An Imperial Idyll*, 185; also entries "Dershau, Karl Fedorovich" and "Dershau, Fedor Karlovich," in A. A. Polovtsov, *Russkii biograficheskii slovar'*, vol. 6 (S.-Peterburg: Izdanie Imperatorskago Russkago istoricheskago obshchestva, 1905), 326–27.

40. Among others, the Russian military legend Aleksandr Suvorov, as well as Sentimentalist poet Ivan Dmitriev, invoked Ossian in their writings on Finland. See G. M. Kovalenko, "Finny i Finliandiia v vospriiatii russkikh (s drevneishikh vremen do nachala XIX v.)," in *Mnogolikaia Finlandiia. Obrazy Finlandii i Finnov v Rossii*, ed. A. N. Tsamutali et al. (Velikii Novgorod: Novgorodskii gosudarstvennyi universitet, 2004), 42. For a useful discussion of the Gothic sublime, see David B. Morris, "Gothic Sublimity," *New Literary History* 16, no. 2 (1985): 299–319. For a poststructuralist reading of the Gothic sublime and of the Gothic as "an earlier moment of the postmodern," see Vijay Mishra, *The Gothic Sublime* (Albany: State University of New York Press, 1994), 17.

41. See, for example, Nikolai Polevoi's sketch "Abo. A Fragment from a Letter," published in *The Moscow Herald* in 1827; and Bulgarin's perception of the Vyborg castle as "romantic" and reminiscent of the Middle Ages (Naumenko, *"Zdes', na kontse Rossii ispolinskoi . . .,"* 451–52 and 548).

42. Otto Boele, "Finland in the Work of Jevgenij Baratynskij: Locus Amoenus or Realm of the Dead," *Essays in Poetics: The Journal of the British Neo-Formalist Circle* 19, no. 1 (1994): 25–46.

43. Ia. K. Grot, "Gel'singfors," in *Trudy Ia. K. Grota* 1:62. The article was originally published in *Sovremennik* 18 (1840): 5–82.

44. Baratynsky, for example, commented on the "simplicity of [the Finns'] manners" but compared their level of education to that of the inhabitants of the German provinces (E. A. Boratynsky, *Polnoe sobranie sochinenii*, 2 vols. (S. Petersburg, 1915), 2:15;

cited in Bulkina, "The Russian Warrior at a *Rendez-Vous*," 85). A poet and translator A. E. Gren, in his travel notes on Finland published in 1836, admired the level of literacy among the Finnish peasants, as well as the multilingualism of the Finnish nobility. See Naumenko, *"Zdes', na kontse Rossii ispolinskoi . . .,"* 497.

45. Grot, "O Finnakh i ikh narodnoi poezii," 102.

46. V. F. Odoevskii, *Sochineniia v dvukh tomakh* (Moscow: Khudozhestvennaia literatura, 1981), 141. Hereafter Odoevsky's *The Salamander* is cited from this edition with the page number indicated in the main text in parentheses.

47. For a detailed study of the myth of Finnish and Lapp sorcery in the Western literary tradition, see Ernest J. Moyne, *Raising the Wind: The Legend of Lapland and Finland Wizards in Literature* (Newark: University of Delaware Press, 1981).

48. See Jeremy DeAngelo, "The North and the Depiction of the 'Finnar' in the Icelandic Sagas," *Scandinavian Studies* 82, no. 3 (2010): 257–86; and Kovalenko, "Finny i Finliandiia v vospriiatii russkikh," 36. Kovalenko cites the Russian proverb on Finland from V. Dal', *Poslovitsy russkogo naroda* (Moscow: Khudozhestvennaia literatura, 1989), 1:305.

49. See Bulkina, "The Russian Warrior at a *Rendez-Vous*," 86.

50. But listen: in my native fen,
Among the lonely fishermen
Are hid miraculous traditions:
In timeless hush past human ken
In farthest forest darkness dreary,
There live the silver-head magicians;
In steadfast quest of wisdom eery
All potency of mind they spend.
By their dread voices all is driven
That ever breathed below, above;
Into their awesome will is given
Both life and death, and very love.
    —Alexander Pushkin, *Collected*
        Narrative and Lyrical Poetry,
          trans. Walter Arndt (Ann
           Arbor: Ardis, 1984), 143.

No slushai: v rodine moei
Mezhdu pustynnykh rybarei
Nauka divnaia taitsia.
Pod krovom vechnoi tishiny,
Sredi lesov, v glushi dalekoi
Zhivut sedye kolduny;
K predmetam mudrosti vysokoi
Vse mysli ikh ustremleny;
Vse slyshit golos ikh uzhasnyi,
Chto bylo i chto budet vnov',
I groznoi vole ikh podvlastny
I grob i samaia liubov'.
         —Pushkin, *Sobranie*
           sochinenii, 4:24.

Nabokov interprets "Finn" as a reference to Fingal, Ossian's father (in which case we observe a conflation of the Ossianic tradition with the "Finnish myth"). See *Eugene Onegin: A Novel in Verse by Alexander Pushkin,* trans. and commentary by Vladimir Nabokov, 2 vols. (Princeton: Princeton University Press, 1975), 2:255. Bulkina draws the parallel between the ambiguity of Pushkin's Finn and the name of Baratynsky's heroine Eda alluding to the Scandinavian epic. "The metonymic mechanism [of transferring Scandinavian imagery to Finland] is in obvious contradiction with the military theme . . .: as a result of the 1808 campaign, Finland ceased to be Sweden." Bulkina, "The Russian Warrior at a *Rendez-Vous,*" 81.

51. As D. M. Sharypkin observes, in the European Romantic imagination the Scandinavian setting was associated with the supernatural, terror, and mysticism. D. M. Sharypkin, *Skandinavskaia literatura v Rossii* (Leningrad: Nauka, 1980), 184–85. Russian translations of Scandinavian literary works published in *The Finnish Herald* between 1845 and 1847 abound in gory stories of terror. The Finns were singled out for their superstitious nature and prowess in magic by both their Scandinavian and Russian neighbors. A notable exception in Russian literature is Baratynsky's *Eda,* where the Finnish heroine is not associated with sorcery and paganism—on the contrary, she appears as a proper Lutheran, reading the Bible, linked thus with the contemporary historical context rather than the mythology of the "wild Finn." Bulkina, "The Russian Warrior at a *Rendez-Vous,*" 86.

52. Here Odoevsky directly contradicts Grot's observation about the Finns, who, even when living in isolated areas, are well informed about world events. Grot, *O Finnakh i ikh narodnoi poezii,* 104–5.

53. Interestingly, *The Finnish Herald* reviewed Odoevsky's 1844 *Sochineniia,* criticizing his mystical stories and praising his more "realistic" society tales. However, in their portrayal of Finland, the journal publications relied on the same assumptions and the same rhetoric as the Romantic writer. Odoevsky's *Sochineniia* were reviewed in the first issue of *Finskii vestnik.* "Sochineniia kniazia V.F. Odoevskogo. SP-burg, v tip. E. Pratsa. 1844, v"-8. Tri chasti, str. 390-436-572," *Finskii vestnik* 1 (1845): 33–51 [Bibliograficheskaia khronika].

54. A. Likhachev, "Prikashchik. Fiziologicheskii ocherk," *Finskii vestnik* 5 (1845): 1 [Nravoopisatel'].

55. "O pietizme," *Finskii vestnik* 5 (1845): 18–19 [Nravoopisatel'].

56. See Lavery, *The History of Finland,* 27.

57. On this distinction and its roots in Western Enlightenment theories, see Minard-Törmänen, *An Imperial Idyll,* 219–20.

58. F. Dershau, "Lalli, Finn XII stoletiia," *Finskii vestnik* 1 (1845): 3 [Nravoopisatel'].

59. Dershau, "Lalli," 5.

60. Dershau, "Lalli," 18–19.

61. Dershau, "Lalli," 19–20.

62. Dershau, "Lalli," 21.

63. See, for example, D. Semenov, *Otechestvovedenie. Issue 1: Severnyi krai i Finlandiia* (St. Petersburg: V tipografii Iosafata Ogryzko, 1864), 139–40. This overview of the Christianization of Finland includes the Lalli legend (but here he is referred to as a "nobleman.").

64. N. V. Kukol'nik, *Egor Ivanovich Sil'vanovsky, ili zavoevanie Finliandii pri Petre Velikom, Finskii vestnik* 1 (1845): 5–6 [Severnaia slovesnost']. Hereafter the text of

Kukol'nik's novel is cited from this source with the page numbers given in parentheses in the main text.

65. A source for this plot twist in Kukol'nik's novel could have been Grot's 1840 article "Helsingfors" where the scholar reports that even the Åbo University professors held superstitious beliefs, supported astrology, and accused each other of practicing black magic. He specifically refers to a trial that took place in the early eighteenth century, which is precisely the setting of Kukol'nik's work. Grot, "Gel'singfors," 87. Grot mostly relied on the work of the Finnish historian Gabriel Rein, at least for a later period of the university history.

66. As Hirvasaho observes, here Kukol'nik, as well as Odoevsky in his *The Salamander*, confuse "European black magic with Finnish *koldovstvo* for negativizing ends, since in both cases the sorcery causes or nearly causes (in "Sil'vanovskii") the hero's demise, thereby imprinting Finnish paganism as destructive and devilish." "A Stepchild of Empire," 97.

67. Finland paid high taxes during Swedish rule. According to Lavery, at the end of the sixteenth century, Finland provided about 60 percent of the Crown's revenue (*The History of Finland,* 41). Still, Kukol'nik paints what seems to be a highly idealized and self-congratulatory picture of the grateful Finns' ecstatic reaction to the establishment of Russian rule, which also describes Finns as typical subalterns. They respond to Golitsyn's address with jumps and other bodily movements, surround him, almost in a stampede, to kiss his hand and, on his departure, compose songs glorifying the prince, which they copy from each other "like parrots" (64–65). For a discussion of the official image of a "loyal" and "happy" Finnish subject of the Russian Empire (including in Kukol'nik's novel), see Guzairov, "Pragmatika obraza 'vernopoddannogo finna.'"

68. Adam Nowakowski points out that such a negative representation of the Swedes was somewhat unusual for the time, when Sweden had long ceased being Russia's military rival. "But, when discussing the past and present situation of Finland in the mid-nineteenth century, many authors emphasized that the Swedes ruled under the banner of the exploitation of the Finns and their country. This was done with the goal of presenting the current Russian rule in a favorable light." Adam Nowakowski, "Obrazy Finliandii, Shvetsii i Rossii v povesti Nestora Kukol'nika *Egor Ivanovich Sil'vanovskii, ili Pokorenie [sic] Finliandii pri Petre Velikom,*" *Rocznik Przemsyki* 52, no. 2, *Literatura i Język,* series vol. 20 (2016): 27–37. This article also comments on the stereotypes about Finn's proclivity for magic and their ties to nature employed by Kukol'nik.

69. Guzairov, "Pragmatika obraza 'vernopoddannogo finna,'" 359.

70. Guzairov analyzes an episode from Bulgarin's memoirs where Russian officers stationed in Finland during the 1808–9 campaign jokingly offer their host's ten-year-old daughter a "Russian fiancé." The girl grows pale, trembles, and says, in Swedish, "Death to the Russians." As a grown-up, she marries a Russian man, learns the Russian language, and becomes a loyal subject of the Russian Empire. Guzairov, "Pragmatika obraza 'vernopoddannogo finna,'" 354.

71. Swedish posters presented Narva as Diana and Peter I as Acteon; Russian propaganda portrayed Ingria as Andromede saved from the sea beast (Sweden) by a Russian Perseus. See Sharypkin, *Skandinavskaia literatura v Rossii,* 62.

72. See Kovalenko, "Finny i Finliandiia v vospriiatii russkikh," 38.

73. Hirvasaho notes that "Finnishness in Russian discourse is not an intrinsic identity; a 'desirable' Finn can be appropriated as a Russian" ("A Stepchild of Empire," 110).

74. To my knowledge, the first scholar to discuss this novella explicitly as a text of the "imperial Gothic" was Neil Cornwell, in his "Pushkin and Odoevsky: the 'Afro-Finnish' Theme in Russian Gothic."

75. See M. A. Tur'ian, "Evoliutsiia romanticheskikh motivov v povesti V. F. Odoevskogo 'Salamandra,'" in *Russkii romantizm*, ed. K. N. Grigor'ian (Leningrad: Nauka, 1978), 187; and P. N. Sakulin, *Iz istorii russkogo idealizma. Kniaz' V. F. Odoevskii. Myslitel'—pisatel',*, vol. 1, pt. 2 (Moscow: Izdanie M. i S. Sabashnikovykh, 1913), 75.

76. In his otherwise nuanced and informative chapter on Finland in *The North in Russian Romantic Literature*, Boele interprets Odoevsky's novella in this optimistic vein.

77. For the parallels between Odoevsky's *The Salamander* and Pushkin's unfinished novel *The Moor of Peter the Great* (1827–28), see V. I. Sakharov, "Eshche o Pushkine i V. F. Odoevskom," in *Pushkin: Issledovaniia i materialy*, ed. M. P. Alekseev et al. (Leningrad: Nauka, 1979), 9: 224–30; Cornwell, "Pushkin and Odoevsky: The 'Afro-Finnish' Theme in Russian Gothic"; and Z. E. Babaeva, "Istoricheskaia interpretatsiia siuzheta povesti V. F. Odoevskogo 'Salamandra,'" *Filologicheskie nauki. Voprosy teorii i praktiki* 4 (2012): 27–30.

78. "—Where are we going to sleep?—There, in my land . . .—But your land is here, Jakko . . . This is my land, the pastor told me, which means it's yours as well" (158).

79. In another (border-crossing) scene, the Finnish pastor's wife traveling with Elsa to St. Petersburg is called "a Finnish witch" (chukhonskaia ved'ma) by the St. Petersburg border patrol.

80. Pushkin alludes to the imperial conquest in the prologue of *The Bronze Horseman* by invoking the "poor Finn" in connection to Peter's project of building a new capital but, unlike in Odoevsky's novella, this theme remains as an undeveloped subtext of the work.

81. See, for example, Odoevsky's critique of Bentham and his utilitarian philosophy in his dystopia "A City without a Name" ("Gorod bez imeni," 1839), as well as numerous passages in *The Russian Nights* (*Russkie nochi*, 1844). For a summary of Odoevsky's social and historical views, including his rejection of the mercantile spirit of his time, see Sakulin, *Iz istorii russkogo idealisma*, vol. 1, pt. 1, 556–90.

82. Sakulin, *Iz istorii russkogo idealisma*, vol. 1, pt. 2, 80.

83. See "A Book on Nymphs, Sylphs, Pygmies, and Salamanders, and on the Other Spirits," in *Four Treatises of Theophrastus von Hohenheim Called Paracelsus* (Baltimore: Johns Hopkins University Press, 1941), 227–30.

84. "A Book on Nymphs," 231–33.

85. Tur'ian, "Evoliutsiia romanticheskikh motivov," 189.

86. Sakulin, *Iz istorii russkogo idealisma*, vol. 1, pt. 2, 75; and Tur'ian, "Evoliutsiia romanticheskikh motivov," 188.

87. Sakulin, *Iz istorii russkogo idealisma*, vol. 1, pt. 2, 76; and Tur'ian, "Evoliutsiia romanticheskikh motivov," 189.

88. Tur'ian convincingly argues that in the novella, Odoevsky explores a tension between the conscious and the unconscious and ultimately advocates a synthesis of rational and instinctual knowledge. Hirvasaho also analyzes *The Salamander* to demonstrate Finland's portrayal as the realm of childhood and the subconscious, as well as the otherworldly ("A Stepchild of Empire," 78–85).

89. Cynthia Ramsey suggests that the fire symbolizes the illicit incestuous passion for his "sister" Elsa that Jakko resists. Cynthia C. Ramsey, "Gothic Treatment of the Crisis of Engendering in Odoevskii's *The Salamander*," in *The Gothic-Fantastic in Nineteenth-Century Russian Literature*, ed. Neil Cornwell (Amsterdam: Rodopi, 1999), 166. V. Feierkherd traces the motif of fire to *The Kalevala* where it is associated with the figure of the blacksmith Ilmarinen. V. Feierkherd "Romantizm i realism v dilogii V. F. Odoevskogo 'Salamandra,'" in *Problemy teorii i istorii literatury*, ed. V. I. Kuleshov (Moscow: Izdatel'stvo Moskovskogo universiteta, 1971), 186.

90. On Odoevsky's dialogue, in this scene, with Pushkin's *The Bronze Horseman*, see Sakharov, "Eshche o Pushkine i V. F. Odoevskom," 227–28; Cornwell, "Pushkin and Odoevsky," 80; and Sakulin, *Iz istorii russkogo idealizma*, vol. 1, pt. 2, 329.

91. As Sakulin points out, in the late 1820s and through the 1830s Odoevsky, the faithful Schellingian in the 1820s, becomes increasingly interested in mysticism, which he refers to as "nineteenth-century sorcery" (Sakulin, *Iz istorii russkogo idealizma*, vol. 1, pt. 1, 476). This tendency mirrors the development of German idealist philosophy, especially Schellingianism, which becomes more mystically oriented during this period as well (Sakulin, *Iz istorii russkogo idealizma*, vol. 1, pt. 1, 391–92). The ideas expressed in the salamander's speech can be traced to the Schellingian philosophy of identity, as well as to many popular mystical teachings with which Odoevsky was familiar, such as St. Martin's views on man's fall from the interconnected and unified universe and God (see Sakulin, *Iz istorii russkogo idealizma*, vol. 1, pt. 1, 400ff.). For an analysis of early nineteenth-century mysticism in Russia and its repercussions in literature, including Odoevsky's prose, see Ilya Vinitsky, "*Amor Hereos*, or How One Brother Was Visited by an Invisible Being: Lived Spirituality among Russian Freemasons in the 1810s," *Kritika: Explorations in Russian and Eurasian History* 9, no. 2 (2008): 291–316.

92. Tur'ian comes to a similar conclusion when she observes that the young adept's infidelity to the salamander is transformed, in the final version of the story, into his apostasy from his true nature, which is in conflict with his new St. Petersburg environment ("Evoliutsiia romanticheskikh motivov," 202).

93. Sakulin, *Iz istorii russkogo idealizma*, vol. 1, pt. 1, 342 passim.

94. In his notes about his conversation with Schelling, Odoevsky cites the German philosopher as saying that "she [Russia] is destined for something important" (Sakulin, *Iz istorii russkogo idealizma*, vol. 1, pt. 1, 395).

95. Based on my analysis of the text, I disagree with Feierkherd's interpretation of the novella as the "apotheosis of the Petrine era," whereas Jakko's decline in part 2 is linked to the post-Petrine historical era. Feierkherd, "Romantizm i realism v dilogii V. F. Odoevskogo 'Salamandra.'"

96. Ramsey, "Gothic Treatment of the Crisis of Engendering in Odoevskii's *The Salamander*."

97. Cornwell offers both a colonial and a feminist interpretation of Elsa's revenge and argues that, while "Part II of *The Salamander* may suggest the 'revenge' of . . . Yakko, both for the loss of his glittering Petrine career and for the ultimate failure of his apprenticeship in cultural assimilation; but the ultimate retribution is of course wreaked by . . . Elsa. In St. Petersburg 'the subject of mockery and hatred,' this 'poor child of nature' strikes back in Moscow . . . on behalf not only of the empire, but of

her female sex, that perpetually colonized half of humanity." Cornwell, "Pushkin and Odoevsky: The 'Afro-Finnish' Theme in Russian Gothic," 81.

Chapter 4. Ukraine: Russia's Uncanny Double

1. N. I. Nadezhdin, "'Vechera na khutore bliz Dikan'ki.' Povesti, izdannye pasichnikom Rudym Pan'kom. Pervaia knizhka, Spb., v tipogr. depart. nar. prosv., 1831," in N. I. Nadezhdin, *Literaturnaia kritika. Estetika* (Moscow: Khudozhestvennaia literatura, 1972), 280.

2. Nadezhdin, "Ob etnograficheskom izuchenii narodnosti russkoi," 102 and 112.

3. [I. Sbitnev], "Poezdka v Khar'kov," *Vestnik Evropy* 15 (1830): 222.

4. The following outline is based primarily on Paul Kubicek, *The History of Ukraine* (Westport, CT: Greenwood Press, 2008), chaps. 3 and 4, and on Orest Subtelny, *Ukraine: A History*, 4th ed. (Toronto: University of Toronto Press, 2009), chaps. 6, 10, and 11.

5. This treaty is subject to conflicting interpretations: Russian and Soviet historiography interprets this event as a logical "reunification" of Russia and Ukraine, whereas other historians insist that Khmel'nyts'ky merely sought a military alliance with Muscovy or the protection of the Russian tsar with the understanding that Ukrainian autonomy would be preserved. See Kubicek, *History of Ukraine*, 41. The leader of the 1648 Ukrainian Cossack uprising, in the course of which thousands of Jews and Poles were massacred, Khmel'nyts'ky is a highly controversial historical figure, whose reputation ranges from that of a national hero to a demonic antagonist. For competing cultural narratives, see Amelia M. Glaser, ed., *Stories of Khmelnytsky: Competing Literary Legacies of the 1648 Ukrainian Cossack Uprising* (Stanford: Stanford University Press, 2015).

6. Catherine was also unhappy with Finnish and Livonian autonomy, viewing the special status enjoyed by some regions as "feudal relics" (Subtelny, *Ukraine: A History*, 172). For an in-depth analysis of the gradual process leading to a liquidation of the Hetmanate, see Zenon Kohut, *Russian Centralism and Ukrainian Autonomy: Imperial Absorption of the Hetmanate, 1760s–1830s* (Cambridge, MA: Harvard Ukrainian Research Institute, 1988). In this book, I refer to the Ukrainian version of this study where quotes are provided in the original Ukrainian and Russian: Zenon Kohut, *Rosiis'kyi tsentralizm i ukrains'ka avtonomiia. Likvidatsiia Het'manshchyny 1760–1830* (Kyiv: Osnovy, 1996).

7. For a broad overview of the Ukrainians' participation in Russian culture and empire-building, see David Saunders, *The Ukrainian Impact on Russian Culture, 1750–1850* (Edmonton: Canadian Institute of Ukrainian Studies, 1985). In his book *Ukrainskii vopros v rossiiskoi imperii*, Aleksei Miller discusses various scenarios for the integration and assimilation of the Ukrainians into the Russian Empire. As he shows, in the first half of the nineteenth century, Russian intellectuals' views of these processes ranged from a call for complete assimilation, even through aggressive Russification, to a more moderate position that encouraged Ukraine to preserve its cultural and regional specificity while stressing the inevitability of its political unity with Russia (*Ukrainskii vopros v rossiiskoi imperii*, chap. 1).

8. Yohanan Petrovsky-Shtern, *Anti-Imperial Choice: The Making of a Ukrainian Jew* (New Haven: Yale University Press, 2009), 14.

9. For one such debate, see "Critical Forum on Ukraine," *Slavic Review* 74, no. 4 (2016): 695–737. For a nuanced historiographical overview of various approaches to Ukraine's "colonial question," see Stephen Velychenko, "The Issue of Russian Colonialism in Ukrainian Thought. Dependency Identity and Development," *Ab Imperio* 1 (2002): 323–67. George Grabowicz argues in favor of the applicability of the colonial paradigm to Ukraine while also observing that in Ukrainian history the colonial model merged with the provincial one. George G. Grabowicz, "Ukrainian Studies: Framing the Contexts," *Slavic Review* 54, no. 3 (1995): 674–90. For a useful survey of the debate on Ukraine's colonial status in a comparative perspective, see Vitaly Chernetsky, *Mapping Postcommunist Cultures: Russia and Ukraine in the Context of Globalization* (Montreal: McGill-Queen's University Press, 2007), 46–53.

10. On the trope of Ukraine as a natural paradise and its anachronistic nature, see Shkandrij, *Russia and Ukraine,* 75–76.

11. Gogol', *Sobranie sochinenii,* 6:55–56.

12. N. I. Nadezhdin, "'Vechera na khutore bliz Dikan'ki,'" 281.

13. Shkandrij, *Russia and Ukraine,* 66. Shkandrij's book offers a comprehensive analysis of the image of Ukraine in Russian imperialist discourse. My discussion here focuses only on those aspects that are crucial to the development of Ukraine as a space of the Russian imperial uncanny.

14. To quote Shkandrij, "all in the local culture that can be absorbed by these tropes of anterior time and anachronistic space is in this way aligned with the atavistic, comically quaint or hopelessly provincial" (*Russia and Ukraine,* 76).

15. In his essay "The Uncanny," Freud observes that "the quality of uncanniness can only come from the fact of the 'double' being a creation dating back to a very early mental stage, long since surmounted—a stage, incidentally, at which it wore a more friendly aspect. The 'double' has become a thing of terror, just as, after the collapse of their religion, the gods turned into demons." *The Standard Edition of Complete Psychological Works* 17: 236. In the case of Ukraine, its past image could be seen as threatening, as well as "friendly," because of its internal doubleness. Etkind argues that Russia's unique imperial experience of self-colonizing and exoticizing its own people (which Etkind defines as "internal colonization") created a "crisis of difference" and "monstrous doubles," to use René Girard's terms. "While external colonization finds its symbolic representation in hybrids," writes Etkind, "internal colonization finds it in doubles." (Etkind, *Internal Colonization,* 247).

16. "'Zinovii Bogdan Khmel'nitskii.' Sochinenie Aleksandra Kuz'micha. Epokha pervaia, molodost' Zinoviia. 5-t' chastei. S. Peterburg 1846," *Finskii vestnik* 13 (1847): 1 [Bibliograficheskaia khronika].

17. See Vitalii Kiselev and Tat'iana Vasil'eva, "'Strannoe politicheskoe sonmishche' ili 'narod, poiushchii i pliashushchii': Konstruirovanie obraza Ukrainy v russkoi slovesnosti kontsa XVIII–nachala XIX veka," in *Tam, vnutri,* ed. Etkind, Uffel'mann, and Kukulin, 478–517.

18. The expression "strannoe . . . politicheskoe sonmishche" (a strange . . . political throng) was used to describe the Zaporizhzhian Cossacks in the 1775 manifesto that abolished the Sich. See Kiselev and Vasil'eva, "'Strannoe politicheskoe sonmishche,'" 491. Their primary source is *Svod zakonov Rossiiskoi imperii* (Spb.: V tipografii II otdeleniia Sobstvennoi Ego Imperatorskogo Velichestva kantseliarii, 1830), 20: 190 (#14354). The phrase "narod, poiushchii i pliashushchii, zla ne mystlit"

(a singing and dancing people can't have evil intentions) is ascribed to Catherine II. See Iu. M. Lotman, "Iz nabliudenii nad strukturnymi printsipami rannego tvorchestva Gogolia," *Uchenye zapiski Tartuskogo gosudarstvennogo universiteta* 251 (1970): 34. The phrase was used, in a modified form, by Pushkin in his 1836 note on Gogol's Dikan'ka cycle where he praised the work for its "lively description of the singing and dancing tribe" (zhivoe opisanie plemeni poiushchego i pliashushchego). See Pushkin, *Sobranie sochinenii*, 7:345.

19. M. Maksimovich, "Obozrenie starogo Kieva," *Kievlianin* bk. 1 (1840): 50.

20. A. Ve-skii, "Sila privychki," *Kievlianin* bk. 1 (1840): 177.

21. See particularly Oleh S. Ilnytzkyj's work on Gogol, including his article "Is Gogol's 1842 Version of *Taras Bulba* Really 'Russified'?," *Journal of Ukrainian Studies* 35–36 (2010–11): 51–68; and Bojanowska, *Nikolai Gogol*. Earlier seminal studies include Shkandrij, *Russia and Ukraine*, 105–16; Luckyj, *Between Gogol' and Ševčenko*, especially 88–127; Yevhen Malaniuk, "Hohol'-Gogol'," in his *Knyha sposterezhen'* (Kyiv: Dnipro, 1997), 374–89; George G. Grabowicz, "Between History and Myth: Perceptions of the Cossack Past in Polish, Russian, and Ukrainian Romantic Literature," *American Contributions to the Ninth International Congress of Slavists, Kiev, September 1983*, vol. 2: *Literature, Poetics, History*, ed. Paul Debreczeny (Columbus, OH: Slavica, 1983), 173–88; and I. E. Mandel'shtam, *O kharaktere gogolevskogo stilia: Glava iz istorii russkogo literaturnogo iazyka* (Helsingfors: Novaia Tip. Hufvudstadsbladet, 1902).

22. N. V. Gogol', *Sobranie sochinenii*, 1:133. In this chapter, quotes from Gogol's works are given from this volume with the page number indicated in parentheses in the main text. Andrei Bely refused to equate Katerina's father and the sorcerer, reading the figure of the latter as a demonization of the other by the traditional community and Gogol's projection of his own otherness. Andrei Belyi, *Masterstvo Gogolia: Issledovanie* (Moscow: Gos. Izdatel'stvo khudozhestvennoi literatury, 1934), 55–56.

23. For an illuminating discussion of violence (particularly fraternal betrayal) as essential to maintaining a community in Gogol's "Ukrainian tales," and specifically "A Terrible Vengeance," see Angelina Emilova Ilieva, "Romulus's Nations: Myths of Brotherhood and Fratricide in Russian and South Slavic National Narratives" (PhD diss., Northwestern University, 2005), chap. 1.

24. See Andrei Belyi, *Masterstvo Gogolia*, 57–71, and Robert A. Maguire, *Exploring Gogol* (Stanford: Stanford University Press, 1994), 5–18.

25. Maguire, *Exploring Gogol*, 6.

26. See also Belyi, *Masterstvo Gogolia*, 56. Bely notes the dangerous alterity of the figure, without connecting it to the Gothic genre.

27. As Oleh Ilnytzkyj shows, both in "A Terrible Vengeance" and in *Taras Bulba* Gogol' uses the adjective "russkii" to refer to Rus' and, by extension, to Ukraine, as the adjective "Ukrainian" was not widely used at the time. See Ilnytzkyj, "Is Gogol's 1842 Version of *Taras Bulba* Really 'Russified'?"

28. Notably, a recurrent adjective attributed to the sorcerer throughout the story is *chudnyi* (magic, strange, uncanny). Modern-day meaning of chudnyi is primary positive (delightful, wonderful), but in Gogol's times the semantics of this word invoked strangeness, oddity, surprise, and the supernatural. See "Chudnyi," *Slovar'*

iazyka Pushkina, 2nd ed., 4 vols. (Moscow: Azbukovnik, 2000), 4:980–81. The folk etymology connecting chudnyi and chuzhoi (other, foreign) is at play here.

29. Virtually every analysis of "A Terrible Vengeance" comments on these characteristics of the sorcerer figure, from Bely's *Masterstvo Gogolia* to studies by Shkandrij (*Russia and Ukraine*), Bojanowska (*Nikolai Gogol*), Krys ("The Gothic in Ukrainian Romanticism"), and others.

30. Maguire, *Exploring Gogol*, 11.

31. *Zhupan* was an outer garment worn by the wealthier classes in the Polish-Lithuanian Commonwealth; in his glossary to the Dikan'ka tales, Gogol defines it as a "type of a caftan" (*Sobranie sochinenii* 1:11).

32. Bojanowska, *Nikolai Gogol*, 57.

33. Belyi, "Masterstvo Gogolia," 66–68.

34. Bojanwoska, *Nikolai Gogol*, 58.

35. Shkandrij, *Russia and Ukraine*, 113–14.

36. The mention of the "Christians" (probably implying "Orthodox Christians") in the list of nonowners of the weapons on the castle's walls may be a way of including Muscovites but this reference is too vague, especially compared to the detailed lists of other ethnicities or places.

37. "Before the Carpathian mountains you can still hear Rus' (russkuiu) speech, and across the mountains here and there the native word will still be heard; but over there the faith is not ours, and the language is not ours (a tam uzhe i vera ne ta, i rech' ne ta)" (166). Both Bojanowska and Maguire, as well as Ilieva, comment extensively on the motif of liminality in "A Terrible Vengeance."

38. Belyi, *Masterstvo Gogolia*, 66.

39. Maguire, *Exploring Gogol*, 9. Maguire comments on the etymology of the town's name, suggesting that the bard's tale might be falling "on deaf ears, that fratricide, curse, and revenge are the inescapable lot of humankind" (*Exploring Gogol*, 345). Bojanowska points out the "delightfully Gogolian detail—a blind bard in a 'deaf' town" but concludes that the bard ultimately serves as a carrier of national memory whose "music falls on keenly attuned, rather than deaf, ears" (*Nikolai Gogol*, 61). She also notes Hlukhiv's historical importance.

40. Subtel'ny, *Ukraine: A History*, 171.

41. Maguire, *Exploring Gogol*, 9.

42. This distinction is complicated by the figure of the devil himself, described as a "German" but also as a Russian imperial bureaucrat (Shkandrij, *Russia and Ukraine*, 109).

43. Bojanowska, *Nikolai Gogol*, 71.

44. Shkandrij, *Russia and Ukraine*, 111.

45. Epshtein points out the demonic connotations of artificial light in the St. Petersburg scene of the story, and Bojanowska concurs, stating that "Petersburg in this passage appears eminently demonic." M. N. Epshtein, "Ironiia stilia: Demonicheskoe v obraze Rossii u Gogolia," *Novoe literaturnoe obozrenie* 19 (1996): 129–47; Bojanowska, *Nikolai Gogol*, 68. Shkandrij demonstrates that light and elevation in this scene are associated with power but observes that "here, in the imposing city of light" a confusion re-emerges "over the appearances and realities of power" (*Russia and Ukraine*, 110).

46. Peter Sawczak, "'Noch' pered Rozhdestvom' Mykoly/Nikolaia Gogolia: K voprosu o 'maloi literature,'" *Russian, Croatian and Serbian, Czech and Slovak, Polish Literature* 49, no. 3 (2001): 259–70.

47. Sawczak, "'Noch' pered Rozhdestvom,'" 267.

Chapter 5. On Mimicry and Ukrainians

1. Gogol', *Sobranie sochinenii* 1:100.

2. V. V. Vinogradov, *Istoriia slov: Okolo 1500 slov i vyrazhenii i bolee 5000 slov, s nimi sviazannykh,* ed. N. Iu. Shvedova (Moscow: "Tolk," 1994), 128–29. As Vinogradov points out, *dvoinik* (a double) was in use in Russian dialects in the sense of paired objects, double amounts, or twins, but Pogorel'sky seemed to be the first to use it in literature in the sense of a person's ghostly alter ego.

3. Aleksei Perovsky was rumored to have an intimate relationship with his sister, Anna Tolstaia, the mother of writer Aleksei Konstantinovich Tolstoi. See M. A. Tur'ian, "Lichnost' A. A. Perovskogo i literaturnoe nasledie Antoniia Pogorel'skogo," in *Sochineniia i pis'ma* (Sankt-Peterburg: Nauka, 2010), 566 and 589–92.

4. Tur'ian, "Lichnost' A. A. Perovskogo," 568 and 601.

5. Antonii Pogorel'skii, *Sochineniia i pis'ma,* 9. Hereafter Pogorel'sky's works are cited from this edition with the page number indicated in the parentheses.

6. The novel's first part came out in 1830 and was a great success with the readers. The second part appeared three years later. For a discussion of the novel's reception, see Tur'ian, "Lichnost' Perovskogo i literaturnoe nasledie Pogorel'skogo," 641–47.

7. Vatsuro, *Goticheskii roman v Rossii,* 418–30.

8. Interestingly, when Baratynsky read Gogol's *Evenings on a Farm near Dikan'ka,* published anonymously, he assumed the author was Pogorel'sky, even though he did not quite recognize the latter's manner. See Tur'ian, "Lichnost' Perovskogo i literaturnoe nasledie Pogorel'skogo," 642.

9. In the novel's final chapter, the narrator reappears and indirectly reveals his full name—Anton(ii) Pogorel'sky (itself a fictional construction of Aleksei Perovsky).

10. Romanchuk sees in this episode "the first example in *Monastyrka* of language (writing) that utterly resists circulation and substitution—interpretation—and quite literally embodies recycling. Such a labyrinth of letters, where the only way out is the way you came in, foreshadows the vampirizing linguistic operations that will be enacted by the novel's eponymous hero." Romanchuk, "Mother Tongue," 282.

11. The new Ukrainian gentry of the Hetmanate era included descendants of the old nobility of Polish times, combined with the descendants of Cossack officers, as well as the new Cossack elite. The new Ukrainian *shliakhta* (from Polish "szlachta," nobility) had a certain degree of autonomy from Russian imperial institutions but at the same time did not enjoy the same privileges as the Russian nobility (dvorianstvo)—e.g., the right to attend privileged educational institutions for nobility, obtaining noble status when advancing up the "Table of Ranks." See Kohut, *Rosiis'kyi tsentralizm i ukrains'ka avtonomiia,* 38–39. Pogorel'sky's narrator specifically refers to his hostesses as "shliakhetnye" and mocks their dubious "dvorianstvo," thus recognizing the distinction (165).

12. *Bunchuk* is a pole with a sharpened top, to which horse or yak tail hair was attached. *Bulava* is a staff, often made out of gilded silver and ornamented by precious

stones. Both were used, as Pogorel'sky's narrator mentions, by Cossack hetmans as a symbol of their power. I. Pidkova and R. Shust, eds., *Dovidnyk z istorii Ukrainy* (Kyiv: Geneza, 1993), 1:76–77.

13. Kohut, *Rosiis'kyi tsentralizm i ukrains'ka avtonomiia*, 111.

14. The elite school for girls from noble families, "The Imperial Educational Society for Noble Girls," was founded by Catherine II in 1764 based on the Smolny Convent in St. Petersburg. See Tur'ian, "Lichnost' Perovskogo i literaturnoe nasledie Pogorel'skogo," 671. The institute was typically referred as "monastyr'," or "convent," in the 1820s and 1830s, and its students were called "smolianki" or "monastyrki" (the "Smolny girls" or "convent girls"), because they lived in the buildings that used to belong to the convent. See V. P. Bykova, "Zapiski staroi smolianki. Ch. 1, 1833–78" (St. Petersburg: Tipgorafiia E. Evdokimova, 1898), VII.

15. As evidenced by Aniuta's letter to her Smolny friend Masha: "Nobody calls me Aniuta here . . . My aunt and cousins call me Halechka, almost all the servants call me *pannochka* (young lady), and some address me as Hanna Trokhvymovna, after my father. They are saying it's all the same, Aniuta or Halechka; but I don't like it . . . Please, my dear Masha, never call me Halechka" (168).

16. Romanchuk, "Mother Tongue," 282. Romanchuk's article also links the colonial subtext and the Gothic tropes of Pogorel'sky's novel, operating mostly within a psychoanalytical theoretical framework and focusing on the vampiric linguistic economy in *The Convent Graduate* and Gogol's "Vii."

17. Romanchuk, "Mother Tongue," 283.

18. On this episode and its Gothic connections, see also Vatsuro, *Goticheskii roman v Rossii*, 425.

19. "Russkaia literatura: Novye knigi," *Moskovskii telegraf* 8 (April 1833): 583.

20. Koropeckyj and Romanchuk interpret the figure of Harkusha, an eighteenth-century Cossack-turned-bandit, as a manifestation of Little Russia's "dark side," "the necessary obverse of all that 'singing and dancing' and of those Gothic frights." Koropeckyj and Romanchuk, "Harkusha the Noble Bandit," 296.

21. Vas'ka is a nickname for Vasilii. The repetition of names here also suggests a diffusion of identity.

22. Vatsuro, *Goticheskii roman v Rossii*, 425.

23. Pogorel'sky's mockery of the Diundiks' Gallomania is indebted to the Russian eighteenth-century satiric tradition, but he develops this theme in a more complex context of the empire's provincial Ukrainian space.

24. Bhabha, *The Location of Culture*, 124–25. Bhabha here quotes T. B. Macaulay, "Minute on Education," in *Sources of Indian Tradition*, ed. W. Theodore de Bary, vol. 2 (New York: Columbia University Press, 1958), 49.

25. Bhabha, *The Location of Culture*, 122.

26. Kohut, *Rosiis'kyi tsentralizm i ukrains'ka avtonomiia*, chap. 7.

27. *The Location of Culture*, 126. Bhabha talks about the horrifying effect of this emptiness (129), but he also distinguishes mimicry from the return of the repressed (130). I maintain that colonial mimicry can be uncanny precisely because of the partial presence / familiarity and the effect of doubleness it produces that Pogorel'sky so masterfully explores *avant la lettre*.

28. Vatsuro, *Goticheskii roman v Rossii*, 424. Pogorel'sky's novel contributes to the Russian literary tradition of the province described through the tropes of void and

distortion—a tradition analyzed by Anne Lounsbery. However, here we are dealing not with a generic Russian province but a geographically specific region of Ukraine, which warrants an individualized approach.

29. I am indebted to Oleksandra Wallo for the term "the relay of mimicry" in connection to this analysis.

30. Klara Kashparovna, the narrator notes, came from the German colony Belye Mezhi in the Chernihiv province. Settling German colonists in the former Hetmanate area was Catherine II's project realized by Rumiantsev in the 1760s. The correct name of the colony in that area was Belaia Vezha. Kohut, *Rosiis'kyi tsentralizm i ukrains'ka avtonomiia*, 102.

31. Józef Smaga, *Antoni Pogorielski. Życie i twórczość na tle epoki* (Wrocław: Wydawnictwo Polskiej Akademii Nauk, 1970), 127.

32. Antonii Pogorel'skii, "O narodnom prosveshchenii v Rossii," in *Sochineniia i pis'ma*, 368–72.

33. Bhabha, *The Location of Culture*, 123.

34. See Tur'ian, "Lichnost' Perovskogo i literaturnoe nasledie Pogorel'skogo," 603–5. Etkind analyzes the Perovsky family's service to the empire as an example of internal colonization (Etkind, *Internal Colonization*, 150–55).

35. For an analysis of the Ukrainian nationalist project, see Serhiy Bilenky, *Romantic Nationalism in Eastern Europe: Russian, Polish, and Ukrainian Political Imaginations* (Stanford: Stanford University Press, 2012), chap. 6.

Chapter 6. 'Tis Eighty Years Since

1. "*Getman Ostrianitsa, ili epokha smut i bedstvii Malorossii*, istoricheskii roman XVII stoletiia, Vasiliia Korenevskogo. V 2-kh chastiakh. Khar'kov. V universitetskoi tipografii," *Finskii vestnik* 11 (1846): 6 [Bibliograficheskaia khronika].

2. P. Kulish, "Vospominaniia o Nikolae Ivanoviche Kostomarove," *Nov'* 4, no. 13 (1880): 62. Cited in Ievhen Nakhlik, *Panteleimon Kulish: Osobystist', pys'mennyk, myslytel'*, 2 vols. (Kyiv: Ukrains'kyi pys'mennyk, 2007), 1:27.

3. As Pushkin famously stated in his 1830 note "On Walter Scott's Novels," "The chief fascination of Walter Scott's novels lies in the fact that we grow acquainted with the past not encumbered with the *enflure* (exaggeration) of French tragedies, or with the prudery of the novels of sentiment, or with the *dignité* of history, but in a contemporary, homely manner." Pushkin, *Sobranie sochinenii*, 7:529.

4. This summary is based on various studies of Scott in Russia and Ukraine, which in turn owe to earlier classical studies of Scott's historical novels. See Bahrij, *Shliakh sera Val'tera Skotta na Ukrainu*; Dan Ungurianu, *Plotting History: The Russian Historical Novel in the Imperial Age* (Madison: University of Wisconsin Press, 2007); and Luba Golburt, *The First Epoch: The Eighteenth Century and the Russian Cultural Imagination* (Madison: University of Wisconsin Press, 2014), chap. 4. The concept of "the middling man" comes from Georg Lukács's *The Historical Novel* (1937).

5. O. I. Senkovskii, *Sobranie sochinenii Senkovskogo (barona Brambeusa)*, 9 vols. (St. Petersburg: Tipografiia Imperatorskoi Akademii nauk, 1858–59), 8:49.

6. Fedir Savchenko, *Lysty P. Kulisha do M. Pohodina (1842–1851)*, *Khar'kov* 10 (1929): 19.

7. [V. A. Ushakov], *Severnaia pchela* 119–20 (1830): n.p. Lamenting the lack of distinctly national Russian literature was a commonplace of Russian literary criticism, from Andrei Turgenev in 1801 to Vissarion Belinsky in 1834. For an in-depth discussion of this recurrent theme and specifically of the term *narodnost'*, see David L. Cooper, *Creating the Nation: Identity and Aesthetics in Early Nineteenth-Century Russia and Bohemia* (DeKalb: Northern Illinois University Press, 2010), especially chaps. 2, 8, and 10.

8. Katie Trumpener, *Bardic Nationalism: The Romantic Novel and the British Empire* (Princeton: Princeton University Press, 1997), 15–16.

9. For a detailed discussion of Kulish's life and work, see Nakhlik's *Panteleimon Kulish: Osobystist', pys'mennyk, myslytel'*. For a recent English-language study of Kulish's translations as both linguistic and cultural projects, see Andrii Danylenko, *From the Bible to Shakespeare: Pantelejmon Kuliš (1819–1897) and the Formation of Literary Ukrainian* (Boston: Academic Studies Press, 2016).

10. Among notable exceptions are Viktor Petrov's article "Val'ter-Skotiv's'ka povist' z ukrains'koi mynuvshyny," in Panteleimon Kulish, *Mykhailo Charnyshenko: povist'* (Kyiv: Siaivo, 1928): 5–35; and Nakhlik's discussion of the novel (*Panteleimon Kulish*, 2:99–104).

11. George Luckyj, *Panteleimon Kulish: A Sketch of His Life and Times* (Boulder, CO: East European Monographs, 1983), 10.

12. Myroslav Shkandrij points out this paradox in the context of Kulish's contradictory attitude to popular uprisings. See *Russia and Ukraine*, 182.

13. See, for example, Borys Neiman, "Kulish i Val'ter Skott," in *Panteleimon Kulish. Zbirnyk prats' Komisii dlia vydavannia pam'iatok novitn'oho pys'menstva. Ukrains'ka Akademiia Nauk. Zbirnyk istorychno-filolohichnoho viddilu* 53 (1927): 127–56; Viktor Petrov, "Val'ter-Skotivs'ka povist' z ukrains'koi mynuvshyny"; Bahrij, *Shliakh sera Val'tera Skotta na Ukrainu*. Although Scott playfully distances his work from the Gothic tradition in the introductory chapter of his *Waverley*, his indebtedness to the genre is widely recognized. Similarly, Kulish plays with his readers' Gothic expectations, revealing his awareness of the clichés of Gothic fiction, and yet he deploys them extensively in his novel.

14. Bahrij, *Shliakh sera Val'tera Skotta na Ukrainu*, 187; Neiman, "Kulish i Val'ter Skott"; Petrov, "Val'ter-Skotivs'ka povist' z ukrains'koi mynuvshyny"; Nakhlik, *Panteleimon Kulish*, 2:100.

15. *The History* circulated in a manuscript form among Russian and Ukrainian intellectuals starting as early as the mid-1820s and was believed to be written by generations of Orthodox monks and edited by the Mahiliou Archbishop Heorhii Konysky in the 1760s. It was established by the late 1840s that many "facts" presented in this work were largely fictitious and could not be corroborated by any existing sources; its authorship is still open to debate. For a detailed discussion of *The History* and its key role in creating Ukrainian national mythology, see Plokhy, *The Cossack Myth*. At the time of writing *Mikhailo Charnyshenko*, Kulish still trusted *The History* (he mentions it as his source in pt. 3, 190)—as did many of his contemporaries (Plokhy, *The Cossack Myth*, chap. 3). A few years later, however, Kulish became skeptical about the credibility of *The History* and in the 1870s would refer to its author—again, through a Scottish analogy—as a "deceptive" but "highly talented"

172   NOTES TO PAGES 114–123

"Macpherson of our historiography" (Nakhlik, *Panteleimon Kulish*, 2:42). As Bahrij (*Shliakh sera Val'tera Skotta na Ukrainu*, 188) and Nakhlik (*Panteleimon Kulish*, 2:100) observe, the *History of the Rus'* was not the sole source Kulish had consulted, but it inspired the main plotline of the novel.

16. *Waverley, or 'Tis Sixty Years Since* by Sir Walter Scott, Bart. (Edinburgh, 1862), 2.

17. *Waverley*, 3. For an illuminating discussion of the Walter Scottian temporality in Russian historical fiction of the 1830s, see Golburt, *The First Epoch*, chap. 4.

18. James Buzard, *Disorienting Fiction: The Autoethnographic Work of Nineteenth-Century British Novels* (Princeton: Princeton University Press, 2005), 67.

19. *Waverley*, 318.

20. Panteleimon Kulish, *Mikhailo Charnyshenko ili Malorossiia vosem'desiat let nazad* (Kiev: V universitetskoi tipografii, 1843), pt. 1, 7–9. Throughout this chapter, quotes from the novel will be given from this edition with the part and page numbers provided in parentheses (1:7–9) in the body text of the chapter.

21. Trumpener, *Bardic Nationalism*, 24.

22. See Kiselev and Vasil'eva, "'Strannoe politicheskoe sonmishche,'" 494.

23. Gogol', *Sobranie sochinenii*, 6:59.

24. Panteleimon Kulish, "Otvet G. Senkovskomu na ego retsenziiu 'Istorii Malorossii' Markevicha," *Moskvitianin* 3, no. 5 (1843): 164.

25. Trumpener, *Bardic Nationalism*, 111.

26. Svetlana Boym, *The Future of Nostalgia* (New York: Basic Books, 2001), 13.

27. Petrov, "Val'ter-Skotivs'ka povist'," 20–21. Starting in the mid-1870s, Kulish primarily views Cossack rebellions and wars as culturally and socially destructive, although he credits it with an important role in fostering Ukrainian national identity. For a more detailed discussion of the evolution of Kulish's views on the Ukrainian Cossack past, see Nakhlik, *Panteleimon Kulish*, 2:39–50.

28. Nakhlik, *Panteleimon Kulish*, 2:104.

29. Petrov, "Val'ter-Skotivs'ka povist'," 6–10.

30. Petrov sees this event as a key symbolic moment of the novel, but he interprets it as Kulish's condemnation of Mikhailo's generation for its destructive role in Ukrainian history.

31. One could apply Boym's classification of nostalgia here and argue that, while old Charnysh indulges into "restorative nostalgia"—a type of longing that "puts emphasis on *nostos* and proposes to rebuild [quite literally, in this case] the lost home," the narrator's sentiment here is what Boym terms "reflective nostalgia," which focuses on *algia* (pain) and "lingers on ruins rather than the restoration of the monument of the past" (Boym, *The Future of Nostalgia*, 41).

32. Petrov, "Val'ter-Skotivs'ka povist'," 31.

33. Fritzsche, *Stranded in the Present*, 102.

34. Fritzsche, *Stranded in the Present*, 104–15. In a later work, Fritzsche interprets ruins in a colonial context more explicitly as suggestive of alternative history to the imperial scheme of development. See Peter Fritzsche, "The Ruins of Modernity," in *"Breaking Up Time": Negotiating the Borders between Past, Present and Future*, ed. Berber Bevernage and Chris Lorenz (Göttingen: Vandenhoeck & Ruprecht, 2013), 57–68.

35. Nakhlik, *Panteleimon Kulish*, 2:55.

36. Note a similar distortion of St. Petersburg in "The Night before Christmas," where Vakula commands the devil to fly to "Petemburg" instead of "Peterburg" (Gogol', *Sobranie sochinenii*, 1:121).

37. *Istoriia rusov ili Maloi Rossii, sochinenie Georgiia Koniskogo, arkhiepiskopa Beloruskogo* (Moscow: V universitetskoi tipografii, 1846), 251.

38. For a discussion of the vampiric Jew in the Gothic tradition and the role of the blood libel, see Carol Margaret Davison, *Anti-Semitism and British Gothic Literature* (Basingstoke: Palgrave Macmillan, 2004), chaps. 2 and 4. On the Jewish blood libel in the Eastern European context, see Eugene M. Avrutin, Jonathan Dekel-Chen, and Robert Weinberg, eds., *Ritual Murder in Russia, Eastern Europe, and Beyond: New Histories of an Old Accusation* (Bloomington: Indiana University Press, 2017).

39. See Petrov, "Val'ter-Skotivs'ka povist'," 14.

40. George K. Anderson, *The Legend of the Wandering Jew* (Hanover, NH: Brown University Press, 1965), 11.

41. On the association of the Wandering Jew legend with the one about the Antichrist in medieval Europe, see Anderson, *The Legend of the Wandering Jew*, 38–42.

42. Davison, *Anti-Semitism and British Gothic Literature*, 2 and 9.

43. Davison, *Anti-Semitism and British Gothic Literature*, 4. In her discussion of this theme, Davison is in dialogue with Michael Ragussis's seminal *Figures of Conversion: "The Jewish Question" and English National Identity* (Durham, NC: Duke University Press, 1995).

44. In his polemics with Senkovsky on Ukrainian history, Kulish justifies the Cossacks' violence against the Poles (and, by extension, Jews) by the Polish brutal and discriminatory policies following the introduction of the Union of Brest and stresses the desecration of Orthodox Churches by the Jewish leaseholders ("Otvet G. Senkovskomu," 166–67). This view is influenced by the *History of the Rus'* (see *Istoriia rusov*, 41–42).

45. This characterization probably drew on the famous polemical epistle written, in response to the Union of Brest, by the leader of the Orthodox community in the Commonwealth, Prince Kostiantyn Ostroz'ky, in which "he denounced the bishops as 'wolves in sheep's clothing' who betrayed their flock." Subtelny, *Ukraine: A History*, 100.

46. *Istoriia Rusov*, 251.

47. Petrov argues that Kryzhanovsky, with his elusiveness, falsity, and artificiality, symbolizes St. Petersburg in the novel, and in this he sees Kulish's only original contribution to the development of the "sorcerer" type ("Valter-Skotivs'ka povist'," 15). The direct link between Kryzhanovsky and Petersburg may be a bit forced, but it certainly echoes my conclusion that the rootless character represents the essentially absent imperial center.

48. On Russian nomadic identity, see Kleespies, *A Nation Astray*.

49. This dream might have been inspired by Melmoth the Wanderer's final dream in Charles Maturin's eponymous novel, as well as by the final scene of Lewis's *Monk* where Lucifer carries the sinful monk up and then drops him on the rocks below. As I discuss in chapter 2, von Mey's death in Bestuzhev's "The Castle Neuhausen" is also most likely modeled after these scenes, clearly influential at the time.

50. The sudden appearance of Serbs in this novel set in late eighteenth-century Ukraine had a historical basis. In the early 1750s, the Russian government established "New Serbia" and "Slaviano-Serbia"—military settlements in what is now Central and South-Eastern Ukraine respectively where Serbs (along with other Balkan Orthodox believers) of the Austrian empire were invited to form military regiments intended to guard the Russian borders against Crimean Tartars and Ottoman Turks. V. Kubiiovych, ed., *Entsyklopediia ukrainoznavstva*, 10 vols. (Paris: Molode zhyttia, 1954–89), 8:2908. Shcherbina mentions Serbs in general as the Russian Empire's accomplices in stifling Ukraine's autonomy (2:79). The case of Kulish's fictional Serbs is somewhat different—prince Radivoj flees because of his involvement with the Serbian independence struggle and primarily pursues his own revenge. As Nakhlik stresses, Kulish did not have substantial historical materials at his disposal and mainly drew on Serbian epic songs for his portrayal of the Serbian warriors: Vuk Karadžić's collection, as well as some contemporary studies of South Slavic folklore (*Panteleimon Kulish*, 2:102). The novel abounds with direct references to Serbian folklore, especially the Marko Kraljević cycle, and Kulish provides his sources in the notes to the novel.

51. This technique could have been influenced by Walter Scott's method of differentiating between Scottish Lowlanders and Highlanders by comparing the latter to more "primitive" and Oriental/despotic societies. See Kenneth McNeil, *Scotland, Britain, Empire: Writing the Highlands, 1760–1860* (Columbus: Ohio State University Press, 2007): 54–55.

52. Cf. Rebecca and Lady Rowena, the exotic Jewess (who also heals the wounded hero) and the Anglo-Saxon beauty in Scott's *Ivanhoe* (1820).

53. Nakhlik, *Panteleimon Kulish*, 2:102.

54. I am grateful to Tetyana Dzyadevych for the suggestion about the role of the Serbs in the novel as "Eastern" foils for the Ukrainians. The association between South Slavs and Zaporizhzhian Cossacks is made more explicit in *The Black Council*, which presents a closely knit pair of friends: the unruly Cossack Kyrylo Tur and Bohdan Chornohor (Montenegrin).

55. According to Trumpener, "unlike the early national tale and the historical novel, 'nationalist Gothic novels . . . refuse this happy ending to stress instead the traumatic consequences of historical transformation and the long-term uneven development, even schizophrenia, it creates in 'national characters'" (*Bardic Nationalism*, xiii).

56. Bahrij points out the parallels between the two banquet scenes and interprets the image of the cup in the context of the theme of hospitality and ritualistic dining (*Shliakh sera Val'tera Skotta na Ukrainu*, 167–69).

57. I am indebted to Edith Clowes for the suggestion of the chalice's connection to Holy Grail.

58. S. Shevyrev, *"Mikhailo Charnyshenko, ili Malorossiia vosem'desiat let nazad.* Sochinenie P. Kulisha. Kiev, 1843. Tri chasti. I. 206. II. 190. III. 221." *Moskvitianin* 4, no. 7 (1843): 126–33.

59. Shevyrev, *Mikhailo Charnyshenko*, 127.

60. "Mikhailo Charnyshenko ili Malorossiia vosem'desiat let nazad. Sochinenie P. Kulesha. Tri chasti, 206, 190, i 215. Kiev, v universitetskoi tipografii, 1845 [sic]," *Syn Otechestva* 5 (1843): 2.

61. "Mikhailo Charnyshenko ili Malorossiia," *Syn Otechestva*, 3 and 22.

62. "Mikhailo Charnyshenko, ili Malorossia vosem'desiat let nazad. Sochinenie P. Kulesha. Kiev, v tipografii Universiteta, 1843, v"-8. Tri chasti, str. 206-190-224," *Biblioteka dlia chteniia* 57 (1843): 50–64.

63. "Mikhailo Charnyshenko ili Malorossiia," *Biblioteka dlia chteniia*, 55.

64. "Mikhailo Charnyshenko ili Malorossiia," *Biblioteka dlia chteniia*, 63, 62, 64.

Afterword

1. P. Ia. Chaadaev, *Polnoe sobranie sochinenii i izbrannye pis'ma*, 2 vols. (Moscow: Nauka, 1991), 1: 94–95. Chaadaev originally wrote his "Philosophical Letters" in French.

2. Chaadaev, *Polnoe sobranie sochinenii*, 97.

3. Chaadaev, *Polnoe sobranie sochinenii*, 96 and 91.

4. Boris Nemtsov, "Zachem Putin voiuet s Ukrainoi," *Ukrainskaia pravda*, September 1, 2014, https://www.pravda.com.ua/rus/articles/2014/09/1/7036345/.

5. Oksana Zabuzhko, *I znov ia vlizaiu v tank* (Kyiv: Komora, 2016), 12.

6. See, for example, Iurii Baranchik, "Ukraina pogruzhaetsia v krovavyi khaos. Chto dal'she?," *Russkaia vesna*, June 16, 2011, http://rusvesna.su/news/1509902827. Olga Nikolaeva comments on the rise of reliance on magic and healers in Ukraine (a Finns' prerogative in nineteenth-century Russian imperial discourse). This tendency, in addition to pointing to the general decline of the quality of life and health care, is supposed to indicate contemporary Ukraine's spiritual deterioration. As independent Ukraine distances itself from Russia, it is moving toward paganism and away from "true" Christian Orthodox faith. Olga Nikolaeva, "Na 'poklonenie' koldunam: Ukraina pogruzhaetsia v magicheskii khaos," *Novorossiia*, September 27, 2017, https://novorosinform.org/411335.

7. "Pryvyd brodyt' po Rosii: Henprokuroru RF vvyzhaet'sia maidan," ZNAJ. UA, June 8, 2017, https://znaj.ua/world/pryvyd-brodyt-po-rosiyi-genprokuroru-rf-vvyzhayetsya-majdan?page=35; Dmitrii Florin, "Prizrak molodezhnogo Maidana v Rossii," TSN, June 14, 2017, https://ru.tsn.ua/blogi/themes/politics/prizrak-molodezhnogo-maydana-v-rossii-877813.html.

8. Andrius Saytas and Aija Krutaine, "Ukraine Crisis Stokes Baltic Nerves over Russia," Reuters, March 3, 2014, https://www.reuters.com/article/us-ukraine-crisis-baltics/ukraine-crisis-stokes-baltic-nerves-over-russia-idUSBREA221J520140303; Aleksandr Khrolenko, "Ischeznovenie Pribaltiki," Ria Novosti, August 18, 2015, https://ria.ru/analytics/20150617/1074774736.html.

9. Etkind argues that "magical historicism" is a more appropriate term for post-Soviet Russian literature than "magical realism," as contemporary Russian writers, who widely include elements of magic and the supernatural in their works, are concerned with history rather than with social or psychological reality. Alexander Etkind, *Warped Mourning: Stories of the Undead in the Land of the Unburied* (Stanford: Stanford University Press, 2013), 232–36. For a discussion of Gothic tendencies in contemporary Russian literature, see Ol'ga Lebedushkina, "Our New Gothic," *Russian Studies in Literature* 46, no. 4 (2010): 81–100. For an analysis of the Gothic underpinnings of post-Soviet "neo-Eurasian" ideology, see Dina Khapaeva, "The Gothic Future of Eurasia," *Russian Literature* 106 (2019): 79–108.

10. Etkind, *Warped Mourning*, 220–21. See also Mark Lipovetskii i Aleksandr Etkind, "Vozvrashchenie tritona: Sovetskaia katastrofa i postsovetskii roman," *Novoe literaturnoe obozrenie* 94 (2008), http://magazines.russ.ru/nlo/2008/94/li17.html, as well as the English version of this publication: Mark Lipovetsky and Alexander Etkind, "The Salamander's Return," *Russian Studies in Literature* 46, no. 4 (2010): 6–48, DOI: 10.2753/RSL1061-1975460401.

WORKS CITED

Alekseev, M. P. "Ch. R. Met'iurin i russkaia literatura." *Ot romantizma k realizmu: Iz istorii mezhdunarodnykh sviazei russkoi literatury*, 3–55. Leningrad: Nauka, 1978.

Al'tshuller, Mark. "Neopublikovannaia redaktsiia povesti V. K. Kiukhel'bekera 'Ado.'" *Russkii iazyk* 46. 153/155 (1992): 185–225.

Anderson, George K. *The Legend of the Wandering Jew*. Hanover, NH: Brown University Press, 1965.

Andrew, Joe. "'The Blind Will See': Narrative and Gender in 'Taman.'" *Russian Literature* 31 (1992): 449–76.

Avrutin, Eugene M., Jonathan Dekel-Chen, and Robert Weinberg, eds. *Ritual Murder in Russia, Eastern Europe, and Beyond: New Histories of an Old Accusation*. Bloomington: Indiana University Press, 2017.

Babaeva, Z. E. "Istoricheskaia interpretatsiia siuzheta povesti V. F. Odoevskogo 'Salamandra.'" *Filologicheskie nauki. Voprosy teorii i praktiki* 4 (2012): 27–30.

Bagby, Lewis. *Alexander Bestuzhev-Marlinsky and Russian Byronism*. University Park: Pennsylvania State University Press, 1995.

Bahrij, Romana. *Shliakh sera Val'tera Skotta na Ukrainu ("Taras Bul'ba" M. Hoholia i "Chorna Rada" P. Kulisha v svitli istorychnoï romanistyky Val'tera Skotta)*. Kyiv: Vsesvit, 1993.

Bahrij Pikulyk, Romana Myroslava. *"Taras Bul'ba* and *Black Council*: Adherence to and Divergence from Sir Walter Scott's Historical Novel Pattern." PhD diss., University of Toronto, 1978.

Baranchik, Iurii. "Ukraina pogruzhaetsia v krovavyi khaos. Chto dal'she?" *Russkaia vesna*, June 16, 2011, http://rusvesna.su/news/1509902827.

Baratynskii, E. A. *Stikhotvoreniia. Poemy*. Moscow: Nauka, 1982.

Bassin, Mark. *Imperial Visions: Nationalist Imagination and Geographical Expansion in the Russian Far East, 1840–1865*. Cambridge: Cambridge University Press, 1999.

Baudin, Rodolphe. "Karamzin et la cathédrale de Strasbourg." *Nikolaï Karamzin en France: l'image de la France dans les* Lettres d'un voyageur russe, edited by Rodolphe Baudin, 75–98. Paris: Institut d'Etudes slaves, 2014.

——. *Nikolaï Karamzine à Strasbourg. Un écrivain-voyageur russe dans l'Alsace révolutionnaire (1789)*. Strasbourg: Presses Universitaires de Strasbourg, 2011.

Bazanov, V. *Ocherki dekabristskoi literatury. Publitsistika. Proza. Kritika*. Moscow: Gos. izdatel'stvo khudozhestvennoi literatury, 1953.

Belinskii, V. G. *Polnoe sobranie sochinenii*. Moscow: Izdatel'stvo AN SSSR, 1953–59.

Belyi, Andrei. *Masterstvo Gogolia: Issledovanie*. Moscow: Gos. Izdatel'stvo khudozhestvennoi literatury, 1934.

Ber, K. M. "Ob etnograficheskikh issledovaniiakh voobshche i v Rossii v osoben-nosti." *Zapiski russkogo geograficheskogo obshchestva* 1 (1846): 93–115.

Bestuzhev, A. *Poezdka v Revel'*. St. Petersburg: Tipografiia Aleksandra Pliushara, 1821.

Bestuzhev, Nikolai. "Gugo fon Brakht." In *Russkaia istoricheskaia povest' v 2 tt*. Vol. 1, 134–45. Moscow: Khudozhestvennaia literatura, 1988.

Bestuzhev-Marlinskii, A. A. *Sochineniia*. 2 vols. Moscow: Gos. Izdatel'stvo khudozhest-vennoi literatury, 1958.

Bhabha, Homi. *The Location of Culture*. London: Routledge, 1994.

Bilenky, Serhiy. *Romantic Nationalism in Eastern Europe: Russian, Polish, and Ukrainian Political Imaginations*. Stanford: Stanford University Press, 2012.

Bodrova, Alina. "Rhetoric and Mythology of the 1808–1809 Finnish War in Bara-tynsky's Poem *Eda*." In *Studia Russica Helsingiensia et Tartuensia XIV: Russian National Myth in Transition*, 59–78. Tartu: Tartu Ülikooli Kirjastus, 2014.

Boele, Otto. "Finland in the Work of Jevgenij Baratynskij: Locus Amoenus or Realm of the Dead." *Essays in Poetics: The Journal of the British Neo-Formalist Circle* 19, no. 1 (1994): 25–46.

——. *The North in Russian Romantic Literature*. Amsterdam: Rodopi, 1996.

Bojanowska, Edyta. *Nikolai Gogol: Between Ukrainian and Russian Nationalism*. Cambridge: Harvard University Press, 2007.

"A Book on Nymphs, Sylphs, Pygmies, and Salamanders, and on the Other Spirits." In *Four Treatises of Theophrastus von Hohenheim Called Paracelsus*, 227–30. Baltimore: Johns Hopkins University Press, 1941.

Botting, Fred. *Gothic: The New Critical Idiom*. 2nd ed. London: Routledge, 2014.

Bowers, Katherine A. "Shadows of the Gothic: Adapted Terror in Russian Fiction, 1792–1905." PhD diss., Northwestern University, 2011.

——. "The City through a Glass, Darkly: Use of the Gothic in Early Russian Realism." *Modern Language Review* 108, no. 4 (2013): 1199–215.

——. "The Fall of the House: Gothic Narrative and the Decline of the Russian Family." In *Russian Writers and the Fin de Siècle: The Twilight of Realism*, edited by Katherine Bowers and Ani Kokobobo, 145–61. Cambridge: Cambridge University Press, 2015.

Boym, Svetlana. *The Future of Nostalgia*. New York: Basic Books, 2001.

Brüggemann, Karsten. "The Baltic Provinces and Russian Perceptions in Late Imperial Russia." In *Russland an der Ostsee: imperiale Strategien der Macht und kulturelle Wahrnehmungsmuster (16. bis 20. Jahrhundert) / Russia on the Baltic: Imperial Strategies of Power and Cultural Patterns of Perception (16th–20th centuries)*, edited by Karsten Brüggemann and Bradley D. Woodworth, 111–41. Vienna: Böhlau Wien, 2012.

Brüggemann, Karsten, and Bradley D. Woodworth. "Entangled Pasts—Russia and the Baltic Region." In *Russland an der Ostsee: imperiale Strategien der Macht und kulturelle Wahrnehmungsmuster (16. bis 20. Jahrhundert) / Russia on the Baltic: Imperial Strategies of Power and Cultural Patterns of Perception (16th–20th centuries)*, edited by Karsten Brüggemann and Bradley D. Woodworth, 3–26. Vienna: Böhlau Wien, 2012.

Buhks, Nora. "Le Voyage à l'île de la mort de Nikolaj Karamzin." In *Le Sentimental-isme Russe*, Special Issue, edited by Jean Breuillard. *Revue des Études Slaves* 74, no. 4 (2002–3): 719–28.

Bulkina, Inna. "Russian Warrior at a *Rendez-Vous*. The Sources and Reception of Evgeny Baratynsky's Finnish Poem." In *Studia Russica Helsingiensia et Tartuensia XIV: Russian National Myth in Transition*, 79–93. Tartu: Tartu Ülikooli Kirjastus, 2014.

Burbank, Jane, and Frederick Cooper. *Empires in World History: Power and the Politics of Difference*. Princeton: Princeton University Press, 2010.

Buzard, James. *Disorienting Fiction: The Autoethnographic Work of Nineteenth-Century British Novels*. Princeton: Princeton University Press, 2005.

Bykova, V. P. "Zapiski staroi smolianki. Ch. 1, 1833–78." St. Petersburg: Tipografiia E. Evdokimova, 1898.

Chaadaev, P. Ia. *Polnoe sobranie sochinenii i izbrannye pis'ma*. 2 vols. Moscow: Nauka, 1991.

Chernetsky, Vitaly. *Mapping Postcommunist Cultures: Russia and Ukraine in the Context of Globalization*. Montreal: McGill-Queen's University Press, 2007.

"Chud' i Rus'." *Finskii vestnik* 5 (1845): 1–39 [Materialy severnoi istorii].

"Chudnyi." *Slovar' iazyka Pushkina*. 2nd ed. 4 vols. Vol. 4, 980–81. Moscow: Azbukovnik, 2000.

Clark, Elena Pedigo. "'Many Lands Have I Left behind Me': E. A. Baratynskii's Quest for Happiness in Finland, Italy, and the Homeland." *Poljarnyj vestnik: Norwegian Journal of Slavic Studies* 17 (2014): 1–18.

——. "'There Like Vast Waters Have Come Together Sea and Sky': 'Finland' and Finland in the Poetry of E. A. Baratynsky." *Slavic and East European Journal* 59, no. 1 (2015): 47–69.

Clowes, Edith. *Russia on the Edge: Imagined Geographies and Post-Soviet Identity*. Ithaca: Cornell University Press, 2011.

Cooper, David L. *Creating the Nation: Identity and Aesthetics in Early Nineteenth-Century Russia and Bohemia*. DeKalb: Northern Illinois University Press, 2010.

Cornwell, Neil. "European Gothic and Nineteenth-Century Russian Literature." In *European Gothic: A Spirited Exchange 1760–1960*, edited by Avril Horner, 104–27. Manchester: Manchester University Press, 2002.

——. "Pushkin and Odoevsky: The 'Afro-Finnish' Theme in Russian Gothic." In *Empire and the Gothic: The Politics of Genre*, edited by Andrew Smith and William Hughes, 69–87. Basingstoke: Palgrave Macmillan, 2003.

Cornwell, Neil, ed. *The Gothic-Fantastic in Nineteenth-Century Russian Literature*. Amsterdam: Rodopi, 1999.

"Critical Forum on Ukraine." *Slavic Review* 74, no. 4 (2016): 695–737.

Dal', V. *Poslovitsy russkogo naroda*. Moscow: Khudozhestvennaia literatura, 1989.

Danylenko, Andrii. *From the Bible to Shakespeare: Pantelejmon Kuliš (1819–1897) and the Formation of Literary Ukrainian*. Boston: Academic Studies Press, 2016.

Davison, Carol Margaret. *Anti-Semitism and British Gothic Literature*. Basingstoke: Palgrave Macmillan, 2004.

DeAngelo, Jeremy. "The North and the Depiction of the 'Finnar' in the Icelandic Sagas." *Scandinavian Studies* 82, no. 3 (2010): 257–86.

Dershau, F. "Lalli, Finn XII stoletiia." *Finskii vestnik* 1 (1845): 1–22 [Nravoopisatel'].

Douglas, Mary. *Purity and Danger: An Analysis of Concepts of Pollution and Taboo*. New York: Frederick A. Praeger, 1966.

"Dva slova o Gel'singforse." *Finskii vestnik* 11 (1846): 27–30 [Smes'].

Emery, Jacob. "Repetition and Exchange in Legitimizing Empire: Konstantin Batiushkov's Scandinavian Corpus." *Russian Review* 66 (2007): 602–26.

Epshtein, M. N. "Ironiia stilia: Demonicheskoe v obraze Rossii u Gogolia." *Novoe
literaturnoe obozrenie* 19 (1996): 129–47.

Epshtein, Mikhail. *Bog detalei: Narodnaia dusha i chastnaia zhizn' v Rossii na iskhode
imperii. Esseistika 1977–1988.* Moscow: Izdanie R. Elinina, 1998.

Etkind, Aleksandr. "Bremia britogo cheloveka, ili Vnutrenniaia kolonizatsiia Rossii."
Ab Imperio 1 (2002): 265–98.

——. "Russkaia literatura, XIX vek: Roman vnutrennei kolonizatsii." *Novoe literaturnoe obozrenie* 59 (2003): 103–24.

Etkind, Alexander. *Internal Colonization: Russian Imperial Experience.* Cambridge, UK:
Polity Press, 2011.

——. *Warped Mourning: Stories of the Undead in the Land of the Unburied.* Stanford:
Stanford University Press, 2013.

Etkind, A., D. Uffel'mann, and I. Kukulin, eds. *Tam, vnutri. Praktiki vnutrennei kolonizatsii v kul'turnoi zhizni Rossii: Sb. Statei.* Moscow: Novoe literaturnoe obozrenie, 2011.

Eugene Onegin: A Novel in Verse by Alexander Pushkin. Translated and commentary by
Vladimir Nabokov. 2 vols. Princeton: Princeton University Press, 1975.

Fasmer, M. *Etimologicheskii slovar' russkogo iazyka.* Translated by O. N. Trubachev.
4 vols. Moscow: Progress, 1964–73.

Feierkherd, V. "Romantizm i realism v dilogii V. F. Odoevskogo 'Salamandra.'" In
Problemy teorii i istorii literatury, edited by V. I. Kuleshov, 175–91. Moscow:
Izdatel'stvo Moskovskogo universiteta, 1971.

Florin, Dmitrii. "Prizrak molodezhnogo Maidana v Rossii." TSN, June 14, 2017, https://
ru.tsn.ua/blogi/themes/politics/prizrak-molodezhnogo-maydana-v-rossii-
877813.html.

France, Peter. "Fingal in Russia." In *The Reception of Ossian in Europe,* edited by Howard Gaskill, 259–73. London: Thoemmes Continuum, 2004.

Frank, F. S. *Guide to the Gothic: An Annotated Bibliography of Criticism.* Metuchen, NJ:
Scarecrow Press, 2004.

Freud, Sigmund. *The Standard Edition of Complete Psychological Works.* Translated by
James Strachey. London: Hogarth Press, 1953–74.

Fritzsche, Peter. *Stranded in the Present: Modern Time and the Melancholy of History.*
Cambridge: Harvard University Press, 2004.

——. "The Ruins of Modernity." In *"Breaking Up Time": Negotiating the Borders between
Past, Present and Future,* edited by Berber Bevernage and Chris Lorenz, 57–68.
Göttingen: Vandenhoeck & Ruprecht, 2013.

Gaskill, Howard. "Introduction: Genuine Poetry . . . Like Gold." In *The Reception of
Ossian in Europe,* edited by Howard Gaskill, 1–20. London: Thoemmes Continuum, 2004.

Gellerman, Svetlana. "Karamzine à Genève: Notes sur quelques documents
d'archives concernant les *Lettres d'un Voyageur russe.*" In *Fakten und Fabeln:
Schweizerisch-slavische Reisebegegnung vom 18. bis zum 20. Jahrhundert,* edited by
Monika Bankowski et al., 71–90. Basel: Helbing & Lichtenhahn, 1991.

"Getman Ostrianitsa, ili epokha smut i bedstvii Malorossii, istoricheskii roman XVII
stoletiia, Vasiliia Korenevskogo. B 2-kh chastiakh. Khar'kov. V universitetskoi
tipografii." *Finskii vestnik* 11 (1846): 1–6 [Bibliograficheskaia khronika].

Glaser, Amelia M., ed. *Stories of Khmelnytsky: Competing Literary Legacies of the 1648 Ukrainian Cossack Uprising.* Stanford: Stanford University Press, 2015.

Gogol', N. V. *Sobranie sochinenii.* 7 vols. Moscow: Khudozhestvennaia literatura, 1976–79.

Golburt, Luba. *The First Epoch: The Eighteenth Century and the Russian Cultural Imagination.* Madison: University of Wisconsin Press, 2014.

Grabowicz, George G. "Between History and Myth: Perceptions of the Cossack Past in Polish, Russian, and Ukrainian Romantic Literature." In *American Contributions to the Ninth International Congress of Slavists, Kiev, September 1983.* Vol. 2: *Literature, Poetics, History,* edited by Paul Debreczeny, 173–88. Columbus, OH: Slavica, 1983.

——. "Ukrainian Studies: Framing the Contexts." *Slavic Review* 54, no. 3 (1995): 674–90.

Greenleaf, Monika. *Pushkin and Romantic Fashion: Fragment, Elegy, Orient, Irony.* Stanford: Stanford University Press, 1994.

Grot, Ia. K. "Gel'singfors." In *Trudy Ia. K. Grota.* Vol. 1: *Iz Skandinavskago i Finskago mira, 1839–1881,* 61–100. St. Petersburg, 1898.

——. "O finnakh i ikh narodnoi poezii." *Trudy Ia. K. Grota.* Vol. 1: *Iz Skandinavskago i Finskago mira, 1839–1881,* 100–48. St. Petersburg, 1898.

Guzairov, Timur. "Pragmatika obraza 'vernopoddannogo finna' v ideologicheskikh tekstakh 1809–1854 gg." *Studia Russica Helsingiensia et Tartuensia XII: Mifologiia kul'turnogo prostranstva.* Tartu: Tartu Ülikooli Kirjastus, 2011.

Hechter, Michael. *Internal Colonialism: The Celtic Fringe in British National Development.* New York: Routledge, 2017.

Hirvasaho, Iida Katariina. "A Stepchild of the Empire: Finland in Russian Colonial Discourse." PhD diss., UCLA, 1997.

Hokanson, Katya. *Writing at Russia's Border.* Toronto: University of Toronto Press, 2008.

Holquist, Michael, ed. *The Dialogic Imagination. Four Essays by M. M. Bakhtin.* Translated by Caryl Emerson and Michael Holquist. Austin: University of Texas Press, 1981.

Horner Avril, and Sue Zlosnik, eds. *Le Gothic: Influences and Appropriations in Europe and America.* Basingstoke: Palgrave Macmillan, 2008.

Hosking, Geoffrey. *Russia: People and Empire, 1552–1917.* London: HarperCollins, 1997.

Huddart, David. *Homi K. Bhabha.* London: Routledge, 2006.

Hunt, Lynn Avery. *The Family Romance of the French Revolution.* Berkeley: University of California Press, 1992.

Ilieva, Angelina Emilova. "Romulus's Nations: Myths of Brotherhood and Fratricide in Russian and South Slavic National Narratives." PhD diss., Northwestern University, 2005.

Ilnytzkyj, Oleh S. "Is Gogol's 1842 Version of *Taras Bulba* Really 'Russified'?" *Journal of Ukrainian Studies* 35–36 (2010–11): 51–68.

Isakov, S. G. "O 'livonskikh povestiakh' dekabristov (K voprosu o stanovlenii dekabristskogo istorizma)." *Uchenye zapiski Tartuskogo gosudarstvennogo universiteta 167; Trudy po russkoi i slavianskoi filologii* 8 (1965): 33–80.

——. "O livonskoi teme v russkoi literature 1820–1830-kh godov." *Uchenye zapiski Tartuskogo gosudarstvennogo universiteta 98; Trudy po russkoi i slavianskoi filologii* 3 (1960): 143–93.

——. "Russkie pisateli i Estoniia." In *Estoniia v proizvedeniiakh russkikh pisatelei XVIII—nachala XX veka. Antologiia*, edited by S. G. Isakov, 3–38. Tallinn: KPD, 2001.

Istoriia rusov ili Maloi Rossii, sochinenie Georgiia Koniskogo, arkhiepiskopa Beloruskogo. Moscow: V universitetskoi tipografii, 1846.

Istoriia russkoi literatury v 4 t. Leningrad: Nauka, 1980–83.

Istoriia russkoi literatury v 10 t. Moscow: Izdatel'stvo AN SSSR, 1941–56.

Johnson, Laurie Ruth. *Aesthetic Anxiety: Uncanny Symptoms in German Literature and Culture.* Amsterdam: Rodopi, 2010.

Jones, W. Gareth. "Catherine the Great's Understanding of the 'Gothic.'" In *Reflections on Russia in the Eighteenth Century*, edited by Joachim Klein, Simon Dixon and Maarten Fraanje, 233–40. Cologne: Böhlau Verlag, 2001.

Kahn, Andrew. "Karamzin's Discourses of Enlightenment." In Nikolai Karamzin, *Letters of a Russian Traveller*, 459–551. Oxford: Voltaire Foundation, 2003.

Kantor, Vladimir. *Sankt-Peterburg: Rossiiskaia imperiia protiv rossiiskogo khaosa: K probleme imperskogo soznaniia v Rossii.* Moscow: ROSSPEN, 2009.

Karamzin, N. M. *Istoriia gosudarstva Rossiiskogo.* 12 vols. Moscow: Nauka, 1989.

——. *Izbrannye sochineniia v dvukh tomakh.* Moscow: Khudozhestvennaia literatura, 1964.

Karlinsky, Simon. *The Sexual Labyrinth of Nikolai Gogol.* Cambridge, MA: Harvard University Press, 1976.

Kempbell, Elena. "K voprosu ob orientalizme v Rossii (vo vtoroi polovine XIX veka—nachale XX veka). » *Ab Imperio* 1 (2002): 311–22.

Khalid, Adeeb, Nathaniel Knight, and Maria Todorova. "Ex Tempore: Orientalism and Russia." *Kritika* 1, no. 4 (2000): 691–728.

Khapaeva, Dina. *Goticheskoe obshchestvo: Morfologiia koshmara.* Moscow: Novoe literaturnoe obozrenie, 2007.

——. *Koshmar: Literatura i zhizn'.* Moscow: Text, 2010.

——. *Nightmare: From Literary Experiments to Cultural Project.* Translated by Rosie Tweddle. Leiden: Brill, 2013.

Khlevov, A. A. *Normanskaia problema v otechestvennoi istoricheskoi nauke.* St.-Petersburg: Izdatel'stvo S.-Peterburgskogo universiteta, 1997.

Khrolenko, Aleksandr. "Ischeznovenie Pribaltiki." *Ria Novosti*, August 18, 2015, https://ria.ru/analytics/20150617/1074774736.html.

Kiselev, Vitalii, and Tat'iana Vasil'eva. "'Strannoe politicheskoe sonmishche' ili 'narod, poiushchii i pliashushchii': Konstruirovanie obraza Ukrainy v russkoi slovesnosti kontsa XVIII–nachala XIX veka." In *Tam, vnutri. Praktiki vnutrennei kolonizatsii v kul'turnoi istorii Rossii: Sb. statei*, edited by A. Etkind, D. Uffel'mann, and I. Kukulin, 478–517. Moscow: Novoe literaturnoe obozrenie, 2012.

Kiseleva, Liubov'. "Istoriia Livonii pod perom F. V. Bulgarina." In *Studia Russica Helsingiensia et Tartuensia X: "Vek nyneshnii i vek minuvshii": Kul'turnaia refleksiia proshedshei epokhi.* In 2 parts. Pt. 1, 114–27. Tartu: Tartu Ülikooli Kirjastus, 2006.

Kiukhel'beker, V. "Ado: Estonskaia povest'." In *Mnemozina, sobranie sochinenii v stikakh i proze* 1 (1824); I–IV, 119–67. Hildesheim: Georg Olms, 1986.

Kleespies, Ingrid. *A Nation Astray: Nomadism and National Identity in Russian Literature.* DeKalb: Northern Illinois University Press, 2012.

——. "Caught at the Border: Travel, Nomadism, and Russian National Identity in Karamzin's *Letters of a Russian Traveler* and Dostoevsky's *Winter Notes on Summer Impressions.*" *Slavic and East European Journal* 50, no. 2 (2006): 231–51.

Knight, Nathaniel. "Was Russia Its Own Orient? Reflections on the Contributions of Etkind and Schimmelpenninck to the Debate on Orientalism." *Ab Imperio* 1 (2002): 299–309.

Kohut, Zenon. *Rosiis'kyi tsentralizm i ukrains'ka avtonomiia. Likvidatsiia Het'manshchyny 1760–1830.* Kyiv: Osnovy, 1996.

——. *Russian Centralism and Ukrainian Autonomy: Imperial Absorption of the Hetmanate 1760s–1830s.* Cambridge, MA: Harvard Ukrainian Research Institute, 1988.

Koropeckyj, Roman. "Towards a Cossack Gothic in Slavic Romanticism." In the Forum "Rethinking the Gothic in Ukraine." *Slavic and East European Journal* 62, no. 2 (2018): 255–71.

Koropeckyj, Roman, and Robert Romanchuk. "Harkusha the Noble Bandit and the 'Minority' of Little Russian Literature." *Russian Review* 76 (2017): 294–310.

Kosofsky Sedgwick, Eve. *The Coherence of Gothic Conventions.* New York: Methuen, 1986.

Kovalenko, G. M. "Finny i Finliandiia v vospriiatii russkikh (s drevneishikh vremen do nachala XIX v.)." In *Mnogolikaia Finliandiia. Obrazy Finliandii i Finnov v Rossii,* edited by A. N. Tsamutali et al., 35–42. Velikii Novgorod: Novgorodskii gosudarstvennyi universitet, 2004.

Kovarskii, N. A. "Rannii Marlinskii." In *Russkaia proza XIX veka,* edited by B. M. Eikhenbaum and Iu. N. Tynianov, 135–58. Leningrad, 1926; repr. The Hague: Moutin & Co, 1963.

Kristeva, Julia. *Strangers to Ourselves.* Translated by Leon S. Roudiez. New York: Columbia University Press, 1991.

Krys, Svitlana (Lana). "All-Time Sinner or National Hero? Language and Politics in Oleksa Storozhenko's Ukrainian Gothic." In the Forum "Rethinking the Gothic in Ukraine." *Slavic and East European Journal* 62, no. 2 (2018): 293–317.

Krys, Svitlana. "Between Comedy and Horror: The Gothic in Hryhorii Kvitka-Osnovianenko's 'Dead Man's Easter' [1834]." *Slavic and East European Journal* 55 (2011): 341–58.

——. "Intertextual Parallels between Gogol' and Hoffmann: A Case Study of *Vii* and *The Devil's Elixirs.*" *Canadian-American Slavic Studies* 47 (2013): 1–20.

——. "The Gothic in Ukrainian Romanticism: An Uncharted Genre." PhD diss., University of Alberta, 2011.

Kubicek, Paul. *The History of Ukraine.* Westport, CT: Greenwood Press, 2008.

Kubiiovych, V., ed. *Entsyklopediia ukrainoznavstva.* 10 vols. Paris: Molode zhyttia, 1954–89.

Kukol'nik, N. V. *Egor Ivanovich Sil'vanovskii, ili zavoevanie Finliandii pri Petre Velikom. Finskii vestnik* 1 (1845): 5–82 [Severnaia slovesnost'].

Kulish, Panteleimon. *Mikhailo Charnyshenko ili Malorossiia vosem'desiat let nazad.* Kiev: V universitetskoi tipografii, 1843.

——. "Otvet G. Senkovskomu na ego retsenziiu 'Istorii Malorossii' Markevicha." *Moskvitianin* 3, no. 5 (1843): 164.

Launis, Kati. "From Italy to the Finnish Woods: The Rise of Gothic Fiction in Finland." In *Gothic Topographies: Languages, Nation Building and "Race,"* edited by P. M. Mehtonen and Matti Savolainen, 169–86. Farnham: Ashgate, 2013.

Lavery, Jason Edward. *The History of Finland*. Westport, CT: Greenwood Press, 2006.

Layton, Susan. *Russian Literature and Empire: Conquest of the Caucasus from Pushkin to Tolstoy*. Cambridge: Cambridge University Press, 1994.

Lebedushkina, Ol'ga. "Our New Gothic." *Russian Studies in Literature* 46, no. 4 (2010): 81–100.

Leighton, Lauren. *Alexander Bestuzhev-Marlinsky*. Boston: Twayne Publishers, 1975.

Lermontov, M. Iu. *Sobranie sochinenii*, 4 vols. Moscow: Izdatel'stvo Akademii Nauk SSSR, 1961–62.

Lermontov, Mikhail. *A Hero of Our Time*. Translated by Paul Foote. Revised ed. London: Penguin Books, 2001.

Letellier, Robert Ignatius. *Sir Walter Scott and the Gothic Novel*. Lewiston, NY: Edwin Mellen Press, 1994.

Lewis, Matthew G. *The Monk*. New York: Grove Press, 1993.

Likhachev, A. "Prikashchik. Fiziologicheskii ocherk." *Finskii vestnik* 5 (1845): 1–16 [Nravoopisatel'].

Lipovetskii, Mark, and Aleksandr Etkind. "Vozvrashchenie tritona: Sovetskaia katastrofa i postsovetskii roman." *Novoe literaturnoe obozrenie* 94 (2008), http://magazines.russ.ru/nlo/2008/94/li17.html.

Lipovetsky, Mark, and Alexander Etkind. "The Salamander's Return." *Russian Studies in Literature* 46, no. 4 (2010): 6–48, DOI: 10.2753/RSL1061-1975460401.

"Listki iz skandinavskogo mira." *Sovremennik* 29 (1843): 84–207.

Lotman, Iu. M. "Iz nabliudenii nad strukturnymi printsipami rannego tvorchestva Gogolia." *Uchenye zapiski Tartuskogo gosudarstvennogo universiteta* 251 (1970): 17–45.

Lotman, Iu. M., and B. A. Uspenskii. "'Pis'ma russkogo puteshestvennika' Karamzina i ikh mesto v razvitii russkoi kul'tury." In *Pis'ma russkogo puteshestvennika*, 525–606. Leningrad: Nauka, 1984.

Lounsbery, Anne. *Life Is Elsewhere: Symbolic Geography in the Russian Provinces, 1800–1917*. Ithaca: Cornell University Press, 2019.

———. "'No, this is not the provinces!' Provincialism, Authenticity, and Russianness in Gogol's Day." *Russian Review* 64, no. 2 (2005): 259–80.

Luckyj, George S. N. *Between Gogol' and Ševčenko: Polarity in the Literary Ukraine, 1798–1847*. Munich: Wilhelm Fink Verlag, 1971.

———. *Panteleimon Kulish: A Sketch of His Life and Times*. Boulder, CO: East European Monographs, 1983.

Maguire, Muireann. *Stalin's Ghosts: Gothic Themes in Early Soviet Literature*. Berne: Peter Lang, 2012.

Maguire, Robert A. *Exploring Gogol*. Stanford: Stanford University Press, 1994.

Maiofis, Mariia. *Vozzvanie k Evrope: Literaturnoe obshchestvo "Arzamas" i russkii modernizatsionnyi proekt 1815–1818 godov*. Moscow: Novoe literaturnoe obozrenie, 2008.

Maiorova, Olga. *From the Shadow of Empire: Defining the Russian Nation through Cultural Mythology, 1855–1870*. Madison: University of Wisconsin Press, 2010.

Maksimovich, M. "Obozrenie starogo Kieva." *Kievlianin* bk. 1 (1840): 5–51.

Malaniuk, Yevhen. "Hohol'-Gogol'." In *Knyha sposterezhen'*, 374–89. Kyiv: Dnipro, 1997.

Malkina, V. Ia. "Povesti A. A. Bestuzheva (Marlinskogo)." In *Goticheskaia traditsiia v russkoi literature*, edited by N. D. Tamarchenko, 36–56. Moscow: RGGU, 2008.

Malkina, V. Ia., and A. A. Poliakova. "'Kanon goticheskogo romana' i ego raznovidnosti." In *Goticheskaia traditsiia v russkoi literature*, edited by N. D. Tamarchenko, 15–32. Moscow: RGGU, 2008.

Mandel'shtam, I. E. *O kharaktere gogolevskogo stilia: Glava iz istorii russkogo literaturnogo iazyka*. Helsingfors: Novaia Tip. Hufvudstadsbladet, 1902.

McCabe, Richard A. *Incest, Drama and Nature's Law, 1550–1700*. Cambridge: Cambridge University Press, 1993.

McNeil, Kenneth. *Scotland, Britain, Empire: Writing the Highlands, 1760–1860*. Columbus: Ohio State University Press, 2007.

Merserau, John, Jr. *Russian Romantic Fiction*. Ann Arbor, MI: Ardis, 1983.

Mighall, Robert. *A Geography of Victorian Gothic Fiction: Mapping History's Nightmares*. Oxford: Oxford University Press, 2003.

"Mikhailo Charnyshenko ili Malorossiia vosem'desiat let nazad. Sochinenie P. Kulesha. Tri chasti, 206, 190, i 215. Kiev, v universitetskoi tipografii, 1845 (sic)." *Syn Otechestva* 5 (1843): 2.

"Mikhailo Charnyshenko, ili Malorossia vosem'desiat let nazad. Sochinenie P. Kulesha. Kiev, v tipografii Universiteta, 1843, v"-8. Tri chasti, str. 206-190-224." *Biblioteka dlia chteniia* 57 (1843): 50–64.

Miliukov, P. N. *Glavnyia techeniia russkoi istoricheskoi mysli*. Moscow: Tipolitografiia Vysochaishe utverzhd. T-va I. N. Kushnerev i Ko, 1898.

Miller, Aleksei. *Ukrainskii vopros v Rossiiskoi imperii*. Kyiv: Laurus, 2013.

Miller, Robin Feuer. *Dostoevsky's Unfinished Journey*. New Haven, CT: Yale University Press, 2007.

Minard-Törmänen, Nathanaëlle. *An Imperial Idyll: Finland in Russian Travelogues (1810–1860)*. Helsinki: Helsingfors Societas Scientiarum Fennica, 2016.

Mishra, Vijay. *The Gothic Sublime*. Albany: State University of New York Press, 1994.

Moretti, Franco. *Atlas of the European Novel, 1800–1900*. London: Verso, 1999.

Morris, David B. "Gothic Sublimity." *New Literary History* 16, no. 2 (1985): 299–319.

Moyne, Ernest J. *Raising the Wind: The Legend of Lapland and Finland Wizards in Literature*. Newark: University of Delaware Press, 1981.

Nadezhdin, N. I. "Ob etnograficheskom izuchenii narodnosti russkoi." *Zapiski russkogo geograficheskogo obshchestva* 2 (1847): 61–115.

——. "'Vechera na khutore bliz Dikan'ki.' Povesti, izdannye pasichnikom Rudym Pan'kom. Pervaia knizhka, Spb., v tipogr. depart. nar. prosv., 1831." In *Literaturnaia kritika. Estetika*. Moscow: Khudozhestvennaia literatura, 1972.

Naiman, Eric. *Sex in Public: The Incarnation of Early Soviet Ideology*. Princeton: Princeton University Press, 1997.

Nakhlik, Ievhen. *Panteleimon Kulish: osobystist', pys'mennyk, myslytel'*. 2 vols. Kyiv: Ukrains'kyi pys'mennyk, 2007.

Naumenko, Valentina. *"Zdes', na kontse Rossii ispolinskoi . . .": Finliandiia v tvorcheskom nasledii russkikh puteshestvennikov XVIII–nachala XX veka*. Iaroslavl': Remder, 2010.

Neiman, Borys. "Kulish i Val'ter Skott." In *Panteleimon Kulish. Zbirnyk prats' Komisii dlia vydavannia pam'iatok novitn'oho pys'menstva. Ukrains'ka Akademiia Nauk. Zbirnyk istorychno-filolohichnoho viddilu 53* (1927): 127–56.

Nemtsov, Boris. "Zachem Putin voiuet c Ukrainoi." *Ukrainskaia pravda*, September 1, 2014. https://www.pravda.com.ua/rus/articles/2014/09/1/7036345/.

Nikolaeva, Olga. "Na 'poklonenie' koldunam: Ukraina pogruzhaetsia v magicheskii khaos." *Novorossiia*, September 27, 2017, https://novorosinform.org/411335.

Nowakowski, Adam. "Obrazy Finliandii, Shvetsii i Rossii v povesti Nestora Kukol'nika *Egor Ivanovich Sil'vanovskii, ili Pokorenie Finliandii pri Petre Velikom.*" *Rocznik Przemsyki* 52, no. 2, *Literatura i Język*, series vol. 20 (2016): 27–37.

O'Connor, Kevin. *The History of the Baltic States.* Westport, CT: Greenwood Press, 2003.

"O pietizme." *Finskii vestnik* 5 (1845): 17–24 [Nravoopisatel'].

Odoevskii, V. F. *Sochineniia v dvukh tomakh.* Moscow: Khudozhestvennaia literatura, 1981.

Offord, Derek. "Karamzin's Gothic Tale: 'The Island of Bornholm.'" In *The Gothic-Fantastic in Nineteenth-Century Russian Literature*, edited by Neil Cornwell, 37–58. Amsterdam: Rodopi, 1999.

Panofsky, Gerda S. *Nikolai Mikhailovich Karamzin in Germany: Fiction as Facts.* Wiesbaden: Harrassowitz, 2010.

Peck, L. F. *A Life of Matthew G. Lewis.* Cambridge: Harvard University Press, 1961.

Perepiska Ia. K. Grota s P. A. Pletnevym. 3 vols. St. Petersburg: Tipografiia Ministerstva Putei Soobshcheniia, 1896.

Petrov, Viktor. "Val'ter-Skotiv's'ka povist' z ukrains'koi mynuvshyny." In *Mykhailo Charnyshenko: povist'*, by Panteleimon Kulish, 5–35. Kyiv: Siaivo, 1928.

Petrovsky-Shtern, Yohanan. *Anti-Imperial Choice: The Making of a Ukrainian Jew.* New Haven: Yale University Press, 2009.

Pidkova, I., and R. Shust, eds. *Dovidnyk z istorii Ukrainy.* Kyiv: Geneza, 1993.

Platt, Kevin M. F., Caryl Emerson, and Dina Khapaeva. "Introduction: The Russian Gothic." *Russian Literature* 106 (2019): 1–9.

Plokhy, Serhii. *The Cossack Myth: History and Nationhood in the Age of Empire.* Cambridge: Cambridge University Press, 2012.

Pogorel'skii, Antonii. "O narodnom prosveshchenii v Rossii." In *Sochineniia i pis'ma*, 368–72. Sankt-Peterburg: Nauka, 2010.

——. *Sochineniia i pis'ma.* Sankt-Peterburg: Nauka, 2010.

Polevoi, Nikolai. "Malorossiia, ee obitateli i istoriia." *Moskovskii telegraf* 17 (1830): 85–86.

Polovtsov, A. A. "Dershau, Karl Fedorovich" and "Dershau, Fedor Karlovich." In *Russkii biograficheskii slovar'*, 25 vols. Vol. 6, 326–27. S.-Peterburg: Izdanie Imperatorskago Russkago istoricheskago obshchestva, 1896–1918.

"Pryvyd brodyt' po Rosii: Henprokuroru RF vvyzhaet'sia maidan." ZNAJ.UA, June 8, 2017, https://znaj.ua/world/pryvyd-brodyt-po-rosiyi-genprokuroru-rf-vvyzha yetsya-majdan?page=35.

Punter, David. *The Literature of Terror: A History of Gothic Fictions from 1765 to the Present Day.* London: Longman, 1980.

Pushkin, Alexander. *Collected Narrative and Lyrical Poetry.* Translated by Walter Arndt. Ann Arbor: Ardis, 1984.

Pushkin, A. S. *Sobranie sochinenii.* 10 vols. Moscow: Izdatel'stvo Akademii Nauk SSSR, 1962–66.

Ragussis, Michael. *Figures of Conversion: 'The Jewish Question' and English National Identity* Durham, NC: Duke University Press, 1995.

Ram, Harsha. *The Imperial Sublime: A Russian Poetics of Empire.* Madison: University of Wisconsin Press, 2003.

Ramsey, Cynthia C. "Gothic Treatment of the Crisis of Engendering in Odoevskii's *The Salamander.*" In *The Gothic-Fantastic in Nineteenth-Century Russian Literature*, edited by Neil Cornwell, 145–69. Amsterdam: Rodopi, 1999.

Reizov, B. G. "Val'ter Skott." In *Sobranie sochinenii.* 20 vols. Moscow-Leningrad: Gos. izd-vo khudozhestvennoi literatury, 1960–65.

Riasanovsky, Nicholas V., and Mark D. Steinberg, ed. *A History of Russia.* 9th ed. New York: Oxford University Press, 2018.

Riggenbach, H. "Inzest und Gefangenschaft in N. M. Karamzins 'Insel Bornholm.'" *Vorträge und Abhandlungen zur Slavistik* 9 (1987): 65–97.

"Riugen." In *Entsiklopedicheskii slovar' Brokgauza i Efrona.* Vol. 54. St. Petersburg: Semenovskaia tipo-litografiia, 1899.

Robertson, Fiona. *Legitimate Histories: Scott, Gothic, and the Authorities of Fiction.* Oxford: Oxford University Press, 1994.

Romanchuk, Robert. "Mother Tongue: Gogol''s *Pannochka*, Pogorel'skii's *Monastyrka*, and the Economy of Russian in the Little Russian Gothic." In the Forum "Rethinking the Gothic in Ukraine." *Slavic and East European Journal* 62, no. 2 (2018): 272–92.

Rowley, David G. "Imperial versus National Discourse: The Case of Russia." *Nations and Nationalism* 6, no. 1 (2000): 23–42.

"Russkaia literatura: Novye knigi." *Moskovskii telegraf* 8 (April 1833): 562–84.

Sakharov, V. I. "Eshche o Pushkine i V. F. Odoevskom." In *Pushkin: Issledovaniia i materialy*, edited by M. P. Alekseev et al., 224–30. Leningrad: Nauka, 1979.

Sakulin, P. N. *Iz istorii russkogo idealizma. Kniaz' V. F. Odoevskii. Myslitel'—pisatel'.* 2 vols. Moscow: Izdanie M. i S. Sabashnikovykh, 1913.

Sandler, Stephanie. *Alexander Pushkin and the Writing of Exile.* Stanford: Stanford University Press, 1989.

Saunders, David. *The Ukrainian Impact on Russian Culture, 1750–1850.* Edmonton: Canadian Institute of Ukrainian Studies, 1985.

Savchenko, Fedir. *Lysty P. Kulisha do M. Pohodina (1842–1851). Khar'kov* 10 (1929): 19.

Sawczak, Peter. "'Noch' pered Rozhdestvom' Mykoly / Nikolaia Gogolia: k voprosu o 'maloi literature.'" *Russian, Croatian and Serbian, Czech and Slovak, Polish Literature* 49, no. 3 (2001): 259–70.

Saytas, Andrius, and Aija Krutaine. "Ukraine Crisis Stokes Baltic Nerves over Russia." Reuters, March 3, 2014, https://www.reuters.com/article/us-ukraine-crisis-baltics/ukraine-crisis-stokes-baltic-nerves-over-russia-idUSBREA221J520140303.

[Sbitnev, I.]. "Poezdka v Khar'kov." *Vestnik Evropy* 15 (1830): 203–53.

Schimmelpenninck van der Oye, David. "Orientalizm—delo tonkoe." *Ab Imperio* 1 (2002): 249–64.

Schönle, Andreas. *Architecture of Oblivion: Ruins and Historical Consciousness in Modern Russia.* DeKalb: Northern Illinois University Press, 2011.

——. *Authenticity and Fiction in the Russian Literary Journey, 1790–1840.* Cambridge: Harvard University Press, 2000.

Scott, Walter. *Waverley, or 'Tis Sixty Years Since.* Edinburgh, 1862.

Semenov, D. *Otechestvovedenie. Issue 1: Severnyi krai i Finliandiia.* St. Petersburg: V tipografii Iosafata Ogryzko, 1864.

Senkovskii, O. I. *Sobranie sochinenii Senkovskogo (barona Brambeusa).* 9 vols. St. Petersburg: Tipografiia Imperatorskoi Akademii nauk, 1858–59.

"Sever Evropeiskoi Rossii." *Finskii vestnik* 4 (1845): 21–94 [Materialy severnoi istorii].

Sh. S. "Utrenniaia Zaria, Al'manakh na 1841 god, izdannyi V. Vladislavlevym. Tretii god. S. Peterburg 1841." *Moskvitianin* 1, no. 2 (1841): 567–74.

Sharypkin, D. M. *Skandinavskaia literatura v Rossii.* Leningrad: Nauka, 1980.

Sheppard, Alfred Tresidder. *The Art and Practice of Historical Fiction.* London: H. Toulmin, 1930.

Shevyrev, S. "Mikhailo Charnyshenko, ili Malorossiia vosem'desiat let nazad. Sochinenie P. Kulisha. Kiev, 1843. Tri chasti. I. 206. II. 190. III. 221." *Moskvitianin* 4, no. 7 (1843): 126–33.

Shkandrij, Myroslav. *Russia and Ukraine: Literature and the Discourse of Empire from Napoleonic to Postcolonial Times.* Montreal: McGill-Queen's University Press, 2001.

Simpson, Mark S. *The Russian Gothic Novel and Its British Antecedents.* Columbus, OH: Slavica, 1986.

Smaga, Jósef. *Antoni Pogorielski. Życie i twórczość na tle epoki.* Wrocław: Wydawnictwo Polskiej Akademii Nauk, 1970.

Smith, Andrew, and William Hughes, eds. *Empire and the Gothic: The Politics of Genre.* Basingstoke: Palgrave Macmillan, 2003.

Sobol, Valeria. "Introduction to the Forum 'Rethinking the Gothic in Ukraine.'" *Slavic and East European Journal* 62, no. 2 (2018): 247–54.

——. "'Komu ot chuzhikh, a nam ot svoikh': Variazhskoe prizvanie v russkoi literature kontsa XVIII veka." In *Tam, vnutri. Praktiki vnutrennei kolonizatsii v kul'turnoi istorii Rossii,* edited by A. Etkind, D. Uffel'mann, and I. Kukulin, 186–216. Moscow: Novoe literaturnoe obozrenie, 2012.

——. "The Uncanny Frontier of Russian Identity: Travel, Ethnography, and Empire in Lermontov's 'Taman.'" *Russian Review* 70 (January 2011): 65–79.

"Sochineniia kniazia V. F. Odoevskogo. SP-burg, v tip. E. Pratsa. 1844, v"-8. Tri chasti, str. 390-436-572." *Finskii vestnik* 1 (1845): 33–51 [Bibliograficheskaia khronika].

Subtelny, Orest. *Ukraine: A History.* 4th ed. Toronto: University of Toronto Press, 2009.

Suny, Ronald G. "The Empire Strikes Out." In *A State of Nations: Empire and Nation-Building in the Age of Lenin and Stalin,* edited by Ronald Grigor Suny and Terry Martin, 23–66. Oxford: Oxford University Press, 2001.

Tamarchenko, N. D., ed. *Goticheskaia traditsiia v russkoi literature.* Moscow: RGGU, 2008.

Tarasenko-Atreshkov, Liubim. "Pomor'e. Territoriia byvshego udel'nogo kniazhestva Polotskogo, sopredel'nogo emu Pskovskogo, i Velikogo Novgoroda," *Finskii vestnik* 24, no. 12 (1847): 1–18 [Materialy severnoi istorii].

Terras, Victor. *A History of Russian Literature.* New Haven: Yale University Press, 1991.

Thaden, Edward C., ed. *Russification in the Baltic Provinces and Finland, 1855–1914.* Princeton: Princeton University Press, 1981.

Thompson, Ewa M. *Imperial Knowledge: Russian Literature and Colonialism.* Westport, CT: Greenwood Press, 2000.

Todorova, Maria. *Imagining the Balkans.* Oxford: Oxford University Press, 1997.

Tolz, Vera. *Russia (Inventing the Nation).* London: Arnold, 2001.

Tosi, Alessandra. *Waiting for Pushkin: Russian Fiction in the Reign of Alexander I (1801–1825).* Amsterdam: Rodopi, 2006.

Trumpener, Katie. *Bardic Nationalism: The Romantic Novel and the British Empire.* Princeton: Princeton University Press, 1997.

Tur'ian, M. A. "Evoliutsiia romanticheskikh motivov v povesti V. F. Odoevskogo 'Salamandra.'" In *Russkii romantizm,* edited by K. N. Grigor'ian, 187–206. Leningrad: Nauka, 1978.

———. "Lichnost' A. A. Perovskogo i literaturnoe nasledie Antoniia Pogorel'skogo." In *Antonii Pogorel'skii. Sochineniia i pis'ma.* Sankt-Peterburg: Nauka, 2010.

Ungurianu, Dan. *Plotting History: The Russian Historical Novel in the Imperial Age.* Madison: University of Wisconsin Press, 2007.

[Ushakov, V. A.]. *Severnaia pchela* 119–20 (1830): n.p.

Uspenskii, D. "Ingry, Vaty, Iagriamia, Savolaksy." *Finskii vestnik* 2 (1845): 1–19 [Etnografiia].

Vatsuro, Vadim. *Goticheskii roman v Rossii.* Moscow: Novoe literaturnoe obozrenie, 2002.

———. "Literaturno-filosofskaia problematika povesti Karamzina 'Ostrov Borngol'm.'" *XVIII vek* 8 (1969): 190–209.

Velychenko, Stephen. "Empire Loyalism and Minority Nationalism in Great Britain and Imperial Russia, 1707 to 1914: Institutions, Law, and Nationality in Scotland and Ukraine." *Comparative Studies in Society and History* 39, no. 3 (1997): 413–41.

———. "The Issue of Russian Colonialism in Ukrainian Thought. Dependency Identity and Development." *Ab Imperio* 1 (2002): 323–67.

Ve-skii, A. "Sila privychki." *Kievlianin* bk. 1 (1840): 177–99.

Vinitsky, Ilya. "*Amor Hereos*, or How One Brother Was Visited by an Invisible Being: Lived Spirituality among Russian Freemasons in the 1810s." *Kritika: Explorations in Russian and Eurasian History* 9, no. 2 (2008): 291–316.

Vinogradov, V. V. *Istoriia slov: Okolo 1500 slov i vyrazhenii i bolee 5000 slov, s nimi sviazannykh,* edited by N. Iu. Shvedova. Moscow: "Tolk," 1994.

Wiebe, Katja. "Die Perspektive der russischen Literatur des späten Zarenreichs auf den 'Norden' (Estland und Finnland)." In *Russland an der Ostsee: imperiale Strategien der Macht und kulturelle Wahrnehmungsmuster (16. bis 20. Jahrhundert) / Russia on the Baltic: Imperial Strategies of Power and Cultural Patterns of Perception (16th–20th centuries),* edited by Karsten Brüggemann and Bradley D. Woodworth, 289–305. Vienna: Böhlau Wien, 2012.

Williams, Anne. *The Art of Darkness: A Poetics of Gothic.* Chicago: University of Chicago Press, 1995.

Wolff, Larry. *Inventing Eastern Europe: The Map of Civilization on the Mind of the Enlightenment.* Stanford: Stanford University Press, 1994.

Zabuzhko, Oksana. *I znov ia vlizaiu v tank.* Kyiv: Komora, 2016.

"'Zinovii Bogdan Khmel'nitskii.' Sochinenie Aleksandra Kuz'micha. Epokha pervaia, molodost' Zinoviia. 5-t' chastei. S. Peterburg 1846." *Finskii vestnik* 13 (1847): 1–10 [Bibliograficheskaia khronika].

INDEX

Page references in italics indicate a figure.

Milton Keynes UK
Ingram Content Group UK Ltd.
UKHW011813150923
428767UK00007B/251